WILDERNESS TRAILS
AND A DREAM

The story behind the Olympic Game Farm

By Lloyd Beebe

Lloyd Beebe

Catherine Beebe

ISBN 0-615-12878-5

First Edition, 1996
Second Edition, 1998
Third Edition, 2005

Designed and Printed by:
Olympic Graphic Arts, Inc.
640 S. Forks Avenue
Forks, WA 98331

Dedication

We decided to write a story of our lives. We were thinking of our family, whom we had never taken the time to tell of the many changes in our lives. It has been good to think back and remember.

This book is dedicated to our family and friends, and to all the people that have worked for the Olympic Game Farm, past and present. They have all helped us along the way. There have been too many to name them all, but we will always be grateful to them.

Many thanks to our daughter-in-law, Alice Beebe, for all the work she did to type it and put it on the computer.

To Maggie O'Hara, for the cover picture and help in editing.

A special thanks to Jack Speirs for writing the foreward for "Wilderness Trails and a Dream."

Lloyd Beebe with baby cougar

Foreward

By the time the year 1953 was underway, the airborne entertainment business had already undergone a revolution. People had stopped listening to "The Hermit's Cave" and were looking at "I Love Lucy". Lots of former radio writers were about to get acquainted with the breadline. Including this one. Fortunately, some friends at the Disney Studio figured that a radio writer might be a natural for writing the voice-over narration for the studio's new wildlife production division, the "True Life Adventures." So, with the help of those friends, I was introduced to the wonderworld of Walt Disney Productions.

Thinking back, it seems that by the end of my first day as a staff writer at "The Studio," I realized there were two highly revered names in the True Life unit: Old Mother Nature and Lloyd Beebe.

At the time, True Life Adventures documentaries were usually shot by several "naturalist-photographers" strung out across the world. In general, they filmed wild animals in their natural state and habitat with hidden cameras and cameramen. His remarkable ability to blend with the wilderness, coupled with a great feel and eye for photography, had made Lloyd Beebe a natural. He contributed film footage to several documentaries. They were Academy Award winners.

So when, in 1957, the International Geophysical Year began in Antarctica, the Disney Studio had acquired pretty much exclusive rights to on-the-spot coverage--if there was a photographer who could handle the unbelievable rigors of being on such an icebound spot. There was only one person to even consider, and that was Lloyd Beebe.

In this book, Lloyd is typically casual about his time in Antarctica. For example, his telling of being caught out in the deadly snow condition called the whiteout is not the version I heard--from Admiral Richard E. Byrd shortly before he died in 1957.

The Admiral had been invited to the Disney Studio to view some of the assembled film footage for the first of three documentaries of the I.G.Y.--"90 Degrees South." According to the Admiral, nobody at Little America expected to ever see Lloyd Beebe again. For one thing, in addition to the incredible cold, the territory out there was a maze of crevasses, often thinly frozen over and covered with a deceptive layer of loose snow. Under any conditions they are hard to detect and next to impossible in a whiteout. Anybody dropping into one of them would likely be there, well preserved, into the next millennium. But when the whiteout eventually cleared up, Lloyd walked into camp and was mostly interested in talking about getting something to eat, and getting warm. In that order.

So I ask the reader of this biography to, at all times, keep one fact in mind: Lloyd Beebe is by nature a low key and understated, thoughtful and modest man. For those reasons, don't be taken aback, as I was, to learn from his book of the time he spent hunting cougars for bounty. I mentioned this to a co-writer friend and she said, "Well look who's talking! I've heard you tell about growing up in the West Virginia hills during the Great Depression. And you've said if there hadn't been rabbits and squirrels to hunt you'd have starved. It's a matter of survival."

Enough said about that.

By the time the Geophysical Year had wound down so had the production of wildlife documentaries. Under 30 minutes running time was the requirement for Academy documentaries while a television show needed 46 or 47 minutes. So the purely animal pictures were phased out and replaced by long animal-people True Life Adventures.

And not surprisingly, Lloyd Beebe was right at home in the new format. And equally at home in training animals to fit it. And he even had the right location. On his farm outside of Sequim, Washington was a stream that looked just about like a stream in the wilderness, some trees that looked like the trees in the same wilderness--and he started acquiring animals to complete the picture. You see a film showing a big black bear come out between the trees, drink and then wade across the stream, you can believe you are deep in the heart of the Olympic National Forest.

In case he needed a little more scope, he had the Dungeness River just across the road. And not too far off, was the real Olympic National Forest. Including, if needed, the snowy cap of Mount Olympus.

I don't really know how many pictures he filmed around there or when he started keeping the animals on his farm when the shooting was over. I do know it seems like they were always there. Somewhere around 1961-62 on my first visit to the farm there were two bear cubs playing in the front yard and a cougar kitten lying under a bush gnawing on a giant bone. All three uncaged. I sat on the front porch and watched them, along with Lloyd and his wife, Catherine.

This seems a good time to comment that an old familiar saying states "Behind every successful man there stands a woman." That could have been written about Catherine Beebe. Better still, the rewritten version that says, "Beside every successful man there stands a woman." Catherine does both, she has been behind and beside Lloyd all the way through a long, successful and highly fulfilling career.

Catherine seems timeless, she looks and acts just about like she did when we three sat on the porch and watched the young animals in the yard. Today a larger house sits up on the bluff overlooking the Olympic Game Farm--but a variety of animals young and old still populate the front yard. And Catherine still feeds them all.

During the next quarter century, I watched Lloyd's reputation and his stature grow in the world of animal handling and filming. You'll notice I say "animal handling" instead of "animal training." That's because I'm not at all sure Lloyd ever actually "trained" an animal in the accepted sense of the word. In my opinion, he simply knew animals so well, how they would react and behave in a given situation, so that he would carefully create the situation, put the animals in it and let them do it for the camera.

As I slowly moved from writer to writer-producer, Lloyd was almost always involved in my show. Mostly I got the credit and Lloyd did the work. Time after time I've had people say things like, "In 'Charlie the Lonesome Cougar', how did you get that cat to jump on the log and burl with the lumberjack?" . . Or about a scene in 'King of the Grizzlies', how did you get that bear to take the cowboy's head in its mouth and then walk away and let him keep the whole thing--hair and all?"

No matter the question, the answer was always the same: "I didn't get the animals to do anything, all I did was write a script and give it to Lloyd Beebe."

Frequently there would be an admiring reaction about 'the imagination it took to write a scene like that.'

And my answer had to be about the same, "I guess Lloyd just thought the story could use a little touch of better action than the script called for." Privately, I often thought Lloyd had figured out something different because the animal wouldn't do what I'd written for him to do and he, Lloyd, made the scene better--better because he knew things an animal would do that I didn't know.

Reading this over, I realize it sounds a little like Lloyd made films only for me and the Disney Studio. Not so. I don't know how many animals and sequences he has furnished for commercials and spots in other motion pictures for other companies. But I'll promise you one thing, the "Grizzly Adams" series wouldn't have lasted one season without Lloyd's well-mannered bears. I say well-mannered because Lloyd might well have had a talk with them and said something like "Look, guys, don't eat Grizzly Adams, he's the star of the show. You'd be out of work." He genuinely did--and does--have a knack for communicating with animals.

Oh, he wasn't out on every location, but he supplied the animals and trained the trainers. He doesn't hit the road much these days and the Olympic Game Farm makes a great retirement home, if he ever needs one.

Jack Speirs,
Walt Disney Productions
Writer-Producer, Ret.

Table of Contents

GROWING UP TO 12

Yesterday I had an accident, some bridge timbers fell on my legs and feet. I was lucky to have only broken toes and bruised legs and ankles. Only my left foot was painful. I'm sitting in an easy chair with my left foot on a pillow high on a chair in front of me. I am looking out of a large window overlooking the farm where the buffalo and deer and elk graze, and beyond to the beautiful Olympic Mountains. These mountains have thrilled me most of my life. I realized that I would be sitting down a lot in the next month or two and I would need something to keep me busy.

I got to thinking about all the trails I'd followed and all the challenges I'd met before reaching my goal.

Until this blustery day in January, I'd never had time to keep even a sketchy record of those days leading up to our goal - Catherine's and mine. Catherine is my wife of fifty-five years, my helpmate and wonderful companion. She was watching me look out the window and got up and came back with paper and pencil and suggested that I write down some of the things she knew I was thinking about.

It had never entered my mind that I could write a book. It would, however, be another challenge and would keep me busy. We laughed together as I put down on paper our memories of the adventures, the setbacks, the challenges and the rewards of our struggles to reach one goal after another.

Now in the winter of 1995, I'm sitting down to begin the task of recording the events that led to our ultimate goal: the Olympic Game Farm in Sequim, Washington. Not being a writer by profession, I'm just going to tell the story as it happened along the trails to our hopes and realization of our dreams.

I was born May 2, 1916 in Huntingdon, B.C., Canada to American parents, Charles Edwin Beebe and wife Jessie. There were three children: Violet was the oldest, next was myself, and Jessie was the youngest.

At this time we lived one mile inside of Canada. People who lived close to the line worked on either side of the border, just as though there was no boundary line between Canada and the U.S. Children born on either side of the line could decide whether to be Canadian or American, simply by spending their twenty-first birthday on the side of the line that they chose. They could also choose to be a citizen of both countries and have free run of the border.

Our family moved to a homestead at Sewall on Graham Island. Graham Island is one of the Queen Charlotte Islands along the north coast of British Columbia, Canada. Then we moved to Everson, Washington, where I started the first grade of school. In 1923 when I finished the first grade, we moved again. This time it would be Darrington, Washington. Dad was going to work in the logging camp on the Sauk River.

We lived in a house on one side of the school grounds, three or four acres cleared out of the

Buffalo in the field at Olympic Game Farm.

1

forest. In front of our house was a large fir tree that always had a lot of fir cones, and all the kids had fun throwing them at one another.

We went to Sunday School every Sunday. The main reason I remember the church was that when we came out the door of the church one Sunday, there was a bear cub up in a fir tree. Everyone crowded around to watch it. Finally the big boys climbed the tree and caught the cub. I had to go home with my mother, but how I wished I'd been big enough to help those boys!

Dad worked at the Sauk River Logging Camp. Every day he would ride a speeder on the railroad tracks up to the camp. A speeder resembled a truck that had wheels like a train. A lot of the workers stayed in the company bunkhouses and ate at the cook house there.

We boys spent most of our time playing cops and robbers in the woods by the school. Prohibition was on at this time, and the bootleggers were busy. At times, we boys found big caches of whiskey flasks and always ended up breaking every bottle.

Another game was one like Tarzan. The trees here were only about twenty-feet-high firs and close together. We spent our time in the tree tops. We would bend the top over and grab another tree, one after another. Once in a while the top would break and we would fall down through the limbs and land somehow unhurt on the ground. When that happened, we went on to another tree and continued the game.

The father of my best friend in Darrington was the cook at this Sauk River camp, and Kenneth Willmer invited me to go up to camp for Thanksgiving dinner. I wanted to go, and my father and mother said I could.

One of the reasons I wanted to go to the logging camp was because of the stories my dad kept telling about an Airedale dog that lived at camp. From the time I was little, animals always interested me. This dog was always fighting with porcupines and ended up covered with quills that had to be pulled out. But he never quit fighting them. His name was Jack. At that time I thought he was a great dog.

Thanksgiving came, and Kenneth and I got on the logging train and rode up to camp. Ken and I were running around camp. The bunkhouses were built on pilings, and there were trails underneath the houses where the men took short cuts. You had to bend over to go under the houses. I met Jack when I bent down to go under one of these bunkhouses. He grabbed me by the chin, and I still have the scars on my chin. I think he figured he was protecting the camp. It sure scared me. Jack didn't bother us any more, and that was all right with me!

This was a great Thanksgiving. The cook mixed up various kinds of food in separate tubs. I never saw so much food, and it was impossible to eat all of it.

The kids who lived on farms got sex education because they grew up with chickens, rabbits and other farm animals. Each year I had to help Dad drive the cow down the road for two miles to see the bull at a ranch. I wonder if Dad needed me to drive the cow, or was this just part of the education that he was giving me?

We had a cow for me to milk. My mother probably milked the cow as much as I did. We had more milk than we could use, so I had the job of delivering milk around town for ten cents a quart.

One day four of us boys were playing, and one of the boys had three cigarettes. This boy said, "We can each have a cigarette, because Lloyd don't smoke." I felt left out, so I said, "Yes I do." So we broke the cigarettes up evenly and smoked them. Then one of the boys took a sack of Bull Durham tobacco out of his pocket and said, "We will have a wrestling match and the winner gets the sack of Bull Durham." I won the tobacco; we rolled one cigarette each and smoked it. It was about time for me to meet my dad as he came in from the logging camp. I usually walked up to the track and watched the men get off the train and walked back home with Dad. I was feeling a little sick and shaky from smoking. My mother and father didn't smoke or drink, and I knew they would feel bad if they found out I had been smoking. I decided right then and there that I would never smoke again, and I never did.

Kenneth Willmer was my best friend. Ken was a little bigger than I. His mother always saw that he was dressed up in nice clothes. He must have been more careful about staying clean than I was. Of course, I didn't have the kind of clothes Ken had. My clothes allowed me to do more things. Usually I had on bib overalls. Ken had cream colored corduroys. I liked to go over and help him get his wood in. It seemed to be more fun than doing my own job at home.

2

The big old-growth tree in front of our house dropped a lot of cones all over the ground. We lived right next to the school playground. There were no fences around the house, so it seemed like part of the playground. All the boys of about the same age chose up sides for the cone fight that happened every year.

During the cone fight, I threw a cone that hit Clinton Tollenaar square in the eye. Clinton dropped his supply of cones and came on the run at me. I was still throwing cones; we were all moving around. Ken stepped in front of me. Clinton and Ken started a wicked fist fight. I don't know why Ken got into it, unless he thought he'd hit Clinton. I knew it was my cone that hit Clinton in the eye.

Ken won the fight, but the cone fight was over for that day. We decided to dig a swimming pond. After a weeks' work, we filled it with water. It never became more than a mud hole, but we had a lot of fun in it.

Mom played the violin and she wanted me to play the violin too. She arranged for a woman to come and give me violin lessons regularly. I took lessons for a year or so. The trouble was that we lived on the edge of the school playground, and that was the only spot cleared enough to play games on. The boys were always playing after school and on weekends when I had to practice. Trying to practice the violin and watch the games being played on the playing field just did not work out. Finally, Mom and the teacher decided I might as well play with the boys instead of learning to play the violin. I did much better playing with the boys, although I missed out on a prize my Aunt Cassie promised she would give me when I learned how to play a Minuet.

Aunt Cassie was my favorite aunt, and her husband, Lex, was my favorite uncle. They had the best cherry tree that I knew of. Whenever we went there, we visited their niece, Jessie and her husband, Floyd Massey. They had a big farm with lots of fruit trees and lots of kids to play with - mostly boys. But years later I found out there was one little girl by the name of Catherine.

My folks had a Model T Ford that we traveled in. I don't remember my sisters ever getting any spankings. I know they never got as dirty as fast as I did. We took turns drying the dishes.

I found out that I could catch honeybees and yellow jackets in my cupped hands and carry them around for a long time without getting stung. You could hear them buzzing around as they looked for a way out of the dark. If I had my hands cupped like I might have a bee, my sisters wouldn't let me come near them and would say, "Mom, Lloyd has a bee!" Then Mother would tell me not to scare my sisters. If I didn't have a bee, I would open my hands and show them.

I don't believe it would be possible to have a better father or mother than we had. I just wish I had told them when I had the chance.

Some of the boys in Darrington had bicycles and would take short trips for the day. I didn't have a bicycle, and I knew my parents couldn't afford to buy me one. Some of my friends had old spare parts they didn't want and gave them to me. I put them together and finally had a bike and could go with the other boys.

They decided to go to a town fifty miles away. There were almost no cars on the road, and in those days, parents were not afraid to let kids go places alone. There just wasn't anything to be afraid of other than rivers and a little traffic. At that time, kids, at least around the pioneering part of Washington, were never harmed.

We started out on our trip of fifty miles each way. I only got thirty-five miles with my made-over bicycle before it broke down. I had to push it thirty-five miles back to Darrington. I never could buy parts for that one, but I'd had fun.

My mother sometimes did not know where I was. She worked out once in a while, and always had a lot to do at home. I remember once I was playing in the woods. It was only a quarter mile to the Sauk River through the woods. I played along the river and was a little late getting home. Mom was pretty worried. I got a spanking when I got home. I don't remember if my mother or my dad spanked me. Dad sometimes had to do that when he got home. I got to think about it until he came. Dad usually sent me to my room and said he would be in before long. I knew he would come in to spank me. I also knew that I deserved a spanking. I could think of other times that I'd deserved it, but no one had found out what I'd done. I have always been glad I had a few spankings. They helped me distinguish right from wrong.

I once ran way down the road a mile or more to play with another kid. My mother finally found out where I was and came after me. She had a switch from a tree and walked behind me. Whenever I lagged, she would give me a switch. She followed me all the way. It must have been embarrassing for her. I knew it was for me.

The only bad thing I can remember happened at the Sheriff's house and that was across the schoolgrounds from us. A couple of men came up on his porch with guns, and the Sheriff shot both of them. They were after the Sheriff - I never knew why. But it didn't work out that way.

In 1927, we moved to Arlington, Washington. Dad had a job falling and peeling pilings one hundred twenty-five feet long. On holidays and weekends, Dad paid me so much a foot to peel poles. The money was used to buy school clothes.

I always was around axes, saws and tools, and never did cut myself. We peeled pilings with what they called a spud. It was like a giant chisel four inches wide with a four-foot handle.

One day, Dad and his brother felled some long, slim Douglas Fir poles for piling, and I was straddling a pole where it was bent over another tree five feet above the ground. When I was up to the bad bend with the bark peeled off, I must have been daydreaming, because I set the sharp blade of the spud down hard on the top of the piling, and the tree broke and threw me end over end up in the air. I came down in a bunch of limbs and surprisingly enough wasn't hurt a bit.

Lloyd Beebe, 12 years old, with string of trout caught in Thunder Creek

We lived on a small farm which had two or three sheds, a cow barn and a small orchard. One day, I brought a young squirrel home with me. He got real tame, but my mother decided the squirrel should stay outside. My dad built a cage for him. Everything was okay until one day the squirrel got out. We all went out in the orchard to try to catch him. Dad hollered, "I got him!" When we looked, Dad threw his hands up in the air with the squirrel holding onto his bloody finger. Then the squirrel let go and flew over an apple tree. We decided we didn't want to get bitten so we let him stay loose.

He gave us a lot more enjoyment now that he was on his own. We fed him regularly. Whenever anyone walked through the orchard or the barn he would jump on their head. He would do the same thing with a stranger. He pestered our cats and dog all the time. We would see the cat running for the barn, and it looked like the squirrel had the cat by the tail all the way to the barn and they disappeared inside. Sometimes the squirrel would stand on the porch, and the dog would be on the ground. They would be looking at each other. They were both excited, and all at once the squirrel would land on the dog's back, and they were off and running through the barn and orchard. It was fun for both of them. The dog wanted to catch the squirrel, but never could. The squirrel lived there as long as we did.

There were two boys my age who were neighbors: Arnie and Earl Anderson. Earl was the best marble player in school. He was always my partner in our marble games. We hardly ever lost. Anyone could be a winner with Earl as a partner. We always played for keeps at our school, and Earl had several apple boxes of marbles under his house.

My dad and two of his brothers took a contract to clear some land that was to be under the Diablo Lake on the Skagit River. They would be working for the City of Seattle.

During the summer vacation, for three months I was to go up and camp out with them and be the water boy. As it turned out, I had a great time. It was exciting. We rode up to where the dam was being built and walked up the river a mile or two. There was a very high cable swinging bridge, which we had to walk across the Skagit River Canyon on. It was a long walk and scary.

We had a tent camp in our part of the woods. The trees had to be cut down and cut into logs and limbed of all brush. Worthless trees and pieces of logs had to be piled and burned. My job was to bring the water bag around to all the workers, then go fill the water bag at Thunder Creek, and on every half hour return to every worker.

It was great fishing in Thunder Creek. The best place was to go up Colonial Creek to a wonderful waterfall that fell into a deep pool. It was full of fish. I didn't get to fish below the falls very often. All of these wonderful places are now covered with water and will never be seen again.

If I could find the time, I would fish a little. I left my fish pole at the place where I filled the canvas water bag. I also liked to look for animal tracks. I liked to know who was out there with me.

We lived in a tent and ate in a tent as well. A bear came and started to steal our butter and meat almost every night; we kept butter and meat in different trees.

My dad and uncle told me of a big bear at another crew camp up by Colonial Creek.

It was great to be in the woods day and night with wild animals

They said that a big bear came in every night and people came by before dark to see him. This bear just waited until dark to get in the cook house. It was against the law to kill him. The cook had thrown an ax at him and done all the law would allow.

One night, we all hiked up to this camp to see the bear. There were twenty-five people lined up by the cook house. They were throwing rocks at the bear, who was standing about forty yards away on a high fir log.

No one could hit the bear. The men were giving each other the raspberry. One man had a sling that could throw big rocks, but they didn't come close. A man saw my slingshot in my back pocket. He said that a kid that carries a slingshot in his pocket could hit about anything. Then my uncle told me to come on up in front and take a shot at the bear. I wanted him to be quiet. I said no, that I didn't have a good enough rock. He said that he'd find me a good one, and he had a good one that wouldn't sail. I didn't want to shoot at that bear because I figured if I hit him he could come right after me. But I couldn't get out of shooting at the bear. I didn't think of trying to miss him. I didn't even think that the rock might miss.

They put me in front of everyone, and I drew back the slingshot quick and let the rock fly. It hit the bear square in the forehead as he stood facing me. As soon as the rock hit the bear, I turned and ran through the crowd toward the cook house. The bear was surprised and almost stepped off the log. He didn't go away, and everyone just roared with laughter. They realized that I believed the bear would be after me.

Great horned owl

A question came up among the men whether it was safe for me to be running around through the woods alone, what with cougars and bears around. I was twelve years old, and I didn't worry a bit about my safety. Finally, everyone just quit talking about it. I was able to do as I pleased in my spare time. I was always thoughtful and didn't take too many chances. I had never gotten hurt in any way in the years of growing up to twelve.

5

OUR FAMILY MOVES TO THE OLYMPIC PENINSULA

The end of the summer came, and I had to get back to school in Arlington. What a wonderful summer I'd had!

1928 to 1930 - My father and I talked a lot about some day having a mink farm or another type of farm where we could raise something to help make a living. I was always doing a little trapping of muskrats and skunks in the slough by our house along the Stillaguamish River.

I caught three mink that winter, and I brought them home alive. They were not hurt, as I had checked my traps morning and night. Dad made cages for the mink and we raised them. He thought a mink ranch might be good to have. Looking back now, sixty-five years later, that may have been the beginning of the Olympic Game Farm.

At this time, chinchilla rabbits were getting popular, and I had been raising them and had twenty or thirty of them. One night dogs came into the building where I had them and killed every one. We still had the three mink and some muskrats.

1930 to 1932 - After my eighth-grade graduation in 1930, our family moved to Port Angeles, Washington on the Olympic Peninsula. I didn't know then that this area would be my home for the rest of my life. The Great Depression was on, and my father hoped to get work in the woods logging.

Peeling and cutting pulp wood for the pulp mill in Port Angeles was all the work to be found. It was hard work for not much pay.

I went to work on pulp wood, too. The pay was one dollar and seventy-five cents a cord of pulp wood. We would fall trees and saw them by hand into four-foot-long blocks of wood, then split and peel the blocks into a size that one man could handle. And then we carried them to the road. We had to open up a road so a truck could get in to load the wood. A pile four feet high and eight feet long was one cord of wood. That meant one dollar and seventy-five cents for me. I enjoyed working. One cord a day was about what I averaged. That was considered good for a fourteen-year-old boy. Some trees were hard to split with sledgehammer and steel wedges.

In bad times, everyone tried to help out. On weekends, I worked in the woods with my father. Sometimes I used part of the money I made for myself, but most of it went to help pay for the family's needs.

While I went to school in Port Angeles, I had a job at the Port Angeles General Hospital. It was a new brick building. My job was to be at the hospital at four o'clock each morning to peel several sacks of potatoes, sacks of carrots, onions and other vegetables. When I had finished with the peeling, I put the vegetables on a dumbwaiter which elevated them to the floor above. Then I had to hurry to school.

I had to work fast so I wouldn't be late for class. My fingers were all cut up most of the time, especially my thumbs, as that is where the knife was supposed to stop.

I got one dollar a day to do this hospital job. I was lucky to have this job with the Depression

Our mother and father, Charles and Jessie Beebe, with Jessie, Lloyd and Violet.

on. My father couldn't find a job much of the time. If I didn't have to work at the hospital after school, I could often deliver newspapers on a route for the <u>Port Angeles News</u>.

When I worked steady in the summer during vacations, I paid thirty dollars a month for my board. Sometimes I didn't make more than that, but I would finally pay it. It was a fair arrangement, and I felt better knowing that I was helping. I always had a .22 rifle with me and usually got at least one rabbit each day. This helped with the food bill.

My mother did a lot of canning. If we got a deer or elk each year, she would can every bit of it, as well as salmon, berries and vegetables. We always had a cow for milk and cream. Milking the cow night and morning was usually my chore.

My father helped me get a big cedar log and we made a dugout canoe, as the Indians did. It turned out to be a very pretty canoe. We didn't know the Indians had flat bottoms on theirs. Ours was round like the log, and tipped over so easily that we couldn't take a new passenger without it tipping over as soon as we left shore. We kids spent a lot of time out on the bay and never tipped over. I still don't understand why, unless it was because we knew it would tip if given a chance.

My best friends at that time were Wayne Hathaway and Perry Brackett. We used bows and arrows, and hiked the mountains. We couldn't go to the store and buy food; each one of us would bring his own. I took a loaf of my mother's homemade bread and a quart of her canned wild blackberries.

I remember one trip when I didn't have a good pair of shoes. The oxfords I wore broke open and I slipped right out of them the first steep ground we came to. I wrapped my feet in canvas and got by okay, but I had to keep working on my makeshift shoes. We stayed three days and found a half jar of peanut butter at an abandoned deer hunter's camp. We got pretty hungry, but had a good time.

When September came, school started. I turned out for football and enjoyed it. I liked school work too, but when it came to standing up in front of the class to give reports, it was really scary for me. I felt just like a wild rabbit whose heart beat like a trip hammer when someone caught him. I knew I was quite a bit like a wild animal and could understand their feelings. I got so if I knew I might have to stand up and talk on a certain day, I would miss class and go out on some stream or pond and try to find a place to catch some muskrats or skunks to earn a little money.

I never got over that feeling and always gave excuses why I could not be there at that time. At seventy-nine years old, I still feel the same way today. Apparently I will not get over it.

If someone said that I was good at something, I would quickly deny that I was. Looking back, I believe I did this so I wouldn't be the center of attention and have people looking at me.

That is the only trouble I ever had in school. I made it through each grade easily.

I spent as much time in the woods and along the streams as I could, and it made me feel good and sure of myself.

I also caught five new mink for my dad. We had raised fourteen mink from the original two females and one male, so, in addition to them, we now had twenty-two mink. We also had two orphaned elk calves that the Game Warden had given us, plus two other elk that Dad had bought from someone. We sold all the male mink, except for two that we kept for breeding. That paid for the food the other animals ate. Now we thought, if only we could buy a bigger farm some day, we would be on our way to a better life.

After two-and-a-half years of high school, I decided to quit school and go to work. I knew my parents were having a hard time paying the bills, and I felt I could do the work in a logging camp. This was the Great Depression.

There was no welfare in those days, and my parents wouldn't have accepted it if there had been. During one especially hard time for them, there was an opportunity to work a day or two for the County. It was a job to help the poorest of families. My father went down to sign up for a day or two of work, but he didn't sign his name. He just didn't want to feel like he couldn't take care of his family. We always got by working harder at home and going without some things we needed.

Most people felt the same way as my folks did, and everyone wore clothes with holes and patches in them. No one thought anything of it.

The Depression was a great education that helped us all through life. We didn't feel too worried whenever another recession was talked about, as we knew we could get through it okay.

The first four jobs I got were clearing land. After working two or three weeks, the landowners told me they had no money and couldn't pay me. So I got a job sawing wood for seventy-five cents a rick.

We moved to Forks, Washington to work for Bloedel and Donovan Logging Company

Some people had to shoot deer and elk in order to survive. The Game Wardens would put a poacher in jail; then the County would have to take care of the wife and kids, and there were some men who killed an elk in order that their families would be cared for. The Game Wardens finally just stopped arresting people.

There weren't many cars. You could see a man carrying an elk liver in one hand and a rifle in the other hiking back to town. The next day the family or friends would go back with him to bring the elk down to his home.

The Game and Fishery Warden understood that people needed to catch salmon to live. So he would tell everyone that he always came across the Dungeness Bridge at noon sharp. He was letting people know that they shouldn't be catching salmon at that time. People ate every fish they caught. They didn't use sports fishing tackle, but gaff hooks or spears. The fun of fishing was not on their mind.

My older sister, Violet, got married to a good man named Ralph Stone. I didn't know Ralph, but over the years I realized how lucky they both were to have met each other.

When school was out, I made a trip to Canada to visit my relatives for a week. In the meantime, Dad had gotten a job as a saw filer for a big logging outfit. They had to move out to Forks, Washington right away. When I got back to Port Angeles, they were not there. Dad had left instructions for me on how to find them, so I started right out walking to Forks. It was sixty miles on the road. I never tried to catch rides by holding up my thumb or ever turning around and looking at the driver as a car came up behind me. I just kept walking fast.

Most people in those days would stop and offer a ride to hikers. There were few cars in Clallam County at that time. Anyway, I kept walking long after dark and had gotten forty miles closer to Forks. I came to a gravel pile along the road, and there was a newspaper lying beside it, so I laid down and used the paper to keep myself a little warm.

Next morning at daylight, I continued on towards Forks. I had walked about fifteen miles when a gasoline delivery truck stopped and asked if I could use a ride. I said that I'd like that. The driver's name was Dan Shearer and he lived in Forks. We lived as neighbors to Dan and his family for the next eight years. I always remembered and appreciated that ride. Forks was a small town. All the people knew each other and they all worked in some way with the logging industry.

I didn't have any trouble finding my family. They had rented a house and were moved in. My dad was working steady six days a week as a crosscut saw filer. It was considered a good job. He had always filed the saws we used. The workers already liked the way his saws cut. He had to sharpen about thirty saws a day and also keep them straightened. Saws often got bent when logs rolled or fell down hills. Dad did his work inside a building called the saw shack. There were long rows of saws. Each worker would have at least two saws. There was always another sharp one ready when hard knots and rocks dulled the saw teeth.

No more working in the rain for Dad. It rained one hundred twenty inches a year in Forks. Every morning two or three hours before daylight, workers would gather to get on a train flatcar or a speeder, which took the workers to different areas.

No matter how bad the weather, everyone had to work. There would be twenty or thirty extra people there every morning wanting a job. If someone didn't come, someone else had their tools and their job.

The big woods' boss was called the Push and he always had a helper who was called the Bullbucker. This man had to see that the big boss' orders were carried out. It was a tough job, because the big boss gave tough orders. The Bullbucker had to be a lot tougher than he wanted to be.

My dad talked to the boss about my going to work bucking logs. That was cutting logs in lengths without splitting or cracking them. Now, a good saw filer would keep the workers happy. I am sure that because of him they said they would give me a try.

They gave me a job of windfall cutting. The trees that had blown over had to be cut into logs or they would hang up on other logs when being pulled to the Donkey engine for loading.

Two men felled the trees, and one or two buckers cut them into logs. For this, the fallers got thirteen cents a thousand board feet in the logs. For bucking into logs, they paid nine cents a thousand board feet to the bucker. For windfalls, the price for the bucker was twenty-three cents per thousand board feet.

The bucker had to cut the roots or stumps off these windfall without pay, and windfall trees fell through trees and had some awful bends in them which could pinch or break a saw if you didn't know what you were doing. These windfalls were sometimes very dangerous, as when you took the spring out of them, they could jump sideways and break your legs or cripple you in many ways. Timber fallers used a saw a little narrower than buckers. Their saws were from seven-and-a-half to fifteen feet long.

I was sixteen when I came to work and got my first set of tools: a seven-foot-long saw, three wedges in a cutoff gunny sack and a ten-pound sledgehammer. The sledgehammer handle was stuck through the gunny sack. You threw the sack of wedges over your shoulder with the hammer handle in the front to balance the wedges. The saw went on top of the wedges and was held by the handle by the worker. Then, you picked up the long-

handled ax and the oil bottle in your left hand, and you were on your way. You may just have gone to a flatcar close to camp and jumped on it and then rode out for miles with a train engine pulling a string of log cars to a location where you were assigned a set, which was a blazed area. The two-man team of fallers and two buckers would work until the set was finished.

Seldom were they happy with the set they were given. You could always see another place that looked better, and they would wonder if the boss gave his friends better trees to work on.

There was a wonderful old character named Ivor Iverson. He might have been only fifty-five years old, but he seemed like an old fellow to Wayne Hathaway and

Elk calf waiting for its mother to return

Each September the male elk fight for control of the cows

me. I was sixteen and Wayne may have been seventeen.

We later found out that Ivor always liked a tough job, so he may have offered to get us started right, or the boss thought it best. Ivor liked to show us how to solve any problem that we might have. If someone came in to camp with a story of a windfall across a canyon that couldn't be cut up, Ivor wanted to go cut it. He wouldn't make much money doing it. He always said that he didn't care about making a lot of money; all he needed was just enough to buy the salt for his meat. The boss, therefore, always gave him the tough jobs, and that made Ivor happy.

The boss assigned the three of us to the job of cutting windfalls across a survey line of a new spur line of the railroad. We sometimes started right from camp following the survey blazes and cutting windfalls. When finished cutting our trees, we walked past the other two buckers and started on the next windfall. Sometimes we crossed canyons and had tough trees, but Ivor was always there to teach us how to handle a new problem. Sometimes we had to build platforms to get up to the tree, and figure which cut to make first to take out the bend in a tree. We already knew most everything we needed to know to start, but he always had his eyes on us and knew what problems lay ahead.

It was fun because it was always wild, and the forest was beautiful with only a blaze here and there. We always had a fire to eat our lunch by. We each carried a two-gallon water bag that we filled up each morning from any creek we crossed.

When spring came, the logging camp shut down. There was no other work. I don't remember if the loggers were on strike or what. One day, Ivor came looking for Wayne and me. He told me he had a job for the three of us. It was for the U.S. Forest Service. We would be clearing and building trails in the forest. On the Bear Creek Trail, for one mile all the trees had been blown over and needed to be sawed and moved off the trail. Ivor said the Forest Service had balked at hiring us kids when so many families were out of work, but he stuck with his demand that he wanted us two kids to work with him. He guaranteed that we could do the work, and that they would be happy with the results.

This was like a dream come true to us. We had to carry our camp on our backs, and the work was hard, but we liked to work. There was always good fishing within a short hike, and we fished some every night. Ivor loved to fish, too, and it helped having fish to eat.

We couldn't keep up with Ivor in eating sometimes. We had large cooking pots from the Forestry Service for big crews. Ivor would cook a pot of rolled oats that would take us two weeks to eat; we had it in the form of cold mush for breakfast and supper. Wayne and I eventually had to quit, but Ivor would finish it by himself. Wayne and I would do more fishing so we didn't have to eat cold mush.

We would see cougar tracks and cougar droppings on the trail, and Ivor would say that there was no need to worry. It

When a black bear finds a dead elk, it will help fatten him for the winter.

was when we couldn't see cougar droppings that was the time to start worrying. He didn't have to explain that to us because we knew the cougars hadn't been eating and were hungry.

We worked on trails along several rivers and creeks that crossed mountains. It was very hard work, but we enjoyed it, and the Forest Service was happy with what we had done. The wage was three dollars a day, but because of the amount of people out of work, they paid two dollars and twenty-five cents a day to make more

jobs. Our trail job was over for that summer. My father and all the other loggers were still out of work, and there was no work in sight.

Soon after moving to Forks, my dad bought part of a farm. We were always trying to find a way to help make a living. We still thought mink farming might help, so we bought seventy-five more mink from one of the homesteads on the Hoh River. The rancher was Charles Lewis and his wife, Marie. We paid what we could when we got the mink and paid the rest of the cost of the mink when we could. We had to build a lot of pens for these animals. This was extra work for weekends and evenings after our work in the logging camps when they were operating.

One day, I saw a bobcat kitten. I watched it and saw it go into a mountain beaver hole. I plugged up the hole, and as mountain beavers have more than one den exit, I then covered up all the holes I could see. I started to dig out the hole in the ground where the cat had entered. With a stick I dug out about fifteen feet of the tunnel, and finally caught the bobcat kitten, wrapped it in my jacket and carried it home. Then I began to tame him.

The Game Department gave bear cubs and orphaned deer fawns and elk to us. The Department usually killed these orphans, as there was no place to put them. I liked to

A wildcat watching

have these animals and enjoyed them very much. We soon had more orphaned elk calves. Each new animal meant we had to build a house and a pen for it. We did well with the mink and soon had two hundred female mink. It was a lot of work, but we felt like we were getting an alternate way of making a living instead of logging. When the time and tide were right, we would go to the ocean with nets to catch smelt. We used them as food for the mink. Quite a few people would come to see the mink and our other animals.

The Game Department people have always been good friends of ours. We have always been very careful never to break any of their laws, and have never had any trouble with the Game Departments. The Game Wardens always stopped at our home with their bosses and friends to see our animals.

Up the river valley there were homesteaders who had worked hard all their lives to build a house and clear a little land. Many homesteaders had left, but the ones who remained were self-sufficient and could take care of themselves and their families. Some of them knew little about what was going on in the world, and may not have cared. They had all they could do to take care of their own needs.

There were no roads to their houses. They packed everything on their backs from Forks. There were stories told of them, like the homesteader who came to Forks and saw a movie. When he returned to his home, he said he had been to this place where they squirted pictures on the wall.

I always had the utmost respect for these homesteaders and wished I hadn't been a little too late to be one. I later knew that I had been born at the very best period of time. I have lived from the horses and wheels to seeing man walk on the moon. Most of my life I could walk through the forest and along unspoiled rivers knowing that the next generation would not be able to do this.

Although the future generations will think it is still very wonderful, I can see that I saw the wilderness at its best. I wouldn't have missed the hard times for anything in the world. I have often heard people say, "I wish they hadn't shot off the buffalo." Or, "I wish the miners hadn't damaged the land." Or, "I wish the farmers hadn't fenced the prairies." It always seemed to me that if everything hadn't happened exactly as it did happen to change the distribution of people in taming the west, our parents and grandparents could never have met, and we wouldn't have been born. Other people would be living in the west instead of us, so I am glad things happened as they did.

We now live in Olympic elk country

A BOY AND HIS DOGS

My first cougar hunt with dogs was in the Dungeness River country. I had sent for a dog that was advertised in a magazine. The dog came by freight. He was very old and I later found out he wouldn't bark treed if he did chase something up a tree. I also had a young dog with me that had no experience.

I drove up as far as the road went to a homestead. It belonged to Dad Schmith. He had a very nice log cabin on Knob Hill above the Palo Alto area. There was a foot of new snow. I knocked on Mr. Schmith's door to ask where the Dungeness Trail started.

A voice called, "Who is there?" I could hear him coming to the door, and as it opened, three or four birds flew out from under the eaves and fluttered around Mr. Schmith's head, and he started talking to them, asking what they wanted. I asked him where the Dungeness River Trail left from his place on up the river. Mr. Schmith told me where it was and asked me to come in and get warm and talk a little, so I did.

He told me that as a young man, he traveled on the seas and spent time in Hawaii. He had come from there to the Olympic Peninsula and built the cabin, then returned to Hawaii and married and brought his wife back to the homestead. He now had several sons and grandchildren in the area.

There was a fireplace in the house, and it seemed very comfortable. On the mantel above the fireplace was a human skull. He told me that the skull was his uncle's. I didn't ask him why he had it, and he didn't tell me.

When I asked if he had seen any cougar tracks around, he said yes, that once one had walked right through the other end of his field. I thanked him and went back outside where I had left my dogs and started up the trail. I was just about out of sight of his house when I saw a cougar track cross the trail. These dogs had never smelled a cougar track. I finally got them interested enough to follow it, and they finally started to bark.

The snow was heavy on the brush and trees. As I pushed past tree limbs, the snow kept falling down my neck. The dogs quit trailing and barking by the time I came up to them in a canyon. The cougar had crossed the canyon on a small tree, and the dogs had given up and didn't want to go any further. They were as cold as I was, so we went home.

Wayne Hathaway and I went up the Elwha River to talk to Grant Hume.

Lloyd and cougar killed with bow and arrow.

Grant lived farther up the river than anyone. He had a nice cabin on a bench with a cleared field between the cabin and the river and plenty of windows to look out toward the river.

We used to sit there and watch the deer. Most any evening there might be a hundred deer in the field. The wolves were gone by now. The last of them were killed in the 1920's. Grant told us he had caught several wolves. He said the State of Washington had put a bounty on wolves and cougars in 1905, and also passed a law against killing elk with a gun. The elk were about gone at that time after years of hunting.

Grant told us the elk had increased and there were almost too many now. We sometimes camped near the river for a week and fished.

My father, his brother, my Uncle Steve, and I took a trip to Mount Olympus and then over the High Divide and out to the Sol Duc Hot Springs. That started me traveling in the mountains whenever I had time.

Another time, I went up to Blue Mountain to see A. B. Cameron. He showed me a hide from a wolf he had killed. That is the only Olympic wolf hide I had seen up to that point. This must have been about 1932. Three years before that, the last wolf was bountied in the Olympics. The last wolf was shot and bountied on January 17, 1929. One wolf hide is now in the Sequim museum.

The logging started up again. Ivor, Wayne and I went back to our jobs until next winter.

In our spare time, we went fishing. This was a great place to fish or hunt. There were four great rivers within five miles, and we could go fish a while after work in the summer.

I found another friend from Port Angeles. He was just the same age as I. His name was Hollum Hunley. He had friends in Forks that hunted wildcats, coons and cougars with dogs, so I met them and was invited to go hunting with them. They went out at night. The dogs would chase something, but never get it up a tree.

The next time we saw them, they gave us a story about how we should have been there the night before, as they had caught wildcats. We kept going but finally gave up. I decided they must have been chasing coyotes or bear.

I was interested in getting a dog, and I heard of two young dogs for sale. A man by the name of Lynn Sproul, who lived about ten miles from Forks, had them. They were beautiful dogs and looked fast. They ran deer every time he let them out, so he hadn't let them out any more. These dogs were one year old. They were white with red spots. I had to have them, so we made a deal. I borrowed the money from my Uncle Claude.

The first dog I bought was named Dot. She was beautiful - black with a brown dot the size of a penny over each eye. I had her trained so she didn't run rabbits any more and would bark on a cat trail. One of the new dogs, Drum, was a little shy and didn't like to be scolded. I soon had him so he would look worried when there was a fresh deer or elk track. I led the two new dogs until I could let them loose on a cat or coon track.

Everyone in those days wanted the cougars to be controlled. People gathered up their nickels and dimes to pay small bounties. Some clubs and organizations paid ten or fifteen dollars bounty on cougars. Washington State was talking about putting a bounty on cougars and wildcats.

The Washington State Game Department and all of the people in the area agreed that a cougar would kill at least one deer or elk a week.

Finally, the Game Department decided to establish a bounty of twenty-five dollars on cougars and five dollars on bobcats. The bounty was gradually raised to fifty dollars and later to seventy-five dollars on each cougar. I liked the deer and elk as well as cougars and knew that the cougars should be controlled, as that would save the deer and the elk. There has always been a good population of cougars, even after the bounty was put into effect.

The logging camps weren't busy, so I kept training my dogs. I knew there were cougars up the Dungeness River near Sequim, so I came with Chet Binkie, who was the son of the Game Warden in Port Angeles. We would go hunting and never get any cats or cougars, but we had hopes.

Wayne and Chet took me to a restaurant in Port Angeles where hunters hung out. When we got there, a few sportsmen were there, as well as some well-dressed people. They were making a fuss over the best cougar hunter in this area. They called him "Cougar Mike." Wayne and Chet knew him, and had visited him at his cabin on the Elwha River. When he saw Wayne and Chet he asked if we had caught anything. He said he'd heard that we'd been hunting on the Dungeness. We had to admit that we had been hunting there, but that we didn't get anything.

Mike gave us the ha ha, and said that he had an old cur dog at his cabin that could catch more than our dogs could. Then he turned to these dressed-up people, and they all laughed. Wayne and Chet didn't have a dog, and the remarks may not have bothered them. I had my dogs, and I loved them. I knew they didn't know much, and neither did I. Mike's remarks hurt me very much. I didn't say anything to Mike, Wayne or Chet, but I thought, "Mike, some day I will show you."

The day came in a couple of years when he hated himself for having said those words. All the time I was training my three dogs I had a burning in my chest, waiting to show Mike. He was a nice guy who couldn't help but show off that night.

Cougar

Hunters usually love their dogs. There was an old man with a three-legged dog that was up before the judge for hunting deer. The Game Warden knew this old man and his dog hunted deer. The judge was inclined to let the old man off. He said, "I don't believe this old man and his three-legged dog are going to hurt the population of the deer any." The old man jumped up and said, "That three-legged dog is the best deer dog in this country." The judge said, "If that is true, ten days in jail." The old man later said, "I don't mind the ten days in jail, but I can't stand anyone talking against my dog."

One time there were two young men who came to work in the logging camp. They moved into a small cabin on the edge of town. There were rumors that these men couldn't be trusted. There were other houses scattered through the woods and a few along the road.

When a person wanted to ship packages, they left them at a wide spot in the road and a bus would come by once a day and take them to the next town, and later they would receive the freight bill. Packages started to turn up missing, and people thought it might be the two young men in the cabin that were taking them. Three men decided to find out. They got a suitcase and put a wildcat that had just been caught in the suitcase. They put it at the place on the road to be picked up by the bus. They knew the men would be coming from work soon, and they did come. The car stopped and one of the men got out, picked up the suitcase, put it in their car, and away they went on down the road.

The three tricksters, who had been watching, got in their car and followed at a distance. After driving down the road a ways, the car with the suitcase in it started swaying from side to side and ran straight off the road and into a ditch. The doors on the car flew open on both sides, and the men ran out with the wildcat right behind them.

The men in the second car, who'd been watching, stopped and asked what happened. The young men knew they'd been caught and said, "If you fellows will help us get the car back on the road, you will not see us anymore." The three men said, "Okay, if you are leaving, we will try not to tell anyone about this until tomorrow." After helping to get the car back onto the road, they watched it go to the mens' cabin. The two men quit their jobs and left the area that same night.

The logging was on and off during the Depression. I kept on taking my dogs out, and they got better and better. Dot no longer was interested in chasing rabbits, deer or elk. The other two dogs, Drum and Bugle, were great after they got on the right track, but not too trustworthy. Now I could let Dot loose in deer country and sometimes let Drum with her as long as I let him know I was watching him.

Whenever I saw deer or deer tracks, I would caution him. He got so that if he found deer, he would come

15

back and walk with me for a minute, and I petted him and told him how nice he was.

Bugle was slower to become trustworthy, so I always led him until Dot started on a track. Sometimes Drum would find a track he knew was okay to chase, and would start barking. I was a little nervous until Dot got there to check on the track. If she started to bark, I felt relieved and let Bugle go. At this time I was letting the dogs chase raccoons.

There was no work. It was November, 1937. I was twenty-one. The dogs were doing great, but they would not quit until they caught what they were after. I didn't lose any time by the dogs' running deer, elk or bear. During the month of November, we caught sixty-three raccoons, ten wildcats and three cougars, and I was ready for the cougar bounty that had been established.

There were no jobs at this time. Chet, Percy Conrad and I decided to go up the Dungeness.

We could dig up only enough money to buy a little dried food like beans, rice and flour for pancakes. We knew we could get some kind of meat to go with this food. When we went up to the mountains and got hungry, we ate any kind of meat. If we got a cougar, bobcat or squirrel, we ate them and made soup out of the bones.

Sometimes we found a deer that was freshly killed by a cougar we were chasing, and we ate the deer first. The dogs could eat the cougar or bobcat. If the deer wasn't good fresh meat, many times we would start right in on the cougar carcass and let the dogs eat the deer. There is no better tasting meat than cougar meat. It has no wild taste. Bobcat was our last choice, and we always made stew out of it.

We each had a pretty heavy pack, and it was raining all day. Our packs and sleeping bags were wet. It was about dark when we arrived at Cougar Creek on the north bank of the Dungeness River. There was a little lean-to by the creek. A deer hunter must have made it. It was made of large pieces of bark, arranged like shingles on the roof. The lean-to was only four feet high in the front and two feet high in the back - just enough to sleep in.

We built a fire and decided to dry everything out before we thought of sleeping. Percy was adjusting the bark on the roof so it wouldn't leak. We ate something and went to bed. It was still raining, and we soon found out that Percy's job on the roof wasn't bad on his side, but water ran through everywhere else!

We got up, rebuilt the fire and gave up sleeping for the night. We did stay warm and comfortable. The rain changed to snow, and by morning there was ten inches of new snow on top of the old snow. We ate our breakfast and started up the trail with our packs. As we went up the river, both the old and the new snow got deeper. We were wading in hip-deep snow, and it was getting deeper as we climbed. We knew we had to get up to McCune's cabin, which was three miles farther up the river. The snow got so bad that we would lose the trail. Several times we had to go into the river to avoid the deep snow and wade up as far as we could go, before climbing back out again. I could see that everyone was getting tired, and I wondered if we could get to McCune's cabin. I knew we would be in bad trouble if we couldn't find it in the dark.

We kept going in and out of the river. The young trees were all bent over to the ground with snow. I was the only one of us who had been to McCune's cabin, so the responsibility was all mine. We didn't find any of the trail again. After about three hours of floundering in increasingly deeper snow as we went upriver, we came to the cabin. I'd known we

Cougar

were close, but it was hidden in the trees, and hard to see. Luck was with us, and we came out exactly to where the cabin was.

I knew where the key was, and we got in quickly, lit a candle and started a fire. What a relief! Chet and Percy were beginning to think there wasn't a cabin.

We opened up our sleeping bags and hung our clothes all around the cabin to let them dry. By daylight, everything was dry, so we went to bed and slept all day. It was time to go to bed again, so we did.

We stayed holed up at the cabin for a few days. I knew there would be no deer or cougar here with this much snow. We did catch a bobcat and made a stew.

In a few days the wind began to blow, and the snow came off the trees. All night we could hear heavy thuds on the roof as chunks of snow came off the trees, each one knocking more snow off the trees as it fell through the tree limbs. The snow that fell off the trees packed the snow on the ground and we could get around much better. A mile straight up the hill from this cabin was my secret cave under a house-sized rock. I knew of two families of cougar kittens that had been raised there. There was too much snow to climb the hill now, but I always thought of that cave when I was near. In the big cave under the rock were always new bones to look at.

We decided to move on down the river to a Forestry lean-to river camp. One side was open, but it was a nice place to stay, and there would be less snow.

From this river camp we caught a cougar. This cougar had just killed a deer. We let the dogs eat all they wanted. Percy wanted to go home, so we packed up.

We dressed out the cougar and decided to take him out in one piece. Our load was much less now, with dog food all gone and most of ours as well. We made two packs and kept trading off carrying the cougar. It started to rain and the snow was melting fast.

When we got back to Port Angeles, we hung up the cougar. Chet and I skinned him in their woodshed, and we left him to hang. We both stayed at Chet's house until we had eaten the cougar. The dogs got the bones and scraps, as well as some of the good meat.

Lloyd and successful hunt with dogs Dot, Bugle and Drum

17

DAD'S FIRST AND ONLY COUGAR HUNT

One day I got up early to go hunting on the south fork of the Hoh River. This is beautiful rain forest country, with moss hanging on trees and covering the ground. The dogs always stayed within fifty yards or so as we were traveling through the forest, and I watched them. I could quickly see when they smelled a track, and I had a good idea what kind of track it was. They might have their noses up in the air and smell something on the wind and start in that direction. I can be quite certain if they smell a dead animal that may be a cougar kill.

Sometimes, they can smell cougar tracks that are quite far away and they will be excited, or more often they will smell the ground and ends of bushes, and their tails will be wagging as they smell any track that they know is okay to follow. If they smell other tracks, they are curious but will look up to let me know they are not going to chase this one. They even let me know by their disinterest if a human has walked there lately.

After hiking through the woods for three or four miles, the dogs found a track that they were excited about and followed it. While following behind the dogs, I looked for cougar signs on the trail.

I could see where three cougars had made cougar scratchings in rotten wood by a fallen log. Cougars will urinate in moss or rotten wood or in a trail and make a scratch. They make this scratch using both back feet. Standing on all four feet, they slide their hind feet back, one at a time, until they have two grooves in the ground side by side and piles of moss or ground at the back end of the scratch. Altogether the scratch may be only a foot long. It is a way for cats to leave messages for others to follow.

As there were three fresh scratchings, I could tell there were three cougars and they were full grown. One was probably a female in season, and the other two would be males following her.

After following the tracks for two miles, the dogs' barking suddenly became a steady roar, and I knew they had come to the cougars and were at a fast run. I saw that the cougars had killed a deer and her fawn and had been eating on them. After about a half mile of running, the dogs started to tree bark.

Tree bark is a steady and shorter bark that says, "We got him up this tree." As the dogs barked treed, they were looking up the tree, and most of the time could see the cougar. If they cannot see the animal, they will smell the tree as high as they can and prove to themselves that it went up that tree. I shot this cougar with my pistol, and the dogs took off because they knew there were two more.

After following the dogs up the mountain, we got one more; then they were off on the third track. This cougar had more time, and it was two miles farther when the last cougar was treed. Now I had three cougars at separate locations to skin. Then I found out that I did not have my jackknife in my pocket. This is the only time I ever went hunting without a knife, and all I could do was go home and come back the next day with my knife.

My dad had never gone with me on a cougar hunt, and when I told him what had happened, Dad wanted to go back with me and help with the cougars. The next morning, Dad and I went back to the rain forest, waded the Hoh River and went up the south fork of the Hoh to each cougar, skinned them and brought the hides back across the river to the car.

My dad really enjoyed the trip, and I have always been glad that he went. Dad had worked in the woods and hunted most of his life, but had never seen a cougar in the woods except for these three. I showed him all the cougar signs and tracks and the dead deer as we traveled. As usual, I went to the Game Warden and checked in the cougars. It would take two weeks before we would get the bounty money for them, and we always needed it.

Because of forest fire dangers in summer, the logging camps shut down during the hottest days. Sometimes they would go on what is called the "hoot-owl" shift. That meant starting early in the morning, about four or so, and ending at noon or soon after. The hoot-owl shift was a safety measure that assured that most of the workers were out of the woods at the time of the greatest danger. Fire watchmen would stay on the job and watch for fires that might start.

Woods workers all have two-gallon canvas bags for drinking water. Canvas bags are used because clear glass water jugs can start a fire if the sun shines on the jug of water. It works like a magnifying glass. Any size of clear glass bottle is a fire danger if the sun shines on it.

Lightning storms start more forest fires than any one thing. Forest fires were always bad news for the loggers. They had to stop work and go fight the fires. The fire might be a hundred miles away, but if Forestry officials are looking for fire fighters, you have to go help put the fire out. They did not pay much for fighting fires, so you had a cut in your pay.

Sometimes you worked hard fighting fires. It was always a long day whether you were working or waiting in trucks for the wind to change.

Forest fires burn best and fastest uphill, and the heat makes its own wind as it rises up the hill. The fire may be burning up the hill on both sides of a canyon; then you can get trapped in between the ridges on each side.

During a very hot fire, whole tree limbs will float through the air, still burning for half a mile or more. When the burning limbs come down, they start a new fire. Limbs land in other trees or dry snags and keep on burning. The snags that are burning are cut down as soon as possible to stop the flying sparks from starting more fires.

When you go to work on a fire, the boss may give you the job you do best. A timber faller would cut down burning snags and trees while others would dig fire trails and start backfires to hold the fire from spreading, thus allowing it to burn itself out. Then people came behind with fire hoses and water. Some carried water on their backs. It may take weeks of work to get the fire out, and there will be underground fires smoking for a long time.

When the fire is out, everyone is free to go back home and to the job he was on before the fire.

The logging camp would have signals, like when a fire started or if there was an accident. When a worker was hurt bad or killed, the Donkey engine would blast three loud whistles over and over again. It could be heard for miles around, and the men would take their tools and leave the woods. The camp would shut down for the rest of the day.

Cougar

19

MY DOGS TAUGHT ME MANY THINGS

My dogs taught me to know many things about cougars, bears, deer, elk and other animals of the forest. They made it possible for me to spend most of my time in the forests and mountains. They forced me to learn a lot about taking care of myself in all kinds of country, weather and situations.

When there was no work to earn money, I had to hunt cougars for bounty. That meant I had to go it alone or it wouldn't pay expenses. I had to stay with the dogs and go where they went, across rivers, mountains and canyons. The dogs and I were a team, and we depended on each other to do our part. Every day we learned something. It might be another hollow stump to spend the night in or a log we could cross a river on. The wild animals knew these things, and the dogs following their tracks taught me to use them, at that time and in the future.

There were times when the dogs didn't come back with me, and I knew they had a cougar treed. I could hear them barking at the tree and knew they would be waiting for me, so I would get my light and go find them.

It happened sometimes that I couldn't find the dogs that night, and once it took two days to find them. By that time, they were lying down at the foot of the tree and only barked once in a while. Their voices were hoarse and could not be heard at a distance. They knew I would keep trying to find them. The cougar would still be there on a limb. If there was snow, I could always find them, but without snow, their tracks were hard to follow. And, there was no way I could know what hill they may have gone over. I had to keep on looking. Eventually, I would find them, or they would find me.

One time, to shoot a bobcat I had to climb a big tree in the dark, and I had only the light of a candle to guide me. In the forest the nights are very dark, and sometimes I couldn't see, so I had to feel my way through the woods.

I had a dog with a lot of white on it, so at night I would follow her when I was sure she was on the trail that led back to camp. I knew she would show me the way back. I was without any kind of light, and the dog knew I was depending on her to guide me. She would walk just ahead of me until we got to our camp. If it hadn't been for her, I would have had to build a fire and spend the night in the woods.

I know my parents worried when I went off alone. There were times when I was gone for a week instead of a day, and even two weeks. Once I was gone for a month, and I was never able to get word to them because I was in the wilderness far from any houses.

Almost always before I left home, I would have a feeling that I might stay away for quite a while, and I warned my folks to expect me when they saw me.

If the dogs were after a cat, I often did not get back to my camp until late. If they finally treed a cat or cougar, I would build a fire and stay until morning.

There were times when I got back to camp and went to bed. If the dogs lost the track, they might come in later that night and they'd be tired out. When it was very cold, my best dog, Dot, would sneak down into the foot of my sleeping bag, and I might not know it until morning. That was something she learned to do on a very cold night. I had lost the dogs on a track up on a very rocky mountain. This was one of the few times I couldn't stay with the dogs, as it was too dangerous for me without a light. I wished the dogs had quit the track and come back to camp with me. I felt bad and guilty that I had come back to camp without them. I built a fire and dried out. It was very cold, so I got in my sleeping bag to keep warm. I didn't sleep because I was worrying about the dogs getting in trouble up in that rocky area. My dogs came in late that night, so I got up and put Dot inside my sleeping bag and let Bugle and Drum sleep on top of the sleeping bag. I built up the fire and kept it up all night to help the dogs stay warm. Dot never forgot how warm it was inside the sleeping bag.

One time on the Sitkum Ridge I found a big bull elk that was all tangled up in a large roll of Forest Service telephone wire. He had gotten into this wire on a trail which had a telephone line along it. This was an unused roll of wire that the elk had found, and he must have been playing with it. He was all tangled up and tired out. It took me several hours to untangle him. I didn't have wire cutters, so I had to take my hatchet and a rock to flatten the wire enough to break it into many pieces. The elk was so tired that he got used to me and just lay down. I was able to keep trees between us part of the time. When he was free, he got up and went away. I had tied my dogs up earlier so they would not get hurt.

Another time, I came upon two bull elk who had been fighting. Their horns were locked together. One elk was dead, and the other bull could not get loose. He was standing and was very tired. I took my ax and chopped off the antlers of the dead elk. The other elk then freed himself, and I stepped behind a tree and then went on my way.

Several times a cow elk with her calf would chase a dog back to me, and that was scary. One time, two bull elk chased a dog, and the dog came to me. I yelled and jumped around. Both elk stopped close to me. I shot my gun a couple of times, but it didn't scare them. I was backed up to a rotten spruce windfall, and I got a spruce knot and hit one of the bulls in the forehead. He looked at

Sometimes one elk kills the other one

me for a minute, and then they turned and hurried away.

The dogs were in a bad situation. When an animal that they were not allowed to chase came after them, they would run back to me for protection and to show me that they wouldn't run after it.

The last of November, 1938 I was ready to take a trip to the Skagit to go cougar hunting. Before I left, I thought I would give my dogs a rest. Their feet were a little sore from icy snow and rocks. While they were resting, I decided to go up the Hoh River into the rain forest that I love. On the way back I would stop and visit a few minutes with John Huelsdonk. I had stopped there several times on my way to go coon hunting. John enjoyed telling hunting stories. He showed me a lot of pictures of his dogs and of cougar hunts. He was one of the early homesteaders on the Hoh River and had raised his family and sent them to college. I know it must have been a struggle.

That November morning, I just went on past the Charlie Lewis place. His was the last place before what is now the Olympic National Park.

I hiked on up the trail until just before I got to the Olympic Ranger Station. I saw a track in the snow. There was about a foot of new snow on top of the old snow. I immediately felt there was something special about that track. I thought of wolf; I was familiar with every kind of wild animal track in Washington. As I studied the track, I knew it was a wolf. I painstakingly brushed the snow off of several selected tracks and got on my knees and blew the rest of the snow off until the track was hard and perfect. I carefully followed back on the tracks where he had crossed the river. Looking across to the snow on the other side, I could see where the wolf had entered the river. I then started following the trail that the wolf traveled. I was careful to walk to the side of the track, so I could do it again. I knew it was not just a big dog track. The back pad of a wolf is different from that of a dog. The wolf was heading toward the Bogachiel River. When he went under logs or close to large trees, the fresh snow had not covered the tracks and they were very clear. I followed until the tracks went over the ridge into the Bogachiel River. It was getting dark, so I built a fire and dried off and sat up by the fire, sleeping off and on until morning. I had eight big sandwiches in my pack, as well as a few other things. I went back to the Hoh Trail and crossed the river, following the track. It went downriver one-half mile above the river and finally around the ridge, where it crossed the south fork of the Hoh, and up the hill toward the Clearwater River. I built another fire, dried out and stayed until morning.

I came back to the south fork of the Hoh, then crossed the river to the trail and on down to the main Hoh River. I waded at the crossing above the Lewis ranch. When I got to my car, I went right home. I'd eaten all of my sandwiches and was very hungry. I wrote the date down in a book: November 18, 1938 - Wolf crossed the river below Olympic Ranger Station. It was believed that there were no more wolves after the 1920's. Was this the last wolf in the Olympics, or was this wolf a visitor from the Cascade Mountains or from Canada?

Since that time, we have raised more than one hundred wolves. I continually look at their feet. The same differences between dog and wolf footprints are always there to see. The back pad is much wider on the wolf, and the back corners of the pad curl out the back.

My dad was not making any money, as there was no logging. The bounty money that I was getting went to our family. I was glad to have something to do and to be able to contribute.

I always told my mother and father that I might be gone a day or more and not to worry, even if I knew I was coming back. I didn't want to worry them.

Wolf

22

FIRST COUGAR HUNTING WINTER

The bounty on cougar had been raised to fifty dollars each. At this time, the Game Department man where you lived had to recommend a hunter to the Game Warden in charge of the area you wanted to hunt. The winter before, a team of local hunters had caught nine or ten cougars. They worked for the Forest Service in the summer and left food in Forestry cabins in different locations on the Skagit River to use while cougar hunting in winter.

This part of the Skagit River is in the Cascade Mountains. It is about one hundred miles from the Olympic Mountains.

I loaded up the old car with my three dogs and packs and snowshoes. The Game Warden in my area gave me a letter to give to the Skagit Game Warden, Mr. Splane. The letter said that Lloyd Beebe was a good hunter and worthy of their support.

I drove to Sedro-Woolley about one hundred miles from home and gave my letter of introduction to Maurice Splane, the Game Warden. He thought I was pretty much of a kid, I guess. He said I could hunt up there, but Warren Presentien and Jay Martin would be hunting there and would catch all the cougars. They didn't go after bobcats, so he said I would be able to chase bobcats. I didn't say anything, but I knew my dogs were very good, and that I would do my part.

From Sedro-Woolley, I went to Rockport and boarded a train to Newhalem and Diablo. The City of Seattle got their electricity from the dam there.

From Diablo, there was an incline and a big flatcar with train wheels on it that had been used when the dam was being built. It was the same one that we rode on when I was twelve years old. When we got above the dam, we took the trail for Ruby Creek, about a six-mile walk. I had about an eighty-pound pack on my back.

Ross Dam was being built, and at the head of Diablo Lake up at Ruby Creek were Mr. and Mrs. Osborn. They were watchmen for the City of Seattle while the Ross Dam was being built. They were very nice and invited me to stay in their woodshed whenever I was near. It was open on one side and you could see through between boards on the walls. There wasn't any snow to see tracks in. That suited me just fine, as my dogs were trained to trail just bobcats and cougars. There were no coons in these mountains.

There was no snow, so the dogs and I started hunting and traveling, staying wherever we found ourselves at night. The weather was great and the dogs kept looking for cougar tracks. It made me feel good to see the dogs looking for tracks and deer hurrying out of their way. The dogs would stop and watch them, but didn't chase any, so I was very pleased with them. We caught several cougars.

One day the dogs were after a cougar high up in the rocks almost on top of a mountain. It was late in the afternoon when I heard someone calling. Then I could understand that someone was saying, "Can you help me?" I looked up and saw a boy on a steep rocky hillside. He was making his way down the hill, and I went up to meet him. He was about fifteen years old.

His father was one of the bosses on the dam-building project for Seattle City Light. The boy had climbed up the mountain, but was now lost and didn't know how to get back home. I could see he had come down the wrong side of the mountain. His name was Bob Baker, and he knew he couldn't get back home before dark, even if he'd known how to.

The dogs were barking treed on the rocky hill across the canyon. I couldn't go over to the dogs and have time to help Bob get home, so I knew I had to forget the dogs and that cougar for tonight. The boy had injured his ankle on a rock and it was starting to swell up. I helped him down through the rocks. When we got to the forest below, it was dark.

There was no moon. I was leading Bob down the hill telling him to duck under this limb or step over this log. We had no light, but I knew there was a trail on the hillside above the river. This part of the hillside was very steep and dark. I thought I would be able to feel the flat trail when we came to it. I had just told Bob to duck under some limbs when I stepped off a cliff. I don't know how far I fell, but I thought of a lot of things in my life. I know I turned at least two somersaults. I was just thinking, "I wish I would hit the ground" when I did.

23

I hit on a shale slide on my back, head downhill, and I was sliding downward. The rifle I was holding hit me over the eye. I slid to a stop and yelled to Bob not to take another step, and he didn't.

I scrambled up and around the rocks to the top where Bob was waiting for me. I guided him back down and around the rocks. After a while, I felt a flat place on the hillside and knew it was the trail. We felt our way down it for about six miles, and arrived at Bob's house just before daylight. There had been men looking for him, and some of the searchers were still out.

I found out I had blood all over my face. The rifle had cut me over the eyebrow. Bob's mother said I should take time to go to sleep on the extra bed they had, and I did. I woke up about noon and started back to find my rifle. I found it and I started up the mountain to try and find the dogs. Before I got very far, the dogs came on my track, so we went back to my camp, and I went to bed early.

Martin and Presentien were up the river nine miles waiting for snow. I knew it must be, because the dogs would run deer unless they could put them on a track in the snow.

I started catching cougars. I met the hunters at their cabin a couple of times in the next few weeks. They were still waiting for snow. I packed up and moved upriver from them and built a lean-to of boughs with the front open. Finally, we did get a snow. I was climbing the Hozameen Mountain Trail when I heard the dogs start barking. I didn't go up to see what they were running, because I trusted them by now. Dot always told me what kind of animal she was following when she barked on a trail.

When she followed a coon, she did a lot of squeaky barks. On bobcats, she just made clear barks. On cougar, she would bark in a quivering bawl as though she might have been a little afraid but also excited. I knew it was another cougar. Instead of climbing to them, I just followed them at the level that I was going and listened up the hill. We went several miles like that, and they were finally out of hearing.

I kept going in the same direction, and when I went over a ridge top, I could hear them all treeing, so I took my time getting there. I wanted to keep teaching them to stay at the tree longer.

In a couple of hours after I'd sat on the ridge and listened to them, I yelled so they could hear me. When I got over there, I saw there were two extra dogs. I knew they had followed me up the mountain and then followed the dogs and the cougar track. Believing Martin and Presentien would be along, I just waited until almost dark. I shot the cougar and started to skin it. Every so often, I yelled, in case someone was coming. I was finished when Martin came and answered my yell. He was surprised to see his dogs. Martin said, "You mean my dogs were here when you came?" I told him that all the dogs were there and that I didn't know how it happened.

It was about dark, and we hurried to get on a trail near the river to hike the five miles to my fir bough lean-to. He said, "You've been staying in this lean-to in this cold weather?" I said I had. I built a fire and got supper ready, and we ate it.

He said that he'd better get back, because his partner would wonder what had happened to him. I picked up the cougar hide and handed it to him, telling him that he'd better take the hide with him. He asked if I meant that he could have it, and I said yes. Then he told me that it would be their first cougar hide this winter. They had waited for snow so they could know that they were on the right trail. He said that he'd never seen a pack of dogs where not one of them would chase deer. I had gotten nine other cougars, and thought they might have gotten some had I not been hunting there. I was butting into their business. He left my camp very happy.

One day there was deep snow, and my dogs had crossed a river following three cougar tracks. It was a very cold day and getting dark. The dogs were still within hearing distance on the mountain across the river, and the track was fresh. I hated to get wet wading the river. I noticed a cable that was stretched tight from one big tree to another on the far side of the river. It was almost dark. There was a ladder on the tree that went up to the cable about twenty feet. The cable was much higher over the river. I decided to try to straddle the cable with my legs hanging down on each side of the cable and lying on my stomach and chest. I was able to pull myself forward on the cable. It was very shaky, but if I let my legs hang straight down and laid flat on the cable, my legs would keep me from falling off the cable. It was a risky thing to do, but the dogs had swum the river, and I felt I had to get across to join them.

When I climbed down the ladder to the ground on the far side of the river, I put my snowshoes on and started up the hill where the dogs were. I could not hear the dogs, but finally found cougar tracks and followed them.

This was a fresh track and there were only two cougars and no dog tracks. I kept following them. I had a can with a candle in it which gave me a good wide light to show me the way. I knew the dogs had treed one cougar somewhere, and these two cougars were leaving the area, so I went backwards on their tracks and finally found the dogs' track and one cougar.

The snow was so deep the dogs were having a hard time. The wind came up and the snow started falling off all the trees, and soon I could not see any tracks at all. After looking for hours, I decided that I'd better go back to the river, cross the trail and go up to the mine I had heard about.

I was cold and had snow down inside my clothes. When I got to the river, I waded across and got very wet. By the time I got to the trail, my clothes were frozen stiff. I could have started a fire, but thought I would be better off hurrying to the miner's cabin. It was three miles to the cabin, and when I knocked on their door they got up and let me in.

There were two old fellows there. They had me take my clothes off and put on some of theirs, boots and all. I stayed for an hour and went back to look for the dogs. The miners said they would dry out my clothes and have breakfast ready after daylight. I searched the rest of the night without any luck and returned for a breakfast with the miners. I didn't find the dogs for three days, at which time they gave up waiting for me and came back and found me.

We caught three cougars the next week.

One other day I was hiking around a side hill that had many little canyons. I heard a terrific noise and knew it was from a snow avalanche. I was in the bottom of one of the canyons. I started to run and scramble up toward the ridge between canyons. The noise continued as I reached the ridge. I could hear the trees being broken as the snow slide came down. I couldn't tell which canyon the snow was coming down, but I soon found out when the avalanche and trees came down the canyons on both sides of me. The trees were being pushed over and filling up the canyons. It went on by, about fifty feet from me on both sides. I knew the danger was now over. It had been very scary. I decided to go on down my ridge and see if I could get past the end of the slide. I did, and when I got to the river I waded across and stayed off the mountain for the rest of the day.

One time after traveling all day on a mountain in deep snow, I found a big fir tree lying on the ground. It was old and near the root end, about fifty feet of the log was three feet above the ground. It was dry and there was rotten wood underneath it. The snow was deep on both sides, but there was no snow under the log. I took my snowshoes off and prepared to stay. I cleared the snow near the log and built a fire. The dogs and I had a good place to spend the night. Sometime in the night I woke up. The rotten wood and bark under the tree was on fire. The dogs and I had to get out and stand in the snow the rest of the night. We did have a great fire to keep warm by.

A few days later, I woke up with a fire burning in my camp. This happened on the Skagit River at my lean-to made of fir boughs. It had been a hard day for the dogs and me. We had traveled in the mountains all day. There was a lot of snow, and I was on snowshoes. I was so tired I went to bed in my sleeping bag to rest a while before getting something to eat. Without meaning to, I went to sleep. When I woke up, the table and food were on fire. I had left the can with the candle burning in it hanging over the table, and when the candle burned down to the hole in the can, it fell on a cloth sack of beans and started the fire. What made it bad was that I had laid my snowshoes on top of the sacks of food, and they were all on fire along with my snowshoes. I got up and put the fire out, and decided to go back to bed. While I was in my sleeping bag, I decided I should repair my snowshoes in the morning as best I could and travel the twenty miles down the river and buy a new pair.

I returned a few days later with a new pair of snowshoes and a fresh supply of groceries.

I soon moved back downriver and went to Sedro-Woolley and got those hides checked and bountied. I knew my family could use the money by now. I arrived back in Forks and prepared to come back to the Skagit for another trip.

A LIFETIME OF FRIENDSHIP BEGINS

Hollum Hunley came over with Sigel Silcox, a cousin of his from Tennessee. As we talked, I found that Sigel was dying to go hunting with me. Hollum knew I didn't take people very often. Hollum told Sigel that he would have to run up steep hills, and find himself in trouble, and that I couldn't be waiting for him. Sigel said that he could run up a steep hill, so Hollum and I took him out to a steep hill through the brush and said, "Okay, show us you can run up that hill." Well, he sure surprised me. I could see he could do his share on a trip and might even help.

I decided to take a day and get acquainted with Sigel. We went out to the Hoh River and on to the rain forest, hiked around, and I showed Sigel the country. We stopped by John Huelsdonk's homestead. John got out his pictures to show us. I always enjoyed talking with these people. I knew they had done a lot of things that I would like to do.

Sigel had told me that he would like to talk to some Indians, so we went to LaPush before we went home. There were Indians there that I knew. Sigel got a lot of fun out of talking to the Indians, and we had a lot of respect for them.

I got Sigel outfitted in warm gear and gave him a pair of my snowshoes, and off we went back to the Osborn's wood shed that they'd told me I could use for shelter when I was hunting. Sigel was having the time of his life.

I had been cutting the wood from the trees by their house. Mrs. Osborn said that if I was going to keep sawing and piling wood for them, she'd like me to come to their house and have breakfast in the morning with them. She said that we needed a good meal at least once a day.

There was a Forest Service telephone in their house. Everyone listened in on it. Martin and Presentien had one in their forest cabin. At Granite Creek, a miner also had one, as did a man named Beebe.

Mr. Osborn and the other people listened whenever the telephone rang, and when Martin and Presentien were asked about cougar hunting, they would say, "We only got one cougar this winter." When someone asked what was the matter, they would say, "There's too much competition." It seemed the other people on the line were enjoying it all.

When we got a cougar and came back to the shed, Mr. Osborn would say, "I knew you would catch one after you ate all those pancakes this morning."

On one day, we were very late getting back. Both Mr. and Mrs. Osborn came out to see us when we finally returned, and saw we had caught six cougar that day. He could hardly believe his eyes. He said, "Boy, those pancakes of mine are getting more powerful every day." They both hurried into the house to tell everyone on the telephone line. It had been a terribly snowy day, and we decided to sleep in the next day.

We hunted for two weeks more, and then returned to Concrete and stopped to see my friend, Lloyd Seabury. When he saw how many cougar hides we had to check in, he wanted to take a picture. He got permission to hang the hides on the wall in the school gymnasium. Before we got all the hides on the wall, he said, "We are getting too many for a good picture." He said that seven would be just right. We had nineteen hides with us. After Lloyd Seabury got the picture, he said that he would send us pictures when they were developed, and he did.

We decided to take one day on our way home and hunt on the south fork of the Nooksack River. The dogs struck a track and took off. After about three miles, they started to bark treed. We could see this female had young kittens somewhere. The dogs finally showed us where the kittens were. We crawled down in a hole under a tree and caught two little kittens.

Now we had to find some milk for them. There was a logging camp with a cook staying there to watch the place until the logging operation started up again. I asked him about a couple of cans of milk. I paid for them. Something bothered me about the cook, but I was in a hurry. Later I remembered that the cook was the father of my good friend in Darrington, Kenneth Willmer. Then I felt bad I hadn't told him who I was, and asked about Kenneth.

An article about my hunt appeared in the Seattle Post-Intelligencer about this time. It read as follows:

26

COUGAR HUNTER BAGS 230-POUND ANIMAL
LARGE SPECIMEN KILLED IN SKAGIT

Concrete, April 25 - Lloyd Beebe, credited with being Washington's No. 1 cougar hunter, brought his 1939 total to twenty-three yesterday when he arrived from the hills with his pack of hounds and a 230-pound male mountain lion.

The cougar, an unusually large specimen, was killed on the south fork of the Nooksack River in Skagit County.

Cougars are listed among the most destructive of predatory animals, particularly depleting the ranks of wild deer, and hence the state game department pays a bounty for each one killed.

Sigel went to Seattle, and I said I would catch up. We were so close to my uncle and aunt's home that I decided to drive to Everson and see them. I knew they would love to see the kittens.

I drove to Aunt Cassie and Uncle Lex Morgan's house. My uncle had to have his picture taken with the cougars and dogs, and they all loved the kittens. While we were doing all this, Aunt Cassie had called Jessie Massey. Jessie's daughter, Catherine, wanted to see the kittens, so here came Catherine and her boyfriend. I hadn't seen Catherine since she was five years old and I was eleven when my folks had visited at their home. Catherine and her boyfriend left soon.

I was shy with girls, and I probably wouldn't have done anything about it, but Catherine's mother sent a

Sigel Silcox, Lloyd Beebe and hound dogs.

27

message inviting Norman Beebe, who I had picked up on my way, and me to supper. Norman was my age, but he was not shy with girls. When Norman and I went to the Masseys' for supper, he said, "I think I will ask Catherine to go to the show tonight." Something told me that I'd better act fast. I said, "No you are not. You get your girl from Acme and I am going to ask Catherine, and we will go to the show together." After eating, the four of us went to the show. I told Catherine I would be back to see her, and I did almost every weekend during the summer. I drove from Forks, a four-hour trip each way.

When I got back to Seattle, Sigel was waiting. It was in the evening, and I wanted to show the two cougar kittens to my sister, Jessie. She was going to the University of Washington. We stopped and showed Jessie and her roommates the cougars.

Then we went to a show in downtown Seattle. When that show was over, we went to one more show in another location. It was now late at night. When we got to the car, I could see the trunk of the car was opened, and one of the hinges was broken. The dogs were gone.

The dogs were somewhere loose in Seattle, but where to look? We had spent time in three locations, and had no idea of when the dogs broke out. All we could do was go to each place where we had parked and call. We went all over, up and down the streets. I left Sigel at one place and I just started hiking around Seattle. I called the Police and Fire Departments, but they couldn't help. These dogs had never been on a street in their lives. I just kept walking and worrying, calling and looking.

In the early hours of the morning, I was walking along a street, and I heard a hound barking. The barking and bawling was coming closer, just like when the dogs would follow me in the woods after we had lost each other. Soon they came running on my tracks like they were chasing a cougar. I was never so glad to see them! I'd had all kinds of thoughts as to what might have happened to them.

The dogs were just as glad to find me. They were all greasy from being under cars. I started back to where I had left the car. The dogs jumped in. I tied the broken door down, drove back and found Sigel, who was still looking for the dogs.

After relaxing a few minutes, we decided to go to the ferry and start for Forks. When we counted our money, we had only two dollars and eighty-five cents. The price of the ferry was two dollars and fifty cents for car and driver. We didn't have enough money for the extra passenger. The ferry was just coming to the dock. Sigel said he would lie in the back seat. I gave Sigel all the money I had and told him to buy the ticket, and I got in the back with our nineteen cougar hides and the two cougar kittens. Sigel covered me up with some cougar hides, got the ticket and drove on the ferry. We both went to sleep in the front seat of the car until we landed on the other side of Puget Sound. The price of a ticket to ride the ferry for a passenger was fifty cents, and I have owed that for most of my life. I can't remember ever not paying anything else in my life that I owed.

Catherine and I became good friends with Mr. Peabody who owned the ferry company a few years later. Mr. Peabody got a great laugh out of my story when I told him about owing him fifty cents.

Two weeks later, I was hunting cougars with my dogs on the south fork of the Nooksack River in about three feet of snow. I had a pack on my back and was using snowshoes. I wanted to cross the river, but didn't want to try to wade and get wet. There was a log about ten feet above the river. There was three feet of snow on the log, too. The snow was built out wider than the log. I knew the snow on the log might not hold me, maybe worth a try, so I got up on the log wearing my snowshoes. When I got out to the middle of the river, the snow caved in with me, and I found myself struggling in the river. I made it to shore soaking wet and three miles from my car. It was cold enough that my clothes froze immediately, so I knew I had to run to the car. When your snowshoes are wet, the snow sticks to them and they get very heavy. I broke a limb off a dead tree and kept pounding the ice off the snowshoes as I traveled. It was hard walking, and as I ran I even got warm, but my clothes were still frozen. When I got to the car, I built a fire at the side of the road and dried out.

My father's Uncle Charley lived with us as long as I can remember until he died in 1932. It was always my job to keep him supplied with Cascara bark. Uncle Charley always had a tin can on our stove with what he called Cascara tea. He said it always kept him regular. Every so often he would go to the wood stove and take a drink of his Cascara tea. He would smack his lips as if it was good. No one else could stand it.

Peeling bark from Cascara trees was another way to make a little money, but not enough to live on. The

Cascara trees were only three to five inches in diameter. I had to peel the bark and dry it in gunny sacks, then take it to the store. They would pay about two cents a pound for the dried bark. You had to wander around through the woods to find a tree here and there. It took more time to find trees than to peel the bark.

This was the Great Depression, but I thought it was just the way it was supposed to be.

The logging camps were still not working, so I decided to take the dogs up the Dungeness River to see if I could catch a cougar. Chet Binkie wanted to take a trip, so we both went. It was spring and the snow was gone over most of the area. We stopped in Port Angeles to visit with Wayne Hathaway, who was one of our best friends. Wayne's wife asked us to sit down and eat dinner which she had ready. I had just returned with quite a few cougars to be bountied, and everyone wanted to know all about the trip. After telling them about my winter hunt, I decided it was time to get rid of the burning feeling in my chest that Cougar Mike had put there when he belittled my dogs at the Sportsman's Restaurant, so I told Chet and Wayne about it. Chet and Wayne had forgotten about it, but as I mentioned it, they both remembered and laughed. Wayne and Chet started telling me about the trouble Mike had had to catch any cougars. They didn't think he had caught more than one while I had caught thirty-three cougars. I told them I could never say anything about it to Mike.

Chet and I went up the river to Roy Creek and made camp. We both felt like just lying around for a week or so. After a day of doing nothing, we took a hike and came home tired. Chet said that he felt like he could eat twenty pancakes. I said, "Chet, you know you can't eat twenty pancakes." He said, "If you will cook them for me, I will bet you a dime that I can eat twenty pancakes." I said, "I bet you can't."

We cooked them in a tin frying pan about eight or nine inches in diameter. When Chet got to sixteen, I was getting worried, so the next pancakes were thicker. Chet said that he could eat one more, but didn't believe he could eat twenty because we had run out of syrup to put on them, so I won. We never paid off dime bets either way, but didn't like to lose.

The next day, we caught a cougar and decided to go back to Port Angeles to Chet's parents' house.

Wayne found out that we were there and called and said that Cougar Mike was in town and wanted to take us all to the show tonight. We agreed we would like to go to the show. Mike and Wayne came, and we started out to walk to the theater. It was only three blocks.

As we walked along, Mike was very friendly in his talk and he had his arm over my shoulders like we were old buddies. After the show, when Wayne, Chet and I were together, I commented that Mike had been so friendly that night. Wayne said that the other night, he had told Mike that I had told him that I had an old collie dog that could catch more cougars than his dogs could. I hated to hear that he had told Mike that. I never would have done that.

Mike was shocked, too. Then Wayne reminded Mike of the time in front of a crowd of people that he had told us that he had an old cur dog at his cabin that could catch more cougars than my dogs could ever catch, and the laugh he gave me. Well, Mike couldn't believe he had ever said that to me. Wayne said, "Yes, you did. Chet and I were both there." Now I knew why Mike had been so friendly on this night. I still liked Mike, and I didn't feel that burning in my chest anymore.

A young Lloyd Beebe holding mink

29

A HILLBILLY MARINE

Many years later, Sigel Silcox wrote a book. When he sent one to me, he wrote under the title:

"A Hillbilly Marine by S. G. Silcox.

Don't let the shock get the best of you, Lloyd."

Sig, like me, would be the last person you would think of who would write a book. He may have had something to do with my starting to write a book. The following I took out of Sig's book:

> For any person who has not lived on the Olympic Peninsula, this is, in my opinion, one of the finest places to live in the United States. From Forks, in one hour, you can be out on the ocean fishing, up at a Hot Springs swimming (all year round), fishing in clear water streams, hunting bobcat, elk, deer, bear, and cougar, or on a trail with a horse or pack on your back climbing the Olympic Mountains. You can climb clear to the top of the glacier with flowers blooming through the snow and along the edge of the icecap. You can visit the Rain Forest. This is really a place of wonder for a person who loves outdoor life as I do. When I have stood on top of a mountain, whether it be the Olympic or the Continental Divide in the Rockies or Mount Baker and Jack Mountain on Skagit River north of Seattle, I could see as far as the eye can see, and there was not one sign of civilization. This is a feeling that I can never explain. Here it is God's World that no man has left his mark on.

> Shortly after arriving on Olympic Peninsula, I met a young man who became a friend. Today he is still a very good friend. Every time I go West, I always stop at his place near Sequim, Washington, and visit with him. His name is Lloyd Beebe. Lloyd was about five feet ten inches of solid muscle. He could carry the heaviest pack load of any man I ever met. He had tremendous chest muscles from bucking a saw, sawing logs in the woods. Lloyd and I became good friends, and we would often go cougar and bobcat hunting on Olympic Peninsula.

> One time I remember we visited an old man and his wife on the Upper Hoh River near where today the rangers have a tour to take visitors through the Rain Forest. This is a good spot to take pack horses and head for the Olympic Glacier. If I remember, it is about an eighteen mile walk. The man and woman we visited had moved from Council Bluffs, Iowa, and had carried everything they owned over the mountains on the backs of horses and on their own backs, fifty-one years before I met them. This was a remarkable visit, and we stayed for about three hours talking to him and his wife.

> At this time in 1938, they were still two or three miles from a road where wagons and cars could travel. They had raised four children and all had graduated from college. This man was truly remarkable. He showed us scars on his body he received while he and a dog were fighting a bear, bare-handed. He was known as the Iron Man of the Hoh, Hoh being the name of the river he lived by. The story is told of someone meeting him on the mountain while he had a cook stove on his back. They asked if it was heavy. 'Not bad,' he replied, 'but that forty-eight pound sack of flour in the oven keeps moving and throwing me off balance.'

Here on the peninsula I met the first Indians I had known. On the reservation at LaPush, it always rains. There is a story about the missionary trying to convert the Indians to Christianity. He was preaching to them about Noah and the flood. As he came to the part, 'and it rained for forty days and nights and the earth was covered with water' an old wise Indian stood up and said, 'That's a damn lie! I saw it rain for six months and we had no flood.'

One evening as I got home from working in the shingle mill, Lloyd Beebe came to get me to help him take a bear from the trap that a trapper had caught. It was a small bear, but the trapper was afraid to take it from the trap. Lloyd knew about the exact spot where the bear was, so, with hatchet and hunting knives, we started out. We parked the car and waded the river clear up to our armpits. The water was ice cold. We soon found the bear and began the process of removing him from the trap.

We cut poles about eight or ten feet long, and pressing the bear to the ground, we got his foot loose from the trap. Lloyd decided we should take the bear home and try to doctor his foot. After a long struggle, we had him tied and gagged. But, still a fifty-pound bear was very difficult to carry. When we reached the river, Lloyd wrapped the bear over his shoulders and waded the river. Try this some time with ice water up to your armpits and a fifty-pound bear kicking and scrambling on your shoulders.

The winter of 1938 was one of the greatest experiences of my life. Lloyd loved the mountains. He loved to hunt cougar and at that time the State of Washington had a bounty of seventy-five dollars for each one killed.

When my dad's father died, I sure missed him. It made me remember that my grandfather had made my first bow and arrows for me. When I was twelve years old, he had taken me to town to get a B.B. gun. We walked to town, as we didn't have a car. When we were looking at guns, Grandpa said that we should do this right and get a single shot .22, and that is what he bought.

He did so many things for me. As I grew up, he built dog houses for my dog, and when I was grown, he built big dog buildings with several inside dog houses for each of my hound dogs. The last one we moved from Forks to Sequim when we bought the farm. That dog house was in use almost as long as I had cougar dogs, and it kept reminding me of the good things my grandfather had done for me. I hope he knew how I appreciated all these things.

Lloyd and his hound, George

31

THE MOST IMPORTANT AND BEST
DECISION OF MY LIFE

We were back working in the logging camps again, and I thought it was time to ask Catherine to marry me. She said yes.

I had to ask her father about that. He dodged me for several weeks. When I did ask him, he said that he gave his permission. Catherine was only seventeen years old, but had cooked and worked for years at home. I thought a lot about it before I asked her. I knew I was honest and felt sure I would do everything to make it work out and do my part. I was sure it would last forever. I felt Catherine would be just as true and sure as I was. I always gave my dogs credit for leading me back to Catherine again. November 28, 1939, we got married, followed by a lifetime of agreement on each decision.

The logging camp was on strike at this time. I would have to go cougar hunting for a while. I kept working in the logging camps, too. Sometimes we got paid; sometimes we didn't.

We stayed at my parents' for a month or two. Then we rented a house in the town of Forks. It was a nice house, and it had all the furniture. An old couple owned it. They were teachers at the LaPush Indian Reservation about fifteen miles away. They came to town once every week or two to get groceries and would spend the night in a room in the back. They only charged twelve dollars a month for the house. They rented it to us because we didn't smoke or drink. They were very nice people. They may have been a little eccentric. For years, everyone in town had seen them in the house dancing with a broom for their enjoyment.

Lloyd and Catherine, married November 28, 1939

There was no work, but people at that time went to work when they got an idea. Our idea was to build a house of our own. We took my saws and ax and went to the woods to cut cedar shakes (also called split shingles). We found a great cedar tree that had been blown down and started cutting it into sections. The tree was seven feet in diameter. After sawing the log in thirty-inch lengths, we split it in blocks to be carried to the car, and we took home enough to make shakes for the roof and all the outside walls.

We had neighbors across the street who would sit in the window and watch what we were doing. If it was interesting, they would come over to the fence and get a better look. They were nice, and we liked them. They just didn't have anything better to do.

All the time that I wasn't working in logging or cougar hunting, I was splitting shakes for the house to be built. After splitting them, Catherine would square them up on a table saw. The cedar log had been perfect, and the shakes were too.

The neighbors watched as we worked. Everyone in town seemed interested and ready to help if there was something they could do. The County road crew offered to bring gravel. The cougar hunters that didn't hunt any more stopped to talk.

One day we came back from a trip to Port Angeles. We stopped in at a farm and bought a dozen live chickens. Catherine was a farm girl, and she was out in the yard wringing their necks to get ready to take the feathers off. When she looked around, there were all the neighbors leaning over the fence watching her. They had never seen anyone do that.

When we got all the shakes ready, we decided it was time to build our house. We had our house pretty well framed up and the roof on. All the frames for rooms were up with no boards on any of the partitions dividing the rooms. You could walk through anywhere: no boards on any walls outside or in. The windows, doors and fireplace were all wide open. I was working again now. It was summer, and we moved in so I could work every night and weekend. It wasn't too long before we had it all closed in. It was almost a year later that it was finished. It was a very nice house.

Catherine had three brothers. Ross was married to Evelyn. Hank was still talking about how he was going to rule the roost when he got married, and his wife would toe the mark. It never worked out that way. Kenneth was the youngest of the brothers. Everyone knew he would turn out to be the businessman of the Massey boys.

They sent word to us that Catherine's friends and all the Massey friends were anxious to have a charivari for us next time we came back to the Massey farm at Nooksack. They suggested we might as well come prepared and get it over with.

I guess there are people now who might not know what a charivari is. In those days anyone getting married would be given a charivari. All their friends and relations, and anyone who heard about it was welcome to join in. A big crowd would gather out of sight and be sure everyone was asleep. It is supposed to be a surprise, but people knew it would come some night. The crowd would start banging circular saws, wash tubs or anything that would make a big noise, hopefully scaring everyone until they all got up out of bed. Often they had charivaris when a couple finished a new home and moved in.

The people who were being charivaried were expected to have candy bars, cigars, anything they needed to make a party out of it. It was to get acquainted and to have fun.

We decided we had better go visit Catherine's folks and let everyone have their fun. The first night we got there, we all stayed up a little just to make them wait. We knew they had people spying on us. We turned out the light just like we were going to bed, and waited and watched out the big windows in the direction they would come from. We could see more cars than usual getting lined up about one-half mile away and a little behind a hill. There were cars coming and turning off their lights until they all got there.

Finally, cars began pulling out into a line and coming up the road, and we knew they would be here soon. We let them park and everyone got out and crowded around the house, and then started to make a lot of noise. We let them keep on with the noise for a while, then pretended to get up out of bed and go out and see what was going on. Everybody came into the house because there was food and goodies to eat. We all had a good time, and the people thought they'd surprised us. When we went back to Forks, we were relieved to have that over with. We had already had a charivari at Forks.

CATHERINE GETS HER WISH

There was one thing Catherine especially wanted to do. She had listened to so many stories of mountains and cougar hunting that she wanted to go with me. She'd had trouble with her appendix, and thought it might be a problem when we were in the mountains. A day or two later, she came home from town and said that she was getting her appendix out the next week. Dr. Ford was the only doctor in Forks. He came from where Catherine was raised, and had been their family doctor at Nooksack.

Catherine got her appendix out, and then she said, "Now I can go with you on a cougar hunt."

The first chance we had was when the logging camp was shut down. We started out for the Skagit River. We went to Rockport on the river. First, we went to see Mr. McGilvary, an old-timer who had a cabin above Ruby Creek. It was small, but a great place for us to make our headquarters for a month in the mountains. Mr. McGilvary was very nice, and he said that we would be welcome to stay in his cabin as long as we wanted to.

At Rockport, we got on the train for Diablo. The lift elevator that we could usually ride on was not working. The only other way was to put our packs on and hike up the mile-long steep trail to the top of the ridge.

When we started up the hill, there were two young men starting up just behind us. We got about halfway up when one of the men said that he would like to carry Catherine's pack the rest of the way up the hill.

We were going for a month. My load was heavier than Catherine's, but she, too, had a big load to carry. When the young man got Catherine's pack on, he was surprised. At the top of that hill, he gave the pack back to Catherine and said, "That is heavy, and if you ever have any kids, I would like to have one for a pack horse."

We hiked on up to where they were building Ross Dam and crossed the river and continued past Ruby Creek. We then climbed up to McGilvary's cabin on the hill facing Ruby Creek. The cabin had only one room, big enough for a bed, and there was a small space to cook our meals. It was a well-made cabin, and we were lucky to have it to stay in. There was plenty of dry wood cut and piled under the cabin. Mr. McGilvary had warned us about the dynamite and caps under the cabin.

We had the dogs with us, but this was to be a fun trip and vacation - a real honeymoon. The inside of the cabin was covered with newspapers, so we read all the articles.

The first few days, we looked over the country close to the cabin, with me explaining some of the stories I had told her earlier. By this time, Catherine was turning over a page or two of the newspapers on the wall to see and read what was on the other side.

We decided to go up Ruby Creek to the Forest Service barn and cabin at Granite Creek. There was a place for horses, and a small cabin on one end. That night we stayed there. I told Catherine about the two miners who had lived there when Sigel and I had stopped several times before.

The next morning, I got up early and took a hike up the mountain behind the cabin. When I got back that afternoon, Catherine had company. I had told her that Ole might stop in. He lived around the woods somewhere. Ole was a man that used to live at Forks several years before this. He was a logger.

One time after a drinking spree, he was walking along a street in Forks at night, and picked up a rock and threw it through the window of a house, hitting a little baby. He felt so bad when he sobered up that he said he shouldn't be around other people, so he came up here in the mountains and never went to town where people lived.

Ole came into the cabin and saw Catherine instead of me. He was so surprised that he started to back out, apologizing. Catherine said, "Come on in, Ole, Lloyd will be back pretty soon." I knew Catherine would have added some to the evening meal, so we all ate and had a long talk.

After a few days, we went back to McGilvary's cabin, which was our main headquarters. The next day, we started for the Canadian border where my brush lean-to was, but we would stay the first night at the boundary cabin.

The dogs started to bark on a bobcat track that was old, but I told Catherine to wait there on the trail for me, as I would not be gone long. It turned out to be many hours later after dark. I had been to the boundary cabin where I left the dogs. I found some dried apricots, so I took a handful of them; they sure tasted good. I filled my pockets with some for Catherine, and then I went back down the trail to get her.

We stayed there all night and ate more dried apricots, as there was a wooden box full. The next morning after daylight, we were going to eat more apricots, but in the light it was easy to see the worms all over them and in the wrinkles of the apricots, so we didn't eat any more.

This day, we went on upriver to my brush shelter to stay a few days.

The next day, we walked up the Skagit River trail to the Canadian boundary. All along the Canadian and U.S. boundary line there is a one hundred foot wide strip that is cleared of all trees and logs. This cleared strip of land goes up and over mountain peaks as far as you can see.

The next day I went hunting with the dogs. I warned Catherine to follow the river trail down to our camp because the upper trail was too rocky and dangerous. The trail was two hundred yards above the river at this place.

It was after dark when I got back to camp. Catherine was just building a fire, and I wondered why she'd waited so long to do so. "When did you get back?" She didn't tell me then, but confessed later that she'd ignored my warning and had taken the dangerous upper trail and had had a very scary time of it. She had gotten back to camp only a few minutes ahead of me.

The dogs had chased a cougar, and I could hear them barking treed from our camp. I wanted Catherine to come with me to where they were. She had heard the dogs as they came down the hill past camp and was expecting me. We traveled about one-half mile to where the dogs and cougar were, and sat down and watched them for a while.

We didn't have a good flashlight for seeing the cougar, but I was lucky, and we got it and carried it back to camp. It had been a long day for both of us, and after skinning the cougar and hanging it in a tree, we ate supper and went straight to bed.

The dogs' feet got sore from running on the rocks. We didn't have anything to make dog shoes out of except Catherine's new high-top leather shoes. She agreed that I could cut them up. I made dog shoes and tied them on the dogs. The first day, the leather stretched and the shoes came off and were lost. Years later, every once in a while, Catherine reminds me that I cut up her new shoes.

The next day, we cut the best meat off the cougar and fried it all up and put it in a package in the rafters. We used up the last salt we had cooking the meat.

The next morning we found that one of the dogs had climbed up and gotten the meat. We decided to go back to McGilvary's cabin.

We were hungry even as we started out, and when we got to the Forestry cabin with the wormy apricots, we shook the worms off and ate them anyway. Then we hiked nine or ten miles back to McGilvary's cabin and had a big meal before going to bed.

Next morning we cut wood to fill up the wood shed to pay for the wood we had used.

Catherine had turned over all the papers on the four walls of the cabin so she could read what the newspapers had to say on that side. She said she had the other side memorized.

Catherine said, "You know, tomorrow is Christmas." We went out and got a grouse and had our Christmas dinner. The weather got cold and we stayed around the cabin for a few days and read all the old newspapers on the wall.

We spent about a month on this trip and had a great time, but it was getting colder, so one day we got up very early to make the trip back home. The train left Diablo at 8 am, and we had ten miles to get there. We got up early and arrived at Ross Dam at 4 am. We came by flashlight. We found the bridge, but signs said it was closed because of ice. This was a hanging footbridge that spanned the Skagit River. We hesitated to wake up the watchman at that early hour, and sat down by his house waiting for him to come out. We and our four dogs huddled together to try and keep warm. It was a bitter cold morning. Besides being cold, we were worried because we had a train to catch and were afraid we'd miss it. So finally, after some hours, we woke up the watchman. He said we could go across the bridge, that he had just forgotten to take down the signs and the barricade. Now we were so late that we had to run as fast as we could go with our packs. We made it and caught the train to Rockport, where we'd left our car.

We looked up Mr. McGilvary and thanked him for the use of his cabin. Then we stopped at Catherine's parents in Nooksack, and on to Forks. We were both very happy with our vacation.

The logging camp was back at work again. Chet and Wayne came out to work at camp. They stayed at our house for two months. Catherine cooked and made their lunches, and washed their clothes. She liked to cook, and we three fellows liked to eat. There would be several kinds of pie every day. I think Catherine was pleased that we ate them up every day.

Wayne soon rented a house in Forks, and his wife, Margaret, came out from their home in Port Angeles to join him. Then we were neighbors. I had stayed at their house when I was working close to Port Angeles. Chet stayed with us for a while longer.

There was a nice insurance salesman who would come in the evening after we got home from work who was trying to sell Chet and me life insurance policies. We would tell him hunting and fishing stories until he got discouraged and would go home. Next day he would stop in again. We were having fun with him, and would think of something to do each time he came. We put a big block of wood in the fireplace and target practiced with .22 pistols. He finally quit stopping in.

The last of September in 1942, Catherine and I walked to the theater to see a show; it was only four blocks away.

While we were at the show, Chet and Hollum Hunley had come to our house and discovered that we were gone. They were sure Catherine was in the hospital having a baby. They went to the hospital and asked about Catherine, whether everything was all right.

The nurse told them that Catherine was not there. They were so sure she must be in the hospital that they insisted on seeing her. The nurse insisted that she was not there. She said, "If you don't believe me, you can go in and see." So both of them went to all the rooms and couldn't find Catherine until after the show was out and we came home.

A SON IS BORN, A SEARCH FOR A NEW
AND BIGGER FARM BEGINS

A few days later, Catherine did go to the hospital to have a baby. Hollum had told me that when his son was born he didn't ask permission to go in with his wife, but just went with her to the delivery room. So, I did the same and walked right in when Catherine was rolled into the delivery room. I stood quietly and watched. On September 28, 1942, we had our first son, Melvin Lloyd Beebe.

In the last few years, I had spent twelve months as woods scaler and a year as saw filer. I preferred to be in the woods, so went back to the falling and bucking. But I had a close shave with logs rolling and began to think about getting out of the logging.

I had watched from the filing shed for years as the loggers came in and out of the cook house. They were older than I and bent out of shape. Many drank too much. Some of the loggers would save five or six months worth of checks and then go to town. They would be back in a week ready to start saving their money for the next trip. When asked if they had a good time they would say, "I must have. My money is all gone." The women at the bars and other crooks would get it all. Then they would send them back to work.

Almost every one of the loggers had a dream of owning some day a little stump ranch (a few acres of land). Some of them got it. We wanted some land, too, so every weekend we were over on the east side of the Olympics looking for a good farm or piece of land. Our trouble was the same as most people's, no money.

We found exactly the place we wanted. It was located in Sequim, seventy-five miles east of Forks. My parents and Catherine and I decided to buy it together. Dad had a little money, and we could sell our house. This farm had eighty-seven acres, most of it cleared. There was a creek running through it and the Dungeness River was close by. There was a great view of the Olympic Mountains. Catherine and I just loved looking at them. We decided that some day when we had enough wild animals, we would call our place <u>Olympic Game Farm</u>.

There were cows and some machinery with the farm. The house had burned down recently, and two bunkhouses had been moved on the land and joined together. Catherine and I were to come and start farming.

I was logging on some dangerous hills at this time, so I told everyone that this week would be my last. Over the years, I had several good friends who were

We moved to our new farm in 1942

killed in this camp on their last day of work before going to their stump ranch. Friday would be my last day of logging.

When I got home Thursday evening, I breathed a sigh of relief because I knew I wouldn't go to work on Friday. I hadn't mentioned it to Catherine. She made my lunch as usual in the morning. When it was time to go to work, I told her that I had never intended to go to work, and that we were going to the farm, and that is what we did.

It was a big job moving all of our animals to the new farm at Sequim, but we had a lot more room for them than before. The grass and brush eating animals, like elk and deer, were much better off, and we could also grow hay and grain for them. We put the mink pens in the orchard area. Having eighty-seven acres suited our purpose much better than our small Forks home.

Our new farm had been homesteaded by one of the earliest settlers. John Weir came from Missouri via Texas. He was a blacksmith, woodsman, sharpshooter and Mexican War veteran, and came to Dungeness in 1858, his family following in 1860. He homesteaded on what is now Olympic Game Farm. He built a log cabin and is credited with building the first wagon and wagon wheels in the Dungeness valley.

The Weir family settled in the river bottom, a mile from the waterfront. There was no road nearer than half a mile. The cabin was about twelve by twenty-six feet in size. It had a split cedar door on wooden hinges and an old-fashioned latch with a buckskin string hanging out. It had a fireplace and chimney of clay and sticks, which was built outside at one end of the cabin. There were no windows. A roof of clapboards completed the picture. There was no clearing. So dense was the forest that they lived there all summer without knowing of the existence of a hill one hundred yards north of the house.

Our view looking to the southwest

38

A GOOD LIFE

When we got moved to our new farm, we started to milk twenty cows morning and night. In between, I plowed fields, put in alfalfa, pasture grass and grain. It was fun. While I was outside, I could see the Olympic Mountains. I had been on all the ridges and peaks that I could see, so I imagined that a cougar or bear was walking up that ridge, or remembered times when I had been. I had everything I needed. Catherine and Mel were all that mattered.

Dad and Mom came to the farm in the fall. They moved a house onto the farm. It faced on Ward Road.

We liked living on the farm. We did have to milk the cows early and late. In between there was always work to be done. If we had to go somewhere, the work would be there the next day. The best part was that Catherine, Melvin and I would be together all day. I always thought of things to be done, but Dad had no hobbies and had a list of things to do also. It was hard to get any time even between milkings. If there was hard work to do, I felt like I should do it. If we wanted to see Catherine's folks in Nooksack, Dad would say that I should go, as I had been working hard, but I knew we had that fence to build or something else that needed doing. All the while I was gone, I couldn't keep from thinking that Dad was wishing I'd get back to build that fence. That kind of spoiled the trip for me.

Every day on the farm I could see the Olympics and I would be just aching to spend a day in the mountains, but I felt like I'd used up my time to see Catherine's folks, and I couldn't take another day off to go to the hills. Dad worked hard, but some things he couldn't do any more. I think he didn't want to be alone with the work any more, and I didn't blame him for it. He had worked hard all his life.

The only thing I could think of was to take my dogs out once in a while after I'd finished milking. It would be a short day for hunting, but it would be great to hike in the forest. Catherine knew I longed to go to the mountains, and she would tell me to go, but I didn't feel that I should.

Our farm payments were only one hundred twenty dollars per month. The milk check sometimes wasn't enough to make it. We had to raise our food and meat, never spending any money on a show or a meal out. Neither Catherine nor I minded going without money. Our fun was saving the money each month for the payment. We would hear stories that the man who held our mortgage on the farm would say, "It won't be long before I will get the farm back. They won't be able to pay for it." We knew that some way or other we would get the money for each payment. Every day we felt closer to winning the battle.

We enjoyed our life on the farm. I just couldn't keep my eyes off the Olympic Mountains. I felt like I could tell right where the cougars were on ridges and sidehills as the weather changed.

Once in a while I would go hunting between milkings. We were having a hard time making the farm payments. Some days I caught a cougar or two. The bounty on cougars was seventy-five dollars each, and it helped us make the payments.

We had a dog on the farm to help with the cows. Shep would sleep on our porch and wait for the alarm to ring to get us up for milking cows every morning. When he heard the alarm,

Our cow dog, Shep, babysitting two bear cubs in his spare time

Shep would go out in the field and bring the cows up to the barn, and by that time we would be there to let the cows into the barn and lock them into their stanchions. The cows always went to their own place in the barn and started eating their portion of grain.

Shep had watched me get the hounds and go hunting for cougars, and he always wanted to go with us. I told him I would take him some day. One day when Shep was begging to go with us, I said, "Okay, you can go," and let him get into the car with the other dogs. He was real happy.

We got to the mountains and there was about one foot of snow. We found the tracks of three cougars. The dogs treed them one at a time. It was hard going in the snow and very steep. By the third cougar, Shep was all in, but continued to go with the hounds. He could just make it back to the car and lie down. He had done very well.

A few days later, I got up to take the hounds cougar hunting. Shep was nowhere to be seen. Catherine found him hiding under the washing machine on the back porch. One trip was enough for Shep. He didn't want to ever go again.

When I thought everything was right for hunting, I would go and Catherine would milk the cows for me in the morning so I could get an early start. Sometimes I would not get back in time to milk at night, but she did that for me too.

The elk season was on, so Bert Wallis and I went elk hunting with our bows and arrows about eight miles up the Bogachiel River. We took a rubber boat with us to carry our elk if we got one, and Wayne Hathaway wanted a big black bear hide. Other friends wanted bear meat. I told them I would watch out for a bear.

We hunted a day or two, and I got the big bear that Wayne needed. I skinned the bear and put the hide in a sack, and gave the bear meat away. Bert and I were living in a little shelter of clear plastic like a tablecloth. Bert said he couldn't eat the food we ate out on a hunting trip at home, but it didn't bother him here.

The next day, I got a bull elk and it started to rain. This is rain forest country, and it rains one hundred twenty inches a year. The river was coming up fast. The elk was only one hundred yards from the river, so we thought it would be great to take the big bull elk out in one piece. We wrestled, dragged and rolled the elk to the river. It was a lot of work, but we got it into the boat and tied it down as tight as you could on a rubber boat.

The river was in flood now, but we couldn't wait. We had split seats out of a cedar tree that lay across the boat, but with the elk in there they held the elk off the bottom a little. We also had made some oars for the boat.

We pushed off and away we went. We were making good time, as the river was running fast. We had such a load that the boat was riding low in the water, and we couldn't change position in the river very quickly.

We were going around a corner in the river when we could see part of a tree sticking out of a rapids. The log would jump out of the river and then go back down. We got there when the log jumped up and we flipped over. I was running the boat and Bert had grabbed both seats, one under each arm. I grabbed a limb of the tree that tipped us over.

I hung on a little while. The limb was more like a knot and I could just get one hand on it. It was hard to hang on. I looked for Bert and saw that he was okay. He had a board under each arm, and they held him up. I watched until he got to shore. I was wondering how Bert could get one of those cedar boards to me.

Then my hand slipped off the knot, and I was in the rapids in too many clothes to swim. I just let myself come to the top once in a while and go down, and when I felt the bottom, I would jump up and take a breath when my head came out. I finally could touch bottom and kept working to shore a little as I drifted down.

When I finally found a place that was shallow enough to sit down, I did, and rested. Bert was on shore and I could see the elk and boat down the river. The elk's horns were dragging and hung up. We went on down to the elk, and after a while, we were able to turn the boat over and get the elk on top.

We had lost our packs and bear hide and could have drowned. We went on down river with the boat and elk. Coming to a log jam, we had to take the elk off and float it under the logs. The heavy rain hadn't stopped all day. When we got down to where our car was, my father and his hunting partner were watching us come down the river.

When we got to shore and got out, my father said, "You two look like drowned rats." We didn't tell anyone what had happened. It would just worry them next time we went hunting. I never did tell my parents events like

40

that. I am not sure I told Catherine for some time. We had a good time. It is such a wet wonderful area. Bert and I went on other hunting trips in other years.

These next magazine and newspaper articles are always exaggerated, but they are nice to read after you are too old to do the things that they say you did.

An article was written in September of 1948 by Damon Howatt of Yakima, Washington titled The Woodsman of the Dungeness. It appears below:

> High in the mysterious heavens the Archer of the Ancients, Sagittarius, must have smiled a knowing smile 31 years ago because it was then in the merry month of May that Lloyd Beebe was born.
>
> True enough, the month of May is the exclusive domain of Taurus and Gemini, but what would they know of 'The Sport of Man Since Time Began?' Sagittarius knows.
>
> Almost one thousand miles west of Wyoming the Woodsman of the Dungeness operates a dairy farm of 85 acres along the Dungeness River near the town of Sequim on the Olympic Peninsula in western Washington.
>
> Beebe is an unassuming young man with a pair of Jack Dempsey shoulders and a Frank Buck propensity for getting along with the wild animals. He knows the deer, bear, cougar and elk better than they know themselves and is as much at home in the wilderness domain as they. Asked if he had ever been lost, he replied, "No, but lots of times I didn't know where I was."

Lloyd with bow and arrow and five cougar. This photograph appeared in the magazine "The Feathered Shaft", in September of 1948.

A NEW WAY TO GET BACK TO THE WILDERNESS
AND ANOTHER SON IS BORN

1945 - I saw my first movie camera today. I had been thinking of a way to get back into the forest and mountains. There were people at this time coming to Port Angeles to show pictures of wildlife.

I didn't know anything about photography, but I did feel like I knew about animals, forests and mountains. When I went to see some wildlife films that came by, I would wonder whether I could learn to do that. After a few days work on the farm, my confidence would come back. I talked to Catherine about buying a camera. Catherine and I talked this photography idea over a lot. She believed in me and went along with it, even though we both knew we would have a struggle on our hands to finance this project and live also.

We never went ahead with something that cost a lot of money until we both agreed that it was worth a try. In that way it was up to the one of us who got the idea to convince the other. Sometimes there was a delay; never a big argument. I usually thought a month or two about these things to feel as sure as possible before I suggested something that might change our life.

It did seem foolish, because we would have to borrow the money on our car. The camera cost three hundred dollars, and the car wasn't worth much more.

I didn't dare tell any of our friends that I was going to see if we could make some money on pictures, so I let everyone think it was to be a hobby. They couldn't understand. They all said that there wouldn't be any money in it.

Melvin as he looked in the show "The Little Archer"

Whenever I could afford a roll or two of color film, I would get it. Then there was other equipment like reels and cans. I took pictures from time to time and kept learning.

I had a tripod, but not a steady camera tripod. I saw a good one in Port Angeles and decided I would get it. When I asked the price, it was one hundred seventy-five dollars. That was a disappointment to me, so I went home and thought how I would never own one of those tripods. Before the week was out, I decided I couldn't get pictures as good as the competition with poor equipment. I finally decided to buy the tripod.

We knew a lady named Patsy Sinkey who took movie pictures for the Washington Game Department on our farm. By the house I had a young cougar, a deer fawn and a bear cub that played together. She suggested we make a short movie with my son Melvin. He played with these animals all the time. Melvin was really good with his bow and arrows. We called the picture The Little Archer. We sold The Little Archer to Warner Brothers. I got just enough money to buy a better camera with my half.

Now followed two years of borrowing money on my car for more film and film equipment. Hunting cougars when time for this was available, paying off the car again, then borrowing more money on the car to buy film, cans and reels. I had always thought I could take my film on tours if I had to, but I knew I could never stand up and talk with my film.

The Peninsula Profile published an article on February 23, 1951. It appears below in part:

PENINSULA'S GREATEST WOODSMAN HAS 118 COUGAR KILLS TO HIS CREDIT

Although he hunts predatory animals and probably will do so as long as he has hounds to run and he can follow them, Beebe always respects the animals he hunts.

He is a good hunter. He thinks so much of physical condition that he never uses tobacco, intoxicating liquor or even coffee. He is a clean-cut and perfect physical specimen, a woodsman tuned to the tempo of travel that no other around here can equal.

I have often been around where hunters and woodsmen gather. Always, right away, the boys talk about Beebe. Never yet have I heard anyone advance any champion to equal him in this area.

It is seldom you find so many accomplishments and so much mental, and physical balance in one man, as in this young woodsman. His friends hope the hounds will bay at the foot of many more Olympic Peninsula trees and that Lloyd will be there to see the snarling cougar.

Lloyd, the hunter and cameraman, Mrs. Beebe, the lady archer and housewife, and Melvin, 'The Little Archer', make a family group hard to beat.

So what if the dairy herd on the banks of the Dungeness are milked by other hands sometimes while the Beebe family takes to the hills? They can milk cows any day, but out in the woods they're in a world of their own.

June 12, 1951 - Another son, Kenneth Lynn Beebe was born.

Our friend, Patsy Sinkey, wrote an article around this time. Excerpts appear below:

MODEST HUNTER BRINGS FAME TO DUNGENESS

"That's where Lloyd Beebe lives", any resident of the area will tell you, proudly. (And if you've been reading your newspapers and magazines and motion picture journals during the last four years, you will know that Lloyd Beebe has hunted more big-game animals than any other man in the Pacific Northwest.)

But Lloyd Beebe

Ken Beebe ready to go milk the cows

Lloyd with deer that a cougar killed

himself goes along with unruffled, quiet patience trying to avoid the limelight which has suddenly been focused on the privacy of his home and family.

"I can't understand why everyone is so excited", he protests, as program arrangers try to run him down for radio interviews and journalists find their way to his little white gate.

"I'm just struggling along like a lot of other people who have a special dream; someday, I hope that I can stop milking cows and spend all of my time out in the wilderness shooting animals with a camera."

Endowed with endless patience and endurance, he was a successful hunter right from the first. One year, he gathered bounties on thirty-three cougars, and on one memorable day, he killed six great kings of the mountains.

When you consider that each cougar is estimated to do away with fifty deer per season, you can understand that a catch of thirty-three cougars is a safeguard for approximately 1,650 deer!

Even a bull elk is no match for the strength and cunning of the big cats.

And now, after two decades of exploring the ways and habitats of creatures of the wilderness, Lloyd Beebe has come to find his greatest satisfaction in capturing their story on motion picture film, so that the rest of the world may know about them, too.

True fame, genuinely earned, does not always come to a man during his lifetime; and seldom does it come to such a young man as Lloyd.

However, he is now making pictures for no less a producer than Walt Disney! He has helped make animal sequences for Warner Brothers and with a still camera he has captured wildlife studies, sufficiently unusual to rate publication in several outdoor magazines.

Dressed comfortably in blue jeans and blazer jacket, you will come upon him in unexpected locations, his camera trained on a rock pile where a marmot may appear, or hidden at the edge of some gathering spot for elk or bear.

If he sees you coming, he may step off the trail and quietly wait for you to pass, for Beebe is no lover of the praise and adulation of crowds.

His happiest moments are spent with his family, Catherine and Melvin, and a bouncing new son, Kenneth, and his heart is wrapped up in the animal pets who live on his farm and make fine, sympathetic performers for his pictures.

With kindness, modesty and diligence, he has worked hard to earn his equipment and pursue the work that he loves.

Shyly and gratefully, he acknowledges his successes and looks to his future achievements. But Walt Disney down in Hollywood and theater patrons throughout the world know that programs will be wholesome and interesting so long as people like Lloyd bring fame to places like Dungeness Valley!

Walt Disney was starting to show animal films. Disney called his series <u>True Life Adventure Series</u>.

I decided to write Disney a letter. I said in my letter that I had some good wildlife color film. The day the letter arrived, Erwin Verity, the Disney Production Manager, called back and said that they'd like to buy some of my film. I knew they would want to pick and choose the scenes and leave me the rest. I didn't want to do that, so I told them that I would be willing to send all my original film for them to keep until they were ready to choose, and we could decide then. The film I sent was a print from the original.

The original film had never been projected and was unscratched. They called back and asked Catherine and I to come to the studio for a week. We were excited about this new development.

We started out in our old car. Twenty-five miles before we reached Weed, California, the rear end went out of our car. We had to be taken to Weed with a wrecker and then spend two or three days getting the car fixed; then on to Burbank. They had gotten reservations at a motel for us. We stopped there and went to the studio.

The next morning, they treated us great. They said they had been looking all over for cougar film in which the cougars were just traveling in natural setting. All they had found was hunters chasing cougars with dogs or treeing them, nothing to show the cougar doing what comes naturally.

I had a three or four year old beautiful cougar that was a pet and lived by our house. This cougar had grown up with Melvin, played with dogs and was a great friend to us. We used to take him up into the mountains and film with him doing whatever he wanted to do. When we used up our film, we would go back home and wait until we could buy more film. Then we would go shoot a couple more rolls. Some of our film was just what Disney was looking for.

Dad always had a fear that we would eventually get in a lawsuit or something bad with the neighbors. One day, Catherine and I were going to film a few scenes of a couple of cougar dogs. We needed someone to help, so Dad came to help. He brought his 30.30 rifle with him. I told him he didn't need it. He wanted it handy in case. The cougar was used to being tied, so we tied him. The two dogs were chained and barking. One dog got loose, and the cougar slapped at the dog. The rifle shot, and our old friend the cougar was dead. Oh, how we wished Dad hadn't shot - as sad as we were, it was done, so we didn't get after Dad about it. We knew he thought he'd done right. It was a sad day for us; maybe a relief for my father.

I had told the studio that the Woodland Park Zoo had some cougar kittens born there. They told me to see if I could get a few scenes of them.

Catherine and I gathered up a big truckload of logs, moss, ferns, etc. We had already called Frank Vincenzi at the Woodland Park Zoo in Seattle, and he said we could try if we wanted to. We arrived at the zoo. Then we fixed what looked like a den and mossy and woodsy looking place. I had to shoot through a chain-link fence. A crowd of people were all around me wanting to know what I was doing, and they had a lot of other questions.

The studio had sent me a camera that I had never seen before, and telephoto lenses, which

Cougar kitten and hound pup

45

Lloyd taming a wild wolverine

were also new to me. All I could afford with my own camera was one wide-angle lens, which is hard to get out of focus.

We finally finished shooting, picked up all the material we had brought from Sequim, and cleaned up the ground before leaving to go back to Sequim.

We sent the film to the studio. When it was developed, they called and said that some of the film was out of focus. They were surprised because all the film that we had sent to them before had been sharp. Also, there was a pattern of chain-link wire on the cougar from the sun shining through the chain-link fence.

I was very embarrassed by this. They had told me on the telephone to give it another try. This sure made me see how much I had to learn. We had thrown all our brush, logs and ferns away, so we went back to the forest and got another load of them.

The first trip I was to get so much a day plus my expenses. Both trips we worked hard, and we never sent a bill for either trip.

This time, the film turned out okay. It was a lesson I never forgot, and it never happened again. This was the most embarrassing thing that ever happened to me. I never told them at the studio that the reason my film had been so sharp was because I only owned a wide-angle lens, and I had to get close to the animals, so it was hard to be out of focus. I also neglected to mention that I had never seen a telephoto lens before. I didn't know if I had spoiled my chances to work for Walt Disney or not. The people at Disney didn't mention it again, and we went ahead with our plans.

The Disney studio wanted to use some of this in the next film they were going to make. This would be The Vanishing Prairie. They wanted me to start working for them filming The Vanishing Prairie. Part of this show we could do from our place in Sequim.

They also wanted to buy some of the film for a show soon to be started, Yellowstone Cub. We said they could do this, and of course we wanted to go to work for them. It was a dream come true. On this visit to Burbank, we were taken around through every part of the studio. Then it was time to go home and be ready to work for the studio. We returned to Sequim.

My parents were happy for change for them as well. We would have to quit working for the farm until this show was finished, and we didn't know if we'd ever work for them after that.

I knew that I had a lot to learn. Filming cougars in the wild would be impossible. Most people never see a cougar in their lifetime. I didn't have our old cougar friend, Jerry, as he wasn't with us any more. The only thing to do that I could think of was to take my dogs and catch two cougars alive and start to work with them. Looking back, I know that was a very long shot to use wild cougars. We only had to fill in the parts that I hadn't filmed before.

The dogs and I started looking for cougars in the mountains, and it wasn't too long before I had two wild cougars at home on our farm in Sequim. But catching a cat the size of a cougar, I found, was not easy! While Catherine waited below, I climbed the tree where the cougar was and got a rope with a slipknot around its neck. The rope was attached to a pole. Then I got hold of one of his hind feet and tied that to the pole. Somehow or other, between Catherine and I, we lowered it to the ground and finally got it into a cage. Catching the second cougar wasn't any easier! I started working with the cougars every minute I could spare, as well as anything else

46

I could do for the picture.

Jim Simon was sent by the studio to help with the filming. Jim had worked on a film for Disney before, and knew some of the things that I needed to learn. My job was photographer and animal handler, so I had to figure out how to get animals to do the things we needed on film as well as run a camera whenever possible.

We worked on The Vanishing Prairie for three months, and finally finished it. I learned a lot about filming and new equipment from Jim, and he learned some from me. Jim went back to his home in Wyoming, and I went back to milking cows. We wondered if we would ever hear from Disney Studio again. Those wild cougars had done a good job for the show. I think they did a better job than if they had been tame. They already knew all the things they could do, and all you had to do was get them to do them.

Wolverine catches fish in Northwest Territory

A month went by, and the telephone rang one day. It was Erwin Verity, Production Manager for Disney Studio. He said they were planning on a new show in Canada, and they wanted me to go to Canada and get everything ready to make the picture. This picture was White Wilderness.

Erwin said they had to have wolverines in this show, and the Banff Park Rangers promised to catch five wild wolverines. The studio wanted me to take charge and see if I could get them to do anything interesting for us.

They said the Park Rangers had told them you couldn't do anything with a wolverine, especially a grown one.

Wolverine

The plan was to go to Banff, Alberta. The reservations were made for me at the Cascade Hotel. Two wolverines had been caught and were in a park warehouse in metal barrels by the time I got there. I started to build small cages for them, four feet wide, eight feet long and four feet high with a divider in the middle to slide in. There were three metal-covered full-size slide doors, one at each end and one in the middle. Metal covered all the wood. The Ranger said that you can't keep them in a wooden cage, as they'd chew right through log cabins and bite through wire as big as a pencil.

It was forty degrees below zero, and there was no heat in the big warehouse. I knew I could never tame these animals if I stayed in the hotel, so I checked out and with my sleeping bag and warm clothes, I

47

moved into the warehouse and slept on the ground. I got a radio and had it on all day and night so the wolverines could get used to all sorts of noises.

I started to build cages as close to the wolverines as possible and talked to them as I worked. I watched them as I worked and made noise and got them so they didn't snarl or jump at me. At night, I kept sleeping closer and closer to them. When I had a pen ready for each wolverine, I slept between them and worked close to them during the days. During the nights, I continued to work with them and gain their trust. If they tried to sleep, I moved or pulled a straw out of their bed to make them aware of my presence. After a couple of weeks, the wolverines decided to go to sleep no matter what I did. They began to think of me as their friend.

In another week, they would eat out of my hand. I began to think they would not bite me, so I decided to break a raw egg in my hand and have it run down my fingers. I opened the door and put my arm in. The first wolverine I called Bill. He came over and smelled my hand, then started to lick up the egg. He cleaned the egg off between my fingers and all over my hands, and then backed off.

I kept repeating that. The second wolverine was ready to try that a few days later. The Park Rangers heard that the wolverines were getting tame and they came to see them clean my hand when I fed them. Nobody else could get near them. If anyone approached their cage, they would snarl and lunge. I kept working with the wolverines. The Rangers caught a third one for me to tame.

Wolf lets wolverine have the caribou

While working with wolverines, I discovered that they were very intelligent animals. They didn't appear to be guided only by their instincts, but were able to figure things out.

It was during the shooting of this movie that we used the buzzer-reward system for the first time. It worked so well that we used it from then on when filming the wild animal sequences. The animals learned quickly that where the buzzer sounded there would be one of their favorite foods.

48

OUR FAMILY IS TOGETHER AGAIN

The Banff Park Rangers told me they had a cabin about eight miles inside the park that Catherine and I and the boys could stay in. They said it was called Hillsdale. One of the Rangers showed it to me. It was an old, one-room cabin in a beautiful location on a river bottom. There were moose and elk tracks all over. I could see they had been there almost every day. I said we would love to use it a couple months or more. We would be moving the wolverines after I found a permanent location.

When I got back to Banff, I called Catherine in Sequim and told her I had found a place for us to stay in a cabin, a perfect place for the boys until we moved to a permanent place. Catherine said, "We will come up on the train", and she would let me know when to meet them in Banff.

In a few days, I met my family at the train station. We went right to the Hillsdale cabin. We had some fixing

Ptarmigan along the Bow River, Canada

up to do. There were blocks of wood for chairs. It was a wild area; every evening and morning elk and moose came around the cabin.

I picked out a great place to build a fence around a small hill. It was a beautiful spot with the Bow River down below and the Rocky Mountains on each side. This spot was outside the park near Canmore. I never saw a lovelier spot.

I started to build bigger and more comfortable houses for the wolverines. I thought we might buy a trailer, and Catherine, the boys and I could live in it close to the wolverines.

I went back to Sequim with the family, bought a new Jeep station wagon, stopped at Spokane and bought a good second-hand trailer, and we went on up to Canmore, Alberta, Canada. We cut a road good enough to get our trailer up to this beautiful spot. We had to winch the trailer up there to a little bench and set the trailer facing the most gorgeous view.

There was a spring where we got our water about a quarter mile away from the trailer. We went through the woods. There was no trail, so we didn't want the boys to go after the water. We all went together to the spring.

As soon as word got out about a movie being worked on, Art Krowchuck stopped in hoping to get a job. He was a nice, likable young man, so I gave him a job helping to build pens and cleaning up. Art had worked as an extra on movies before.

Catherine and I liked him and his wife, and we visited back and forth from then on.

Erwin sent us a message that Tom McHugh was coming up as a photographer to help us. And he, Erwin, would be up as soon as Tom arrived. We didn't have long to wait. Tom came with a trailer, and we set it up on our bench a little past our own. We didn't know Tom but had heard the stories that always followed him. The stories were much the same as the one that had just reached us a few days before.

Tom had done work for Disney on <u>Vanishing Prairie</u> with the sequence of prairie dogs. That had turned out well. Tom had just finished filming in Montana. It seems he had a trailer on that job, too. The Ranger and his wife had Tom eat with them most of the time and had tried to help him as much as they could. Tom had a few items of food he hadn't eaten when he was ready to leave, so he made a list of what he had paid for them. Tom took the list and went to the Ranger's house and wanted to sell them this little box of groceries.

All the stories were of his stingy ways. We found out later that the reason for Erwin's visit to us now was to put Tom straight on this job. Cameraman Jim Simon said that if Tom ever got married the girl would have to buy the license. Tom kept books on every penny and would save one any way he could.

Erwin came soon, and the first thing he did was to call Tom, and we had a meeting in our trailer. Right away Erwin said, "Now Tom, this meeting is to get things started right. I don't want you eating with Lloyd and Catherine unless you get together and set a price per meal for Catherine's cooking." Of course, we said that we didn't need to be paid for Tom eating with us; no one else paid. But Erwin knew more than we did, and it was settled.

Catherine always had great meals for us, so Tom would come and see what was for dinner, and if he stayed for dinner and we had big steaks on a platter, he would move all the steaks around before he took what he thought was the best one.

When Erwin or Winston Hibler or others from the studio were there, Tom would always be checking to see what Catherine was going to feed them. She would often have fun with Tom and say she had a pot of beans or something else. Tom would warn her that you just couldn't feed beans or meals like that to people from Hollywood. He would worry all day about what our company was going to get for dinner. The meal was always great, and he would be there, too.

Tom's mother came to visit him. She stayed at the Banff Springs Hotel. She came out to visit us several times. One day before she was going back to her home, she told Tom and us that she would like to take us all out to dinner on Friday night. We accepted the invitation, and then she said, "Why Tom, that is the first time I have seen you smile since I got here."

We got along fine with Tom, and I learned more about photography. But he never learned that other people had feelings, and was always surprised when he hurt someone's feelings. He just couldn't understand.

Our family just loved living on this bench with our backs to the forest and high mountains. Everything in front of us was beautiful: the most gorgeous Rocky Mountains close across the valley and the beautiful Bow River that we could see for miles in either direction.

Mel and Ken were free to do as they pleased all day. Ken had to stay within sight of the trailer, but he found a way to be by himself. He had a hatchet I had given him. There were jack pines growing all around, and Ken would spend most of his time up in the top of them with his hatchet. Catherine worried about Ken cutting himself. I had stuck out my neck and said that he wouldn't, and he never did.

One day Catherine went to the door to see where Ken was. Just outside the door was Ken with his hatchet held up over his head in a threatening attitude with a black bear standing up in front of him. Catherine yelled and jumped out the door, and the bear left.

When Thanksgiving came, Catherine asked me to go to town and get a turkey big enough for the crowd of people we would have for dinner. I shopped all over and came back with the biggest dressed turkey I could find. When I gave the turkey I had bought to Catherine, she said, "We don't have an oven big enough for that turkey." She had been thinking of a fifteen or twenty-pound turkey. The one I found was weighed in at forty-two pounds! I thought I had done good, but I made a big problem for the cook.

We couldn't find an oven that was large enough. Catherine called Frank Jones, the Ranger in that area, to see if he knew of an oven that was big. Frank said that one of their Forestry cabins had a very big oven. She took it to the cabin and cooked it.

Catherine had invited everyone we knew including the Rangers and their families and our crew. We were living in our trailer, so we put up tables outside facing the spectacular view. People were eating on the beds and tables in the trailer. Everyone had a great Thanksgiving dinner.

We had to have a lot of snowshoe rabbits alive in this show, so I got some snare wire that they sell in Canada. It is a brass wire that is limber and small. It is easy to catch rabbits, but they are always dead the way you set the traps.

I decided to try snares that would not close on the neck, so that a rabbit would be alive when I came to look at the snares.

The way I fixed the loops worked fine, and after a week of checking on the traps three times a day, we had all the snowshoe rabbits we needed. We put them in a big fenced-in area that we'd built for them.

We'd gotten a trailer with a water tank on it, so we could haul water from a creek a mile away. We built a ramp to back the trailer up higher next to the trailer so that water would run into the house. We built an outside backhouse, and we were all set for a year and a half with this as our headquarters. Never had we lived in such a wonderful place. All the family enjoyed it.

Jim Simon came to help, then Tom McHugh. We now had our full crew. Tom had his trailer past ours; Jim rented a house.

We made long trips, but there was always someone there to take care of the wolverines. Catherine and the two boys spent the entire time there. There were trips to Southampton Island to film polar bears, and other trips to the Northwest Territories, and many other places.

When we came with the trailer, I had bought an aluminum canoe and brought it with us. I knew there would be a long canoe trip before we were through with the picture.

The studio sent me to Brochet, Manitoba in the Northwest Territory to film caribou.

All the time since starting to work for the studio, I had used our own money until the studio

Ken became good friends with the Rocky Mountain bighorn sheep

Arctic lemming

would send the money to the bank. Then I would send a bill, and they would reimburse us for the money spent. That way, I didn't waste any time.

I packed up and got on the train for the Northwest Territory. It was very cold weather. I didn't know about it when I left, but I had created a problem by leaving immediately.

Hugh Wilmer, one of the photographers working with us, was to go to Southampton Island, and the studio hadn't sent the money for expenses. Jim Simon was in charge of the money, and he told Hugh that there wasn't any money yet.

Hugh said, "Jim, you gave Lloyd all the money. I know Lloyd got all the money." Hugh went to Catherine and she told him that she had gone to the bank and gotten the money from our personal account. Hugh didn't believe her. His own wife told him that she was with Catherine when she'd gone to get the money out of our account. Hugh still insisted I had taken all the money. This was later straightened out.

When I arrived at The Pas, Manitoba, I hired a plane with skis on it. I had the pilot fly me to Brochet. It is a small Indian town with a Hudson Bay Company trading post.

Little kids had sleds and puppies tied to their sleds. They were training the puppies to pull their sleds. They would run ahead and the pups would follow with the sleds. Grown-ups had their dog teams going in every direction, hauling wood or whatever else they were doing.

There was a Manitoba Game Department man there named Pat Patterson. Pat was to help me get started filming. He took me and my outfit about twenty miles, and we set up the tent. Pat said that this might be a good place to see caribou.

The weather was sixty-five below. The tent was cold, but had a little wood stove in it. I cut boughs from trees and

Wolf overlooking frozen lake

made a place to sleep above the snow. Pat had left me a leg of caribou meat to eat. After a week of filming caribou in small groups, Pat came and picked me up with his dog team.

Then I went out with an Indian for a few days. Again, there were only small groups of caribou.

This is all forest country, and when a herd of caribou comes out of the north and into the forests, they have to spread out to find food until spring, when they get together in a herd and go to the barren land.

After three weeks filming caribou, I took a Game Department plane ride up into the barren lands to try and locate a big herd of caribou, but they were all scattered out in the forest.

When we got back to Brochet, I went over to the Hudson Bay Company store. This was an interesting place. There was a white man running the store; the customers were all Indians.

I won't forget it: One Indian came in, and he couldn't speak much English. He was having a hard time with one item. He kept saying he wanted paper. The clerk could not understand what he wanted. This Indian was getting flustered. He said, "paper, paper, paper, saltie's brother, saltie's brother," and finally the clerk understood he wanted pepper!

Sure enough, when we were near the finish of this show, there was a canoe trip.

I had practiced in the canoe whenever I had time. Catherine would take me to Banff and let me and the canoe out, and meet me when I got down to Canmore; sometimes to other rivers also. There was a Park Biologist named John Tener who was interested in canoes. John would come and talk animals and canoes. It was almost the first of July when John came, and he had an

Canoe trip practice

assignment to map out a new musk ox reserve in the north. The plan was to fly to Yellow Knife in the Northwest Territories. From there, we would fly the canoe and outfit to the Back River, which runs into the Arctic Ocean.

We would have our tent set up on the river in three weeks, so that when the plane came in at the appointed time, it could find us. Then we would be flown into Thelon River, which goes into Hudson Bay. What a trip that would be! I would be filming wildlife pictures for White Wilderness.

We asked the studio about it. In a few days they sent back the answer that they had decided not to take part in this trip. It would be too expensive for the film compared to what they got out of it. I was very disappointed. A few days later, Erwin Verity called and said that the head Canadian in charge of Fish & Game, Land & Mines, and a lot of other things, had called and requested that the studio send me with John.

The Canadian government had done the Disney Studio a lot of favors, and they could not refuse them, so I was free to go.

No white man had been on the Back River since Commander Back was there more than one hundred years before. We flew to Yellow Knife, got aboard another DeHaviland plane with pontoons and the canoe tied to the pontoons. The plane left us eight hundred miles later on the Back River.

John and I had our fishing gear handy from that time on. Every day we would paddle down the river, and the wind usually came up the river. The wind made great waves as it blew against the river, and we had to paddle. For three weeks we went down the river. More than once when we were ready to go down a canyon with high rocks on each side, we would go to shore and wonder what this rapid would take us into. Then we would get back in the canoe and ease our way into the rapids.

John wanted me to run the canoe. I was sure I didn't know as much as I should to be responsible for the canoe. John thought I did, and I didn't think he was any better qualified than I to handle the canoe. Many times when we went down a rapids into a high-walled canyon, I felt the responsibility of my job and fear of the unknown and the river. To capsize and lose your supplies would be tragic. You wouldn't have much chance of getting out.

The flies this time of the year would just about eat you up if you got out of your tent. We could get in the tent at night, though. If the wind didn't blow, the flies were so thick when you opened your mouth that they would be crushed when you shut your mouth.

When walking across the tundra, you would get panicked like the caribou and start running to get away from the flies. The tundra is soft and makes a drumming sound when you run. The flies up ahead rise like a cloud to meet you, and you run right into that cloud of flies. By the end of the day, your coat pockets would be full of dead flies. We would be glad to get in the canoe and in the middle of the river where the wind would often be blowing and there were no flies.

We sometimes went up on hills where we had seen piles of rocks on the ridges. They looked like lines of men on each side of a ravine, the line getting closer together near the top of the hill. You could see that these rows of rock men were there to guide the caribou through a saddle in the hill where Eskimos with bows, arrows and spears killed the caribou as they came by their hiding places.

Then there were meat caches, great piles of rocks around a hole in the ground in which the Eskimos put their cache, then piled the rocks on the cache to protect it from wild animals.

After three weeks traveling downriver, we pitched our white tent on a sand bar and waited for the plane. Sure enough, the plane came and took us to the Thelon River. The next day we started down the Thelon River, which goes into Hudson Bay.

We saw many musk ox, and I got some very good footage of them. We fished our way down the river. We'd already had the greatest fishing you could dream of in the Back River.

Along this river, we saw hundreds of musk ox. Some of them would crowd you and

Rock men guide caribou to Eskimo hunters.

54

almost run over you. We had another three weeks of great fishing. Our muscles were hard from paddling a canoe every day, but we never got tired any more. John and I were great friends, and neither of us would ever forget this trip.

The time came to go home. We were about to finish <u>White Wilderness</u>. Catherine and I and the two boys hooked up our trailer and started back to Sequim.

Rock men on ridge

THE BIG DECISION

About the time we unpacked and got moved into our house, a phone call came from Disney Studio. Erwin Verity was on the line. I could tell he had something important to tell me. He finally told me that the Disney Studio was going to take part in Operation Deep Freeze, which would start in October. This operation was the precursor to the 1955-57 International Geophysical Year, and its purpose was to prepare the Antarctic location for the event.

About forty nations would participate in carrying out earth-science studies from the North Pole to the South Pole and at points in between.

They wanted to know if I would go down to the Antarctic to film the operation and represent Disney Studio. He said I was their first choice, and they thought I could do the job. I would be gone for eighteen months, most of the time without hearing from home, and would not be able to send letters or messages.

When Erwin finished, he told me to think it over carefully for a week, then call him back. He said, "It's my job to tell you about this, but Lloyd, I would advise you not to go." So far, I was getting seven hundred dollars a month. They would double my salary for the eighteen months. Catherine and I talked it over for a week, and finally we decided I should do this job.

We had struggled with money for some time. Things had gotten better and better. We didn't know how long the job with Disney would last. We could be sure of eighteen months at fourteen hundred dollars per month. I knew Catherine would save it until I got back, and we would have some money to do something with. We didn't want to be separated for so long, and I would miss a year and a half of the two boys growing up, which I could never get back. Still, if everything worked out, we would probably be much better off. If I was single, I would have jumped at the chance to go.

I knew I could fit right into the job. There would be unknown dangers encountered before I returned. I always felt I could relax at time of danger and be at my best. For the few days before I had to leave, I kept wondering whether we'd all be together again. I didn't expect anything bad would happen to me, but what about my family at home? A lot can happen in eighteen months. My father was having heart problems. I had an idea that Dad didn't want to tell me all he knew about his health, because he knew I wouldn't go if I knew what he knew about his health.

First I went to Disney studio to learn all about the trip and how to take my cameras apart and put them back together. This would be filmed in wide screen, so I had to learn about anamorphic lenses. I took my camera apart and put it back together so it would focus and do everything it was supposed to do. I did this every day for a week. If the camera had troubles in the Antarctic, now I could fix it.

The Disney studio was to design the insignia for Operation Deep Freeze, and also to give the navy photographers a week of training and parties before we set sail for the Antarctic.

All the film and camera gear had to be boxed up and ready. I was to be in Norfolk, Virginia on October 5, 1955 with everything that was to go from Disney. I returned to Sequim for a few days.

The day of departure came. Catherine, the two boys, my mother and dad all went to the Seattle airport. My baggage was put aboard, and then came the bad time. When I looked at each one, I could tell what they were thinking. I'm sure we were all thinking the same thing, that something could happen that I wouldn't get back. My two boys didn't think about how long eighteen or twenty months really was.

We grown-ups knew how long it was. Dad knew he might not last that long. My mother was probably thinking that something might happen to me or to her.

Catherine knew, for we had talked the trip over, and had to go through with it. She knew it would be a long time to be separated. She trusted me and I trusted her. There was no doubt. She would save all the money she could, so the trip would be worthwhile. She would not hear from me for most of the time. I knew it would be a long, lonely stretch for me; at least I would not be worrying about how I was, but she and the rest would worry. As I looked at them before going aboard the plane, I wondered which ones might be gone when I got back. Would they all be there to meet me in eighteen months?

We said our goodbyes, and I went on board. I took a seat so I could see out the window, and waved to them as they looked for me. Soon the plane was in the air, and the trip had begun.

When I arrived at Norfolk, Virginia, I went right to the icebreaker, the Glacier GB4. I was given an area in which to put my equipment, which I did. Then I tied it down so it could not move around in a storm. A few of the Seabees had been to the studio before we left, and they introduced me to others. The wintering-over party were all Seabees, except Chet Twombly, who was the Weather Bureau man. The Seabees said we were to have cold weather gear of the latest design. I could tell they didn't know much about it, though they told me and everyone that they would have down sleeping bags, which would allow them to sleep warm lying on the ice.

I knew that it didn't work that way. When you are in the bag with your weight on the down, it becomes paper thin and very cold. I began to worry about the cold weather gear. I had to decide quickly, so I called Catherine and asked her to send my reindeer hide to use under the sleeping bag, as well as my Arctic clothing.

Catherine did send my things, which I picked up when we went through the Panama Canal. Catherine said when she told Erwin Verity about it that he thought I was crazy. They had told him we were to have the very best. The Seabees would have liked some clothes like mine before we got out of the Antarctic. My clothes were light and didn't get stiff in the cold weather.

The icebreaker Glacier GB4 moves through the Panama Canal locks

Mule pulls ship through the Panama Canal locks

At Panama, we were to pick up the Y.O.G., which was an oil tanker, and tow it to Antarctica to be frozen into the ice for winter. Cameras were much cheaper in Panama, so I bought another still camera.

November 8, 1955 - The loud speaker woke us up at 0500 this morning. Two Navy photographers and I went ashore at daylight to take pictures of the Glacier going through the locks and canal at vantage points. It is beautiful country here. Labor is so cheap that everyone keeps their lawns up nice.

I began to keep a log of this trip.

November 9, 1955 - Film shipped - 24 rolls @ $8.00 = $192.00 - APA Airlines. Just got it in the mail in time. The Postmaster had to wait a few minutes for me and then close the office. I also sent packages of things to the family: two baseball gloves, ball and two alligator bags. Called the family from Panama City. I guess that will be the last call I will be able to make for a long time. Wrote two letters today. The icebreaker Edisto left this morning.

November 10, 1955 - Everyone had to get up at 0430 this morning. It was still dark when we cast off and slowly moved down between the two rows of lights and into the bay. The Y.O.G. was waiting and we tied on and were off for New Zealand. The sea has gradually gotten rougher, and by noon the Glacier is pitching badly. The water is going clear over the Y.O.G. I am glad I am not riding on it. Took a few scenes of the Y.O.G. I feel a little sick myself. After dinner, we all went to see the show, Tanganyika.

Initiation of Crossing the Line

Giving a bad haircut

You get dunked until you give the right answers

November 11, 1955 - Weather is bad. The Y.O.G. is rolling and pitching. We are due to cross the equator tomorrow. The shellbacks have plans for us. This morning they caught a polliwog spying on their meeting. They greased his hair and put him in a straitjacket and chained his feet to a big shackle. My camera gear has to be tied down, or it would be bounced around by the ship's pitching, and by the time I get my camera ready to take a picture like that of the spying polliwog, it is over, and I have to tie down my equipment again.

November 12, 1955, Saturday - The weather is still windy and cloudy. The Glacier had to change speed eight different times last night. The Y.O.G. was taking too much water and had to be pumped out. We varied speed from eight to fifteen knots. Now the Edisto is one hundred forty-six miles ahead of us. We gained forty-four miles the last twenty-four hours. We hope to pass the Edisto in three to four days. The fellows on the Glacier are expecting big things in New Zealand and want to be first.

The Y.O.G. is out of food and fresh water. I thought I had better get pictures of that; also of transferring a man on tow between ships. 11:30 am - Just finished the pictures. Took it in Cinemascope, as might not get another chance to photograph passing men between ships again. It was a beautiful day today, but no flying fish. I would like to get some pictures of them, but until today the sun hasn't been out. Spent more time arranging my equipment so as to have more room and got out some more film. The show tonight is Desperate Moment. Soon it will be a month since I left home and family. Could be eighteen more to go.

Crossing The Line - The boisterous ceremonies of Crossing The Line are of such ancient vintage that their derivation is lost. It is well known that ceremonies took place long ago when ships crossed the thirtieth parallel, and also when going through the Straits of Gibraltar. These early ceremonies were of the roughest sort, and were, to a great extent, supposed to try the crew to determine whether the novices on their first cruise could endure the hardships of a life at sea. Then, as is the custom at the present time, it was primarily a crew's party. At an early date the Vikings were known to carry out their ceremonies on crossing certain parallels. It is highly probably that the custom was passed on to the Saxons and Normans from the Vikings.

At an earlier date, ceremonies of propitiation were carried on. Neptune, the mythological God of the Seas, was appeased by the men of the sea, and marks of

58

respect were paid those of his underwater domain. It is plausible that a part of the ceremony grew out of traditions of other days, even though sailors had come to doubt the existence of Neptune. Nevertheless, Neptunus Rex is today the majesty who rules at these occasions.

Those who have crossed the line are called Shellbacks. The sons of Neptune compose the cast for the present-day ceremonies. It is a curious fact of human nature that men will suffer a severe initiation in order to inflict the same punishment on other men. Sailor men treasure the certificate which testifies that they have crossed the line. Usually, the ceremonies of the modern Navy are picturesque, and, with the exception of the discomfort of a good wetting in the tank, a slight shock of electricity from the Devil and the shaving chair, the initiation cannot be called extremely rough. Officers of the Navy could, at one time, buy off by giving the Neptune party so many bottles of beer. Unless the ceremonies are very crude it is tradition that the younger officers undergo the initiation.

The eldest and most dignified member of the Shellbacks is selected as Neptunus Rex, and his assistant is Davey Jones. Her Royal Highness Amphitrite is usually a good-looking young seaman who makes a fine appearance in the dishabille of seaweed and rope yarn. The court in general consists of the Royal Doctor, Royal Dentist, the Devil and other names that suit the fancy of the party. The Bears have the task of rounding up the uninitiated, and also standing the Dousing Watch in the tank.

The night before the ship crosses the line, it is the custom that Davey Jones appears on board with a message to the Captain from His Majesty, Neptunus Rex, stating at what time he wants the ship hove to for the reception of the Royal party. He also issues subpoenas for certain men to appear before him. This reception usually takes place at night, and may be most impressive. The ship is stopped, and amid a glare of lights and a whirl of water, Davey Jones emerges from the hawse pipe or is hoisted in over the bow to deliver his message. He is usually received by the Captain and Officer of the Deck on the bridge.

The following ritual took place on the U.S.S. Glacier on the evening of November 12, 1955:

VIA SEAWEED CABLEGRAM
TO OUR LOYAL AND TRUSTY SHELLBACKS ABOARD THE GOOD SHIP GLACIER:

Greetings and Salutations. We anticipate with Royal pleasure your return to our Royal Realm aboard this fine staunch ship. Davey Jones reports you have the Midwest plowdiggers, Newport prissies, San Diego turkeys, Pedro pelicans and San Francisco native-sons but last and not least those Greenpoint, etc. zoot-suiters. Don't be too trusting, however. Deadeye Dick, our Seaweed Radio Sleuth, has heard faint rumblings over the foam waves of secret gatherings by polliwogs in numerous parts of the ship. Scandalous remarks have been made concerning the Royal Princess and her Mermaids, as also the parentage of our Royal Babe, as to earn our utmost wrath and vindictiveness. Show them the errors of their ways in not paying proper respect to King Neptune by delving deeply into the mysteries of our Realm and paying honor to our Royal Court as all good Sailors of the Seven Seas have done who are members of our Ancient Order of the Deep. Tend all polliwogs well. Let none escape.

(Signed) Neptunus Rex

This afternoon my name was called out over the loud speaker. I knew what was up as I was to go down to the crew's mess; that is the shellback headquarters.

They were holding court on all polliwogs, one at a time. I had to get down on my knees to the court. Of course they said to straighten up, get that smile off your face. They charged me with four different things: first, monopolizing Disney's cartoons, second, impersonating Mickey Mouse, third, taking pictures of secret meeting, and fourth and worst of all, taking pictures of shellbacks at the House of Love in Panama.

If I pleaded not guilty, they would ask if I would like this man to act in my behalf as Counsel. The first time I said yes. My Counsel immediately said, "He is guilty. He pleads guilty, Judge," so after that I pled guilty to all charges. They made me act like Donald Duck, among other things. When they let me go I was told Davey Jones would come on board tomorrow, and he would hold the initiation then.

November 13th - At 9:30 last night, we crossed the equator. All day yesterday the shellbacks were working on a pool to dunk us in, and as soon as it is finished this morning, they will start in. First the Jolly Roger flag was run up. The shellbacks had agreed to let me take pictures first and then go through the initiation last, so I got my camera and started taking movies.

All the polliwogs lined up, about three hundred fifty of them. About ten of them had to lie on the deck in front of the court of Davey Jones, which included several princesses, a queen and king, and others. It was a sort of assembly line.

As the polliwogs moved along on their stomachs, heads down and toward the court, shellbacks would pound on them if they didn't stay close together or if they raised their heads. As they passed the court, three or four at a time would be ordered to rise and sing some song to the court.

Then down again to inch along to a pair of electric shoes. You have to put on the electric shoes and stand before the Court to answer questions. When you gave the wrong answer, you got a shock! While standing in them, you would have to tell who you were, and they would not let you go until you said you were a low-down slimy polliwog, or something like that. Then you removed the shoes and crawled over to the baby, who was a three hundred pound man dressed like a baby. This baby spread a thick layer of axle grease over his belly, and as you passed him on hands and knees, you had to kiss his belly. Of course, the baby grabbed your head and rolled it around in the grease.

From there, the polliwogs gradually moved up, always on their bellies, with screaming shellbacks pounding on them with clubs made out of canvas and soaked in water.

Next came a chair to sit in while they fed you terrible looking food. Some got sick. From there, you crawled to a stockade affair that you put your neck and wrists into, then it was locked down and a couple of shellbacks pounded on the polliwogs' butts for a minute or so.

From this, they had to crawl to a chair on the deck above the pool. The Royal Barber took over here. He sure made some funny looking haircuts. Almost everyone had to get their head clipped as short as the clippers would cut the next day to make an even haircut. As soon as the Royal Barber had finished, a couple of shellbacks grabbed the chair and dumped the polliwog into the pool. Two more fellows were there to ask them questions and keep dunking them until they got the answers they wanted.

From there, they were paddled all the way over to a long tunnel made of canvas. In this tunnel was slimy garbage and an extra big pile where you came out. The tunnel was just big enough to crawl through on their stomachs, so the top of the tunnel was on their backs. As the polliwogs progressed through, they were paddled until they came out.

Then the last of the initiation was getting washed off with a big water hose of sea water. To get all the grease off was your own problem, and it didn't come off easy. When I had taken enough pictures, I went up to the head of the line and went through the initiation. They were waiting for me, and the Navy photographers were ready to take pictures of me at each stop along the way. They said they were going to send some to Erwin Verity.

Even the shellbacks were glad when it was over, as it was a lot of work for them too. There were a lot of black and blue and bloody spots on some of the men after it was all over. There are always some who get too rough.

NEW ZEALAND AND NEW FRIENDS

November 19, 1955 - Pictures were taken of everyone today singly and in groups. I took a few snapshots for myself and a few scenes of inspection on the 02 level deck; also of a navigator taking a sighting of the sun. We had to set our clocks back again tonight. Every two or three days, we have to set them back one hour. The movies are shown out on the deck in good weather. Tonight the movie is Captain Kidd and the Slave Girl.

November 20, 1955 - Today the weather is beautiful but windy, and the sea is rough. The ship is pitching continually. At 10 am I went to church on the flight deck; the chairs would hardly stay in place. There were about thirty of us there.

November 21, 1955 - It is very rough today, and we have been forced to slow down. The swells are about thirty feet high. Quite a few of the men are sick. So far, I have been okay. I took pictures of the Y.O.G. disappearing between swells. I hope they are steady enough. Four or five whales showed up today, and we watched them for half an hour.

November 22, 1955 - The tow shackle broke last night for the second time. The weather is real rough, and we can only go eight knots an hour.

It was Thanksgiving day when we ran into heavy weather and were forced to slow the ship's pace. A banquet for the men on the Y.O.G. tanker was made ready. Men on the Glacier loaded 20 mm ammo cans with turkey dinner, buoyed them and floated, or high-lined, them back to the little tanker being towed to the Antarctic for freezing in the ice at the fuel farm.

By the time they had finished their Thanksgiving dinner, we had passed Easter Island of Mutiny on the Bounty fame, and were nearing the Roaring Forties. First there was a report of the sea worsening, then strong winds came up and mountainous seas. The winds developed into gale force.

The hatches were all closed, and the loud speakers said not to go out on the deck unless it became necessary to tie down loose equipment. The Glacier was hard pressed to keep steerageway and avoid losing its precious tow. The Glacier could only travel three-tenths of a knot per hour and rolled at fifty degrees.

After the storm was over, a crewman on the Y.O.G. jokingly said that his ship had pushed the Glacier sixty-five hundred miles from Panama.

The ship commanders throughout the task force took advantage of every chance to hold emergency drills and to be prepared for any contingency in the ice. Hulls with imaginary iceberg ruptures were patched up time after time. Non-existent fires were fought and brought under control.

Even the cooks got into the act when combat drills were held - feeding men at their battle stations. They tried to bring food to the table, but eggs and all food slipped off the trays to the floor of the ship. They gave up and brought sandwiches, and we all tried to sit in a corner on the floor.

The chairs and everything that wasn't tied down slid from one side of the room to the other with each roll of the ship. The safest place to be was in our bunks; there were straps to keep a person from being thrown out of bed. Loose bottles and whatever else would slide back and forth under the bed.

The Glacier rolled sixty degrees, and the floor looked like the wall as the ship rolled from side to side. There was a steady crashing of glass. After several days of rough weather, they broke out the U.S.A.F. college courses. There were enough college courses on board for the wintering-over group alone to complete eighteen college degrees.

The voyage to Antarctica wasn't all work, drills, initiation and study. Acey-Deucey tournaments were played and champions were crowned; also, there were bridge tourneys. Everyone had a chance to write letters.

We spent a lot of time lying on our backs on the ship's deck. Throughout the night, many of us tried to recognize certain stars or groups of stars. Some people knew a lot about them, and those of us who didn't learned from the men who could recognize stars and tell us about them. In the daytime, we watched the flying fish that would sail alongside the ship as it pushed through the water.

When we arrived at Christchurch, New Zealand, Ken and I and a couple of other fellows got off and headed for town. There was a short train ride to town. It was funny how quickly people recognized us as Americans. People were amazingly friendly, even on the train. They would ask if they could help us spend the time while we were in New Zealand.

When we got to town, we went window shopping. Every item had a price on it, but it was in pounds instead of dollars, so we were trying to figure what it meant in dollars.

As they drove by, people would stop and ask what we were doing that night. They would invite us for dinner or to see home movies of the area. Some wanted us to go with them for a ride so they could show us the country.

We did accept an invitation for dinner and home movies of fishing in New Zealand. We went back to the ship later.

On the Glacier, I got acquainted with a man who owned the Snow Cat factory from Medford, Oregon. His name was Archie Pierce. He was a nice fellow, and was going to the Antarctic to see how his machinery was working in the snow. That afternoon, a pilot ship came out to the Glacier, and a couple of people came aboard. We had gotten word that the Glacier would pull out the next day for a weeks' cruise and would stop at the other end of New Zealand the following week.

Archie and I thought it would be nice to go in with the pilot boat and ride a bus up through the island and meet the Glacier next week. That would give us time to see New Zealand. The pilot boat was ready to go, so we had no time to ask the captain if we could go with him. We just piled over onto the rope ladder and called back to people on the deck that we would see them next week at Port Lyttleton on the other end of New Zealand.

We each got a room in a hotel in Christchurch. We could see Scott's statue from our room. Scott was the last man to visit the South Pole, but all the men on that expedition died before they could get back.

That night, I was sitting in my hotel room when the telephone rang. A voice said, "Is this Commander Beebe?" I couldn't hear him very well. I finally understood that this man was asking about Commander Ebbe.

He told me that he was Commander Richard E. Byrd, the famous Antarctic explorer and in command of this expedition. I told him that I was not Commander Ebbe, but was Lloyd Beebe, so he said that he was sorry and hung up.

In a few minutes, the telephone rang again, and once more it was Commander Byrd. He said, "Who are you?" and I told him who I was and that I was on the expedition to photograph motion pictures for Walt Disney Studio. Commander Byrd said, "It is fortunate that I called you. Why don't you come over and have dinner with me tonight?" I told him I would love to, so it was arranged for 8 pm in his room.

I waited a few minutes and went to his room, and we had a nice talk. He said he was not too well, and that he was the only one on the trip who didn't have to pass a fitness test.

It wasn't long before the hotel waiter came with two huge dinners - steaks that were as big as I had ever seen. Commander Byrd told me that I would have to eat his dinner, too, that he wouldn't want anyone in the Navy to know that he couldn't eat his dinner. He sat at the table and watched me eat those two big meals with his encouragement.

We talked for a couple of hours, and discussed many things. I heard some of his life and he asked me a lot of questions. We got along very well. I could see he was lonely and wanted to talk more. He seemed tired, so I went back to my room, happy to have met Commander Byrd. I didn't realize then that he would invite me to eat with him in his room aboard the Glacier many times, even after I left the ship. Whenever Commander Byrd went to locations or whenever there was room, he would send me a message inviting me to go.

Commander Byrd seemed lonely and would stand by himself on the stern of the Glacier on our trip. When I had time and knew he would like company, I would go down and join him. There weren't many things to do. It was interesting to just watch the wake of the ship go by.

December 10, 1955 - We are expecting to set sail at 1330 today. It has been a nice stay in New Zealand. The people here have been wonderful. Yesterday when I returned from Christchurch, the people were swarming the dock by the Glacier. It was visiting hours. I went aboard and got my camera. After taking four rolls of movies of the ship and the people, I wrapped my film shipment of twenty-eight rolls and had supper. The boys on the ship had girlfriends, and soon a dance was going on the flight deck. The music was coming out over the loud speaker. It was so nice that I hated to break away, but had letters to write. About 0300 the next morning, I had to quit letter writing. I still had to write Erwin, and mail the film before the last mail at 1200.

Dr. Mears and the Hepburns came aboard as I was writing to Erwin the next morning. I showed them around the ship. It made me late, and I was unable to finish Erwin's letter. I hated that.

People were all over the dock to say goodbye to us as we left Port Lyttleton. I was surprised when Ken's girlfriend came aboard with a small package for Ken, Ed and me - not to be opened until Christmas. Something to eat, I think; her mother made it. Also she asked if we would like a copy of the newspaper reporting the departure of the Glacier sent to our homes. We told her we would. I was kept busy taking pictures as we pulled away and had no time to think of leaving.

As I took pictures, I was surprised to notice some of the officers and men with tears running down their cheeks. Everyone was sorry to leave New Zealand. We were treated in such a friendly fashion. Many boats followed us several miles, playing band music, singing, waving goodbye and blowing whistles.

December 14, 1955 - It has been quite a nice day, seeing whales and also our first iceberg. We were all getting ready for bed when it was announced over the loud speaker that an iceberg was sighted. Most of us went up to the 02 deck to watch it for a while.

Earlier in the day, it had been announced that ice could be sighted from the 02 deck, forward. Ed and I were in my little room, so we went up to see the first ice. Seemed like everyone was going up there with cameras to take a picture of it. When we got there, we saw a bucket full of ice cubes. Needless to say, cameras weren't clicking, but there was a lot of joking and laughing.

Last night the show was Student Prince. I thought it was pretty good. Before the show started, a couple of the officers brought out a tape recorder. They had made a broadcast recording of what they called the New York Monitor.

This is your reporter, Upchuck O'Roark aboard the assbuster, I mean icebreaker, U.S.S. Glacier, interviewing some of the passengers.

Of course, the ones who were interviewed were the ones who were sick on the trip. That is to say, someone impersonated them. It was real funny. Next while he was interviewing someone who was supposed to be Lieutenant Hillfrank, a letter came on board by carrier pigeon. Of course, reporter O'Roark asked if he could read it. The boys had been gone so long he knew they would like to hear something to cheer them up. It started out something like this:

Dear Frank, (Then told him how lucky he was to be going on this trip.) By the way, I was over to your house last night to a party. It sure was a humdinger. We offered to help pay for the drinks, but your wife, Nancy, wouldn't hear of it. She said that Claude had given her ten dollars to do as she pleased with. I guess you know Claude is staying at your house now. He says that he saves a lot on lunches and gas that way. You should have seen the imitation of Gypsy Rose Lee that Nancy put on. She sure has got the figure for it. It finally got late, and we had to leave, but Nancy and Claude were still going strong.

It sure is too bad about Nancy wrecking your car. We sure do admire her for being willing to mortgage the house to pay for the damage. Too bad she forgot to pay the insurance.

I sure do envy you on that trip to the Antarctic. My wife is working now and getting fifty dollars a week. It helps out, along with the one hundred fifty dollars I bring home. I can see across to your house. Claude and Nancy are having cocktails. Claude is wearing that dinner jacket you wore so much.

I can't remember just how it went, but it kept on and on. Everyone got a kick out of it. The Monitor then took off for New Zealand to interview the Mayor and other officials. They had a lot to say about sending their wives and daughters to far distant places. Everyone enjoyed that, too.

The movie tonight was <u>The Limping Man</u>, not very good. We expect to see Scott Island tomorrow.

After leaving New Zealand, we had smooth sailing for a while. Commander Byrd spent a lot of time at the stern of the ship watching the whales. He was always dressed in his fur suit to keep warm. I spent a lot of time with him. Often he would send word to me inviting me to eat with him in his room or at the officers' table. He may have felt left out. The young officers probably thought of him as from another generation and stayed with those of their own age. Anyway, when on the deck, he was always alone unless I was with him.

The icebreaker U.S.S. Glacier

Ship convoy

ARRIVING ON THE WHITE CONTINENT

December 15, 1955 - Scott Island and Frankland Island - This morning there is a parade of icebergs going by. They look like big homes. Some of them tower one hundred feet above the water. Seven-eighths of an iceberg is under water, so that means seven hundred feet of ice is below the surface of the water.

I got busy taking pictures of the icebergs and cape pigeons. They are beautiful white birds; some have black on them. The first one hundred feet of film I thought I shot I had no film in the camera. I ended up with four hundred feet of film for the day. I might shoot fifty rolls of movie film by the time we reach Little America via McMurdo. The camera battery got cold and slowed up this morning.

I got out the Yardley silver-cell batteries and made new cable with switches to fit my tripods. They sure are nice; we would be lost here without them. One seal lay on the ice as we entered the pack ice. The Glacier is shaking and shuddering as I write.

December 16, 1955 - Now that we are in the pack ice, the Glacier is doing what it was built to do. The ice is two or three feet thick here, but not solid all over; there are spots of open water here and there. One thing I am thankful for is that the ship is not rolling and pitching any more, as the ice keeps the water smooth.

The Glacier shudders and shakes as it plows into the ice. I expected to see icebergs in the pack ice, but the icebergs were in open water, and there doesn't seem to be any in the pack ice. Every once in a while we see a seal, usually near a crack in the ice.

I have kept busy taking pictures as we move along.

December 17, 1955 - The ice is getting thicker as we move along. It is now about five or six feet thick, but not completely solid. Cracks appear in the ice, and we follow them. It must be a little tough on the seals and penguins, who appear often as we go through the ice. The chunks of ice being pushed around must surely get some of them. I see blood on the ice as we run over three penguins. Two live ones came up later.

Sunday, December 18, 1955 - I stayed up all last night. It is light twenty-four hours a day now. The light is better at night for some pictures, as the sun is low. We arrived in McMurdo sound at 3 am. It was a beautiful sight coming in as we passed through the ice past Beaufort Island. We could see Mt. Erebus in the clouds, by far the most beautiful sight of the trip with its volcanos smoking. Through field glasses we could see penguin rookeries along the shore at Point Crossier, where the Emperor penguins have their rookery. We didn't go much further, as we hit solid ice.

After three tries, we only got one hundred fifty yards. It was solid, and the ice had no place to go. The captain decided to stay here and wait for the Edisto.

Monday, December 19, 1955 - Penguins were waiting for us and coming across the ice from every direction to look at the ship. Everyone waved their arms and got a big kick out of the penguins as they waved their arms back as if saying hello or goodbye. I got down on the ice with my camera and took pictures of the Glacier in the ice. Some of the fellows in front of the ship were playing with the penguins.

We are still thirty-five miles from the proposed air landing field that is our mission. The helicopter went to look for the landing field location. When it was found, I asked to go, and went out the next trip. We saw Scott's cabin at Hut Point. I took pictures of the putting in of flags to mark the strip location. We went to Shackelton's camp. Sir Ernest Henry Shackelton was a British Antarctic explorer during the early 1900's.

As soon as we got back to the ship, I replenished my packsack with film, hiked two miles to a penguin rookery and exposed nine hundred feet of film.

The weather was poor, but we were to leave early the next morning. I arrived back home at the ship at 0430 Monday morning after forty-six hours of picture taking without sleep. I went to bed for two hours, and Dick Byrd came to my room to get a key to the room where I kept my camera. He had left some things in there.

Dick is Admiral Byrd's son. He said his dad was going to visit Scott's cabin, so I got up hoping to go with Admiral Byrd and take some pictures of him. It snowed and the flight was called off. I have never seen a more mixed-up affair. Plans were changed every few minutes.

Now we are going to wait for the icebreaker Edisto to come in tonight. A few of the other fellows are getting

Admiral Richard E. Byrd and Admiral Dufek

off on the ice and transferring to the <u>Edisto</u>. I was the only one allowed to go to the penguin rookery last night, as the ice is shifting and may move out at any time.

December 21, 1955 - We left just before the <u>Edisto</u> came, so I could not cover her arrival. We are to take up station for the arrival of the air flight due in from New Zealand. Just heard that the radio equipment which was headed to the <u>Little America</u> airstrip from the <u>Glacier</u> by Snow Cats and snow weasels had to turn back. They were unable to cross a crack in the ice. The planes have left New Zealand, but there will be no radio contact to <u>McMurdo Air Field</u> to home in on until they arrive. <u>McMurdo</u> was another operation like <u>Little America</u>.

December 28, 1955 - We were cruising along the coast, and at 12:30 in the morning we came to the Bay of Whales. We could see poles sticking above the snow at <u>Little America</u>. The <u>Glacier</u> broke ice until there was a small bay of open water in which to park ships. At 1330, I was taken by helicopter to <u>Little America</u>. Four trips later, Admiral Byrd, Jack Bursey, Ed Goodale and Commander Dustin flew in and erected the flag. After taking pictures of the ceremony, I had my picture taken standing on the radio tower, which is only twelve feet tall now. Originally it stood seventy-five feet, but snow and ice have increased since it was used.

This <u>Little America</u> was where Admiral Byrd and his Antarctic expeditions had spent the winters many years before our arrival. We dug a ways to get down to the level of all the old tunnels and rooms where the men had lived during the winter.

There were tunnels and passageways to get from one room to another. Some of the passageways were almost closed, and I had to crawl through them and eventually came out to a room. There were letters and papers still on the tables and beds. There were little storage places with quite a few things in them.

I looked around as much as I could, and then picked up a couple of things and returned to the surface. Admiral Byrd and party were still there, so after more ceremonies, we got back in the helicopter and returned to the ships.

I walked back to <u>Little America IV</u> four miles away. I really appreciated Admiral Byrd's letting me go to see the first <u>Little America</u>.

Robert Falcon Scott was a British naval officer and Antarctic explorer. Shackelton was a member of Scott's expedition from 1901 to 1903. All five members of Scott's 1912 expedition died from lack of food, frostbite, illness and blizzards when they were only a few miles from their depot.

Another time we went to Hut Point to see Robert Falcon Scott's cabin. There were dead husky dogs still there on the ground, frozen.

When the helicopter came for us, we were taken back to the <u>Glacier</u>. It was decided to search farther along the coast. We came back to Kainan Bay to build <u>Little America V</u>. We arrived at 10 pm. I took pictures of ice breaking from the ship until 4 am.

I went to bed at 4 am after working all night. I got up every hour to check on camera batteries being charged until 7 am; missed breakfast until 1630. The captain stopped the ship and let me over the side. I took pictures of offloading snow weasels, sleds and Snow Cats onto the ice.

I then walked four miles with the survey party that was to survey the trail to the <u>Little America</u> campsite, if

66

they found one. Took pictures of putting flags along the trail and checking for crevasses under the snow. Blew out one crevasse with dynamite. George Moore was lowered on a rope to measure a crevasse. Then on to the Little America site.

The helicopter was coming back and forth unloading equipment. We raised a tent at the Little America site; flag and pole all good scenes. Commissioning ceremony of Little America was one of them. Also one of erecting a tent. The first message was sent and received at Little America V on radio.

We returned to the ship by helicopter and were all tired out. Will go to bed now for a couple of hours - 2010. The Glacier is breaking heavy ice and it is hard to write.

There were the wanagans to be put together. The wanagans were bunkhouses for the trail crew that will travel to Byrd Land and maybe other destinations. It takes one bulldozer to pull one and build roads.

While the Arneb and Grenville Victory kept well to seaward of the coast, the Glacier and us men aboard hugged the coastline, exploring every foot of the shelf ice to learn whether or not there was a better landing site for Little America Station than the one planned at Kainan Bay.

One day a helicopter took off from the Glacier's flight deck with Admiral Byrd aboard. The destination was Little Americas I, II, III and IV. I was on this flight, too. Here is how the old Little America bases looked to Associated Press reporter Saul Pett, who took the same helicopter from the Glacier:

> No one here today (December 28, 1955) will ever forget the strange macabre scene. Sticking up from windswept snow were tops of two steel radio towers built at the first Little America in 1928. Towers were originally seventy-five feet high; today only about eight feet of their peaks show.
>
> Also protruding from the snow like tips of fingers frozen in death were five wooden poles which were used for radio wires at the second Little America between 1933 and 1935.
>
> The second settlement was built directly over the first. Thus, the buildings of Little America I lay packed in ice and snow about sixty feet below us.
>
> Tops of poles and towers were all we found of surface at 0300 today in clear, bright light with the sun well up over the horizon.
>
> To picture the rest of the scene in all directions, imagine a flat broad Kansas wheat field. Remove all signs of human, animal or plant life. Cover it all over with snow reaching into flat infinity north, south, east and west. Drop the temperature to about four degrees below and bring up wind from the south to forty miles per hour.
>
> Imagine wind cutting into your face like steel needles, and imagine it whipping thin powder of snow like a death veil across white nothingness, and you have a picture of what Little America looked like today.

That day, the Bay of Whales was ruled out as a landing site for Little America V. Because of the ice barrier break up reported earlier by Atika, the lowest shelf ice to be found was a sheer thirty feet above the sea, which would have posed problems for unloading the ships.

The next day, the small force stood off Kainan Bay, the site that was recommended by Atika. Admiral Dufek looked at Kainan Bay and said, "This is the spot." There was an area of eight hundred-foot-thick ice within five miles of the water's edge. There was a "U" between high barriers to the right and to the left to protect the ships while they were being unloaded.

Best of all, there was a gentle slope from the barrier to the sea which would allow tractors a line of least resistance in hauling cargo upward from the ships. There were some crevasses (cracks in the ice disguised by snow on top) to be filled or bridged between shipside and campsite, but overall, Kainan Bay was a perfect landing site.

LOOKING FOR A HOME

The Glacier worked like a demon for thirty hours breaking ice to cut a channel into the landing site. She would plunge into the pack ice, ride up on it until I wondered if she would end up parking on top of the ice floe, but finally she would crash back down through the ice. I kept filming, and it was very exciting.

I would be right at the bow sometimes. She just pointed her nose to the sky until it would finally crush the ice with her weight and come down with a crash and a splash as the water would fly with chunks of ice. For the next thirty hours, no one could have slept. I just filmed and watched over the side.

We were having twenty-four hours of daylight here. The Glacier would back off and charge at full speed again and again. She cut by boxes: down a line, right angle, straight right again, straight until about an acre-wide section of ice was sliced neatly out like a slab from a pie and could be washed seaward by her propellers.

Before the ships were tied up, every available man was assigned to one of two ships for handling cargo. Booms had been uncovered, a brow boom was rigged for lowering. Four landing boats were in the water to fend off loose and drifting ice cut free by the icebreaker, lest these packs floated in with the tide and injured the ships' hulls.

By 0440 December 30, 1955, both cargo ships were tied up to the ice, their hawsers connected to deadmen, coffin-like boxes buried in the ice to anchor the ship.

Here at Little America there was a big problem.

Lloyd standing on top of "Little America's" seventy-five foot tower, now only twelve feet above the snow's surface.

Building "Little America V"

Temperatures above freezing threatened to melt the ice from under the temporary supply dump located between the ships and the base site. In addition to this drastic situation, the meteorologist predicted that a storm would hit the area within forty-eight hours.

It was the same week that LCDR Jack Bursey and six volunteers made all preparations to leave for the six hundred mile overland trip into Marie Byrd Land to mark off a safe trail to be followed by tractor trains taking material to 80 degrees/S, 120 degrees W to build Byrd Station. They left January 14th.

All those who could be spared from their other work joined the big effort of clearing all materials from the bay ice and getting them to the safety of the ice barrier where Little America V was taking shape before they fell through the ice or got blown away.

Crews worked silently, but frantically, to meet the challenge; one work gang assigned to unloading sixty-ton sleds from mid-supply at the base site from midnight to noon was comprised of a Lieutenant, two Yeomen, two radio men and two journalists. This crew unloaded five sleds in one shift.

After everything was moved from the threatened area, buildings were erected to house men at Little America during the same crucial hour.

I tried to film every project, first at the unloading, then hiking to Little America V, filming sleds and equipment along the way, then hiking back to the ship after filming the house construction. I went back and forth from the unloading to Little America. Finally, I tired and curled up on a pile of supplies for a short rest period.

Seabees, cargo handlers and ships' personnel from Arneb and Grenville Victory had worked steadily in two shifts from 0500 December 30, 1955 to midnight, January 9, 1956, when the Task Force Commander ordered a day and a half of rest and recreation for the Little America crew.

I didn't get time off because I then had baseball games and other recreation to cover on film. I guess that isn't harder than playing baseball on ice.

The day started with sightseeing rides to Little America for the people living on the ships. There were a few journalists and other people here for the summer. Five new red houses had gone up at Little America, and tons and tons of materials had been hastily unloaded just before the storm threat died. There was a steak dinner served aboard ship and an afternoon of baseball.

Picture a normal man wearing twenty pounds of clothes above heavy shoes, put a baseball bat in his hand and a three-foot cardboard in front of him for a plate. Comes the pitch, and he hits the ball perfectly using all his muscles. The ball soars over the head of the last outfielder and stops dead in the snow. Batter falls on his face four times on his way to first base only to find that he has been thrown out by the outfielder.

Commander Paul Frazier said he gave up golf when in the Antarctic Tournament a penguin took a fancy to five balls in a row.

Football was played much the same as at some colleges in the snow. The only thing unusual about the game was that everyone forgot to keep score after each side had made fifteen touchdowns.

The Admiral judged a beard growing contest, which the Grenville Victory crew won just before the cook announced the seal meat steaks were ready. Inhibitions aside, this dark seafood-tasting food was better than most people expected.

All the while, refreshments were served on Antarctic ice. Double-feature movies rounded out the day's merry-making, and crews returned to the work of unloading ships and building the base with renewed vigor at noon, January 12, 1956.

The first thing will be to build a road to the Little America site, while at the same time unloading equipment from the ships; Glacier first, and then the Arneb.

I try to get film shots of everything going on. It is daylight for twenty-four hours

Building "Little America V"

69

every day now. We are sleeping when tired in any equipment or on a pile of supplies. I then get up and carry camera, tripod and my pack of film to the next location. I took pictures of the christening of <u>Little America</u>, setting up the flag and putting up temporary tents at the site for the officers to get out of the wind.

There are several crevasses on the road to <u>Little America</u> that the bulldozer had to fill with snow. Bulldozers are pulling big sleds loaded with the insulated panels for the houses at <u>Little America</u>.

After the sleds got by, I took time to go into one crevasse and took a few pictures, but had to get back out and try to keep up with all the things going on along the <u>Little America</u> road. Before <u>Grenville Victory</u> had gotten out of sight on the horizon, an all-out effort was started to unload the <u>Arneb</u>. Three holds were being worked simultaneously when at midnight January 16, 1956 this announcement came over the loud speakers: "Make emergency preparations for getting under way."

A storm centered almost directly between New Zealand and Antarctica was causing ground swells in the Ross Sea. These swells had worked under the bay ice for several hours, and had literally undermined the whole area where cargo was being unloaded onto waiting tractor sleds alongside.

No sooner had the last tractor sled raced to the safety of the ice barrier than the bay's ice began to crack. Men stood by <u>Arneb's</u> deadmen ready to cast off. <u>Arneb</u> was a small icebreaker.

Luckily, the section that broke, some twenty-five thousand square feet of ice, was inside <u>Arneb's</u> deadmen. The mike-work boats were rushed between <u>Arneb</u> and the edge of the bay ice, plied their bows to the floating pack and shoved it clear of the ship's stern. Now it was simply a matter of bringing the <u>Arneb</u> back to the ice shelf.

The ground swells continued to work their way under the ice, so no more cargo was unloaded. Meanwhile, an eerie fog covered the ship, caused by cold air passing over warmer water and ice. The fog threw a blanket of hoarfrost over every line, boom, antenna and every man's beard.

By 8 am, the fog had cleared enough to see a few hundred yards out on the bay ice, and several large ruptures were seen. Boats took crews ashore, who hastily slipped the ship's mooring lines from the deadmen, for by now the jagged ditches in the ice were growing wider by the minute. As quickly as sections of ice broke free, they were washed away by the current.

Crevasses are mostly covered with a certain depth of hard snow. The snow flows along the surface of the ground. You can't see where you are walking. This snow, as it comes to an open crevasse, starts to build a bridge of hard crust and snow until you can't see into the crevasse. You look for any sign of a slightly sunken surface or a crack.

Ice breaking off the Ross Ice Shelf

When alone, I always wore snowshoes, so there was less chance of breaking through. I had my old snowshoes with me from home. Most others wore skis. With camera and other things I had to carry with me, the snow shoes seemed best. I didn't fall like others on skis in lumpy snow areas.

Finally, the cook house was set up and I could go in to regular meals. I still didn't show up if I was too far away. I never had a drink of water for the first month. I just ate snow. In fact, that is where all fresh water comes from in the Antarctic. You have to melt snow to get it.

After the cook house got going, there was a snow detail that brought snow in, and it was melted down to water for the

Little America people.

I never went back to the ship after landing and offloading my equipment, just wandered like a stray dog from one thing to another, sleeping or eating when I had a chance, and never sleeping in a bed. There was a tent at Little America with things to eat, but no hot food.

Almost every day was sunny, and sometimes windy.

When too tired to continue, I would crawl into a vehicle to sleep, once in a while on a pile of equipment, sometimes on snowshoes or skis around where the equipment was left.

I often went away from an operation to get long shots of Little America or anything that might be going on. When crossing new areas, you must watch for crevasses. The wind blowing on the top of the snow makes a thin hard surface sometimes, and once in a while the thin surface will settle for hundreds of feet in all directions from your weight, and make a terrible noise when this happens, "Korump". It is scary as you are constantly worried about crevasses.

When walking with other people, sometimes the fellow next to you would break through and fall to his armpits. The man next to him would jump onto a solid surface, get hold of the man and help him back out of the hole. After helping to get him out, you could look down in that hole for one hundred or more feet into a crevasse.

The Seabees finally got the Little America buildings up. As soon as they were finished, some people moved in.

There were two rows of bunkhouses with an alleyway to connect all buildings, with chicken wire and burlap on the walls of the alleyways. This was so the blowing snow would not fill the alleyway and allow them to stay open over the winter.

I was assigned to the first building on one end of the alleyway, left-hand side on entering. The building was divided into small cubicles, big enough for two single beds and room to dress in, and room for very little equipment. Under the bed was the storage area.

Chet Twombly, the Weather Bureau man, was my roommate. I was glad of this, as we were both easy to get along with. We became good friends.

I kept my camera and film in the alleyway just outside of our room. There they would be cold all the time. If you took cold metal into a warm room, condensation would get all over it, and the lenses would get fogged up. Then you couldn't take the equipment out until it was dry.

When Arneb put to sea to wait for all loose ice in the area to wash away, she left forty-three Seabees and a handful of staff personnel and Army observers high and dry on the eight-hundred-foot thick ice barrier at the base camp where, by now, nine buildings had been completed, including eight which were heated, where power was ready to be turned on, and the galley crew was serving meals regularly.

The Arneb returned to the bay ice at Little America V at 8 am, January 18, 1956 to discover the shelf had an entirely new appearance. Nature had removed more ice in eight hours than Glacier had cut in thirty, and in places nature had left as clean an edge for mooring a ship as if it had been planned.

Commander Jack Bursey, who will be leading the trail-blazing party, is in our house at Little America. His cubicle is to the right as we come in from the alleyway. Chet and my cubicle is on the left from the door

Commander Bursey and the six men under his leadership have been getting their gear together. They will have two or three snow weasels, at least one or two Tucker Snow Cats pulling sleds, with fuel for the trip to Byrd Station about six hundred miles inland from Little America. Byrd Station will be one of several scientific stations to be used in the International Geophysical Year.

The Otter plane will fly out to them whenever the weather is good for flying. They will bring supplies and added fuel; also cache the fuel and mark it with trail markers, which are bamboo poles with red flags on top.

The trail blazers will keep putting these flags out, five flags to the mile. They will have to be supplied to the crew with plane or helicopter as their supply is used up.

I would like to have gone with them, but there are just too many things going on at the same time, so I will have to fly out with the plane and spend a day or two at a time. I can't miss any operations.

The day came for the trail party to leave, and Jack Bursey made sure that everything was tied down tight, and the seven-man crew set off across the flat white expanse of Antarctica. We waved, and I kept on filming as they left Little America, then went back to filming the building of Little America and the last of the ship unloading.

From the first day the trail party left Little America, an Otter plane made daily contact when weather permitted. The party made good time the first and second days, with their crevasse detector showing no signs of hidden chasms. On the third day, they came face to face with a gaping crevasse several yards wide and ninety-five feet deep. The chasm ran perpendicular to the trail and ran twenty miles in each direction. The crevasse detector was not working! Now the detection reverted to the old prod and pray technique. The trail party backtracked ten miles, then altered course to clear the canyon, the first of many to be discovered.

They made a painful ascent of the Rockefeller Plateau, encountered more bad weather, more crevasses and leaned more heavily on the small Otter plane as time went by, mile after mile as they went into Marie Byrd Land.

I flew out to the trail-blazing party several times with the Otter plane and pilot, Paul Streich. I would take pictures until he went back to base. One trip we were socked in for fifty-two hours straight with the men on the trail.

Immediately after visibility improved, we took off in the Otter and found what appeared to be a safe trail from the crevassed area to the Rockefeller Plateau. The next day I started filming the two hundred fifty thousand gallon fuel tank to be constructed at Little America V. They needed to hurry, as the ship was scheduled to be here soon to fill the tank.

On February 22, 1956 I wrote the following letter:

Dear Family,

Hi! I wrote a letter to you while out on the trail party from Byrd Land to Little America, or L.A. as we call it. All the paper I had was a small scratch pad so I wrote on that. After carrying it around in my pocket for two weeks, it is hard to read, so I am going to copy it now.

I certainly have put off writing too long, so I will try to write a letter as I sit in a Snow Cat. The buildings at L.A. are coming along pretty good, but none of them are finished, no electricity, water or anything like that. At least not when I was last there.

As there are no windows in the walls, it is quite dark in the buildings and hard to write or read. In my spare time, or when I should be writing you, I have been working around the camp.

I just finished putting together eleven metal lockers. They are about six feet high and three and a half feet wide. It has a full width shelf about a foot from the top, then is divided straight down the middle and on one side is a small clothes closet, and the other side has four shelves. It is a real nice locker for here and holds a lot of things. I guess you know I have it all filled up.

So many things have been going on all at once that I have really been keeping busy since leaving the ship. I've been grabbing sleep whenever I get the chance, not every day though.

I think it was the first of February that I flew to Byrd Land in the Otter plane. It was real bad weather and the plane iced up and couldn't gain any altitude to get above the clouds. We got lost, and after flying around for seven hours almost without seeing the ground, and L.A. trying to fix a homing device so we would know which way to go to get to L.A., the gas tanks registered empty for twenty minutes with the red warning light on the rest of the way in.

The next day we started out again. It wasn't too good weather when we left, but soon cleared up as we got away from L.A., and it was good the rest of the way to Byrd Land.

When we got to the trail party, they had decided not to go any farther and to come back by plane to L.A. As it would take two trips to get everyone back in the Otter, I said that

I would take the second trip. That way I would get more pictures. I had intended to stay with them a few days anyway.

We erected an American flag by the tent and called it Byrd Station. The Snow Cats and weasels were parked by the tent to be left until next year when the station would be built. I took pictures of the first load getting in and taking off after some trouble getting the Otter's skis unstuck in the snow. The L.A. base was to call us on the radio, and tell us when the plane would be back for us. The pilot said it would be about eight hours before they would be back if the weather was good. I kept busy taking pictures of the camp and anything else I could find that was interesting. In fact, I didn't go to bed at all that night. After six hours had gone by, we were informed by the L.A. base that the Otter plane had gone down and to return toward L.A., looking for the downed plane and the men. The base said they would stay in touch with us. We got the vehicles out from their parking place and broke camp. After traveling one hundred thirty miles over the snow without sleep, we had to stop and get some sleep. My eyes were burning from looking at the bright snow and because of lack of sleep. I had driven one of the Snow Cats. The power steering had gone out on it, and it was hard to steer. It is supposed to be impossible to steer without the power steering, but it is such a big country I had lots of room to turn, and soon got used to it, although it is hard on the arms.

The next morning we went on until we met a search party from L.A. There were seven of them in two weasels, and they had changed drivers as they traveled. The trail to Byrd Land had been covered now, and there was no sign of the plane or the men. Orders came over the radio for us to make a camp at the two hundred-mile cache and use it for search headquarters.

Planes from McMurdo would be here soon to carry on the hunt from the air. Three days later, the Otter from McMurdo came and has made several trips over our camp, but has not stopped here. The weather has been excellent, and we all feel like the good weather can't last much longer. The plane hasn't found the men yet.

One helicopter is out here now, but has only enough gas to get back to L.A., so can't search. We felt much better when we heard that a P2V plane was coming from the states, then a few hours later word came that it had gone down on its way. It looks kind of bad for the fellows in the plane. The one good thing is the good weather. We have never had such a long stretch of nice sunny weather this summer.

When we met the search party from L.A., they were surprised to see me and told us that I was on the list of missing. The radio man called in as soon as possible and had my name taken off the list, and let them know I was with the trail party. I sure hope they didn't send the list out to the states. I felt sure they wouldn't for a week or more, as they didn't when the Otter at McMurdo crashed.

The camp here is made up of three ten-man tents tied to the Snow Cats and weasels to keep them from blowing away. There are eleven men here now, including one doctor. The time sure goes slowly for us, as we are wondering why they don't send planes to help, and we can do nothing until the search planes find the Otter. Then we may be able to bring the survivors out with the vehicles if the search planes could not land. I try to take a few pictures every day, sometimes of the wind blowing the tents or the snow drifting along them. I am living in a Snow Cat. It gets pretty cold in here.

Some of the fellows didn't know what to do with their time, so had started to build a snow igloo, and I was getting my camera to take some pictures of them when Vic Young came running from the radio weasel shouting that they had heard a message saying the plane had been found. Everyone ran over to the weasel to wait for the rest of the message to come through.

CLASS OF SERVICE
This is a fast message unless its deferred character is indicated by the proper symbol.

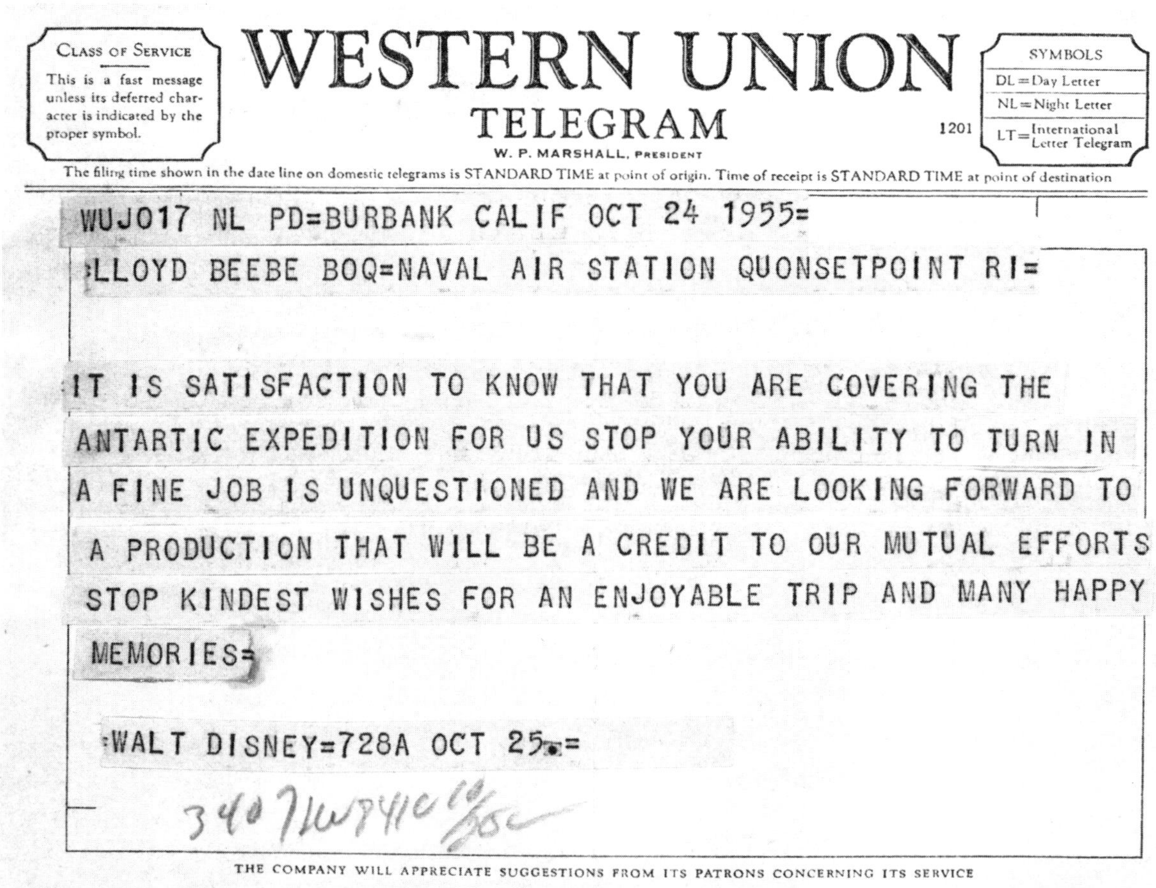

WESTERN UNION
TELEGRAM
W. P. MARSHALL, PRESIDENT

SYMBOLS
DL = Day Letter
NL = Night Letter
LT = International Letter Telegram

1201

The filing time shown in the date line on domestic telegrams is STANDARD TIME at point of origin. Time of receipt is STANDARD TIME at point of destination

WUJ017 NL PD=BURBANK CALIF OCT 24 1955=
LLOYD BEEBE BOQ=NAVAL AIR STATION QUONSETPOINT RI=

IT IS SATISFACTION TO KNOW THAT YOU ARE COVERING THE ANTARTIC EXPEDITION FOR US STOP YOUR ABILITY TO TURN IN A FINE JOB IS UNQUESTIONED AND WE ARE LOOKING FORWARD TO A PRODUCTION THAT WILL BE A CREDIT TO OUR MUTUAL EFFORTS STOP KINDEST WISHES FOR AN ENJOYABLE TRIP AND MANY HAPPY MEMORIES=

WALT DISNEY=728A OCT 25=

THE COMPANY WILL APPRECIATE SUGGESTIONS FROM ITS PATRONS CONCERNING ITS SERVICE

Telegram from Walt Disney

As soon as we heard the position of the plane, we knew we were out of the rescue and had better head back to L.A. Orders soon came over the radio to go toward L.A. fifty miles and set up another camp. The men would be taken from the plane to that point and turned over to us and the doctor.

We did as ordered, but the men were taken to L.A. instead. The helicopter that was out at the last camp with us still had not caught up with us. It was in a whiteout, and after we traveled one hundred ten miles, orders came to wait for it. One weasel went back to the helicopter and the rest of us waited there for two days. Then the copter came and went on to L.A.

That night, seven of us started out in two weasels. After twenty-five miles had been covered, one weasel broke down. Leaving the weasel there, everyone climbed into the other one and started out. It was so crowded that two of us climbed out at the fifty-mile cache and rode on the sled that we were towing. It was cold, but we made it the last fifty miles into L.A.

First we went into the mess hall, but it was an hour too early to get breakfast and I didn't want any coffee, so I went to the B.O.Q., which is our quarters. There I found someone in my bed and sleeping bags all over the floor. The fliers and others who had come on the ship for the rescue work had taken over. I didn't bother to go to bed that day. When night came, I got my bed back.

Until the extra fellows go, it will be a mess in our building, and they can't go until the Edisto and the Wyandot come in a few days. Then all the men not wintering over will go, including Ed Most, who I have mentioned before in my letters.

I can hardly wait. That will mean we can start to put in our own partitions and live like we will for the next year. It will be nice to have a room of our own. There will be two of us in each room. The enlisted mens' room will have four each. Chet Twombly is my roommate. I think I am lucky to get him for a partner. He is about fifty years old and works for the Weather Bureau. He is kind of quiet, and I will be able to go ahead with the things that I want to do.

We are having to double up our bunks now that there is so much company here. These airmen are quite a bunch. When they aren't talking about the flights they made or medals they have or should get, they are telling jokes, but always get right back to talking of their own experiences, all the time drinking beer and wondering why they can't have unlimited amounts of it.

The Chaplain just came in and asked if I would help him with some work in the recreation hall. As soon as I finish this letter, I will help him. He is a nice fellow and stays in the far end of the building from me.

There is supposed to be one more ship in at <u>L.A.</u> after this next one. I won't dare to take a chance on it, though and will get my film all ready to go on this ship. That will take quite a while, as I have to explain every roll of film. I have three full cases of forty-eight rolls each to send and am trying to finish another case by the time the ship leaves here.

Then I will have to write Erwin another letter telling him of my progress so far. Erwin sent Elmo and me a wire a couple of weeks ago wanting a progress report, and he wanted to know when to expect each shipment of film. They are not sending messages out of here by radio yet, so I haven't been able to do as he asked.

One of my cameras went bad on me, so I changed cameras as soon as I noticed it. I will be wondering how many pictures I ruined until I get a report back. That might be two months yet. They haven't seen any of my pictures that were taken in the Antarctic. I will keep my fingers crossed, and how about you keeping yours crossed too? I really am not worrying much, though, as I know I did the best I could and will have close to four hundred rolls shot by the last of February. The <u>East Wind</u> is supposed to come in at that time with our last mail. That seems like a lot of film not to have a report on. If it isn't good, it would be real bad. It is about half the film I came down here with. From now on, it will go more slowly and be harder to find something different.

As the time for the last ship to leave gets closer, more of the fellows are wanting to go home. So far, it doesn't bother me too much, as I know I will not be going, even though I love my family very much. I am staying for them and hope that the money we can save will be worth the separation. This will be the last time, though.

The Chaplain is waiting for me to help him, so I had better go now. I think of you all the time and hope the time will go fast for us.

Lots of love to all.

THE ANTARCTIC NIGHT

The tractor train with D8 tractors and sleds has reached the crevasse area on the <u>Marie Byrd Trail</u>. Seabee driver Max R. Kiel was killed instantly when the thirty-five ton tractor he was driving crashed into a crevasse one hundred twenty-five to one hundred fifty feet deep, about one hundred ten miles from <u>Little America</u>. Max Kiel was a member of a tractor party sledging fuel to be cached on the trail to <u>Marie Byrd Land</u>. He died almost exactly two months after Seabee Richard T. Williams plunged through the bay ice at <u>Cape Royds</u> in a similar tractor.

On the way to Marie Byrd Land

This same day, I went on a snow weasel and arrived at the site of Max's accident, and started to film the accident. No one was doing work; there was nothing that could be done for Max. I crawled up to the hole in the crevasse roof and looked down at the tractor. The door had apparently been open, but was now shut with Max's arm hanging out. These crevasses are wide at the top. Because of the weight of the ice, the walls always come close together at the bottom.

The tractor was at the bottom, both walls tapered tight against it. I got my camera and went back and took pictures of it. When looking straight down through the camera, it seemed like I was slipping right on down to join Max, because of the camera weight and the weight of my body hanging out over the hole in the snow, which was the same size as the tractor.

It was a sad day. Max was one of the best liked of the crew. The tractor train crew all felt bad. After I arrived, they told me that they had all agreed that no one could sleep in Max's bed except me whenever I came out to join them.

I decided to stay with them for a few days, as there were crevasses everywhere. When I went from Max's grave (he would be left in the crevasse), I arrived at the weasel I had come in, and as I stepped to the door, I fell in the snow. I reached in the door, but my hand caught on the window sill.

I fell into a crevasse but hung onto the window sill. I was able to get my camera and tripod off my shoulder and let it down on some snow. I climbed up to the window and got my feet out of the hole in the snow. I could see through the hole one hundred fifty feet or more to the bottom of the crevasse.

As soon as I could, I went back to warn everyone not to walk up to that weasel. The tractor sled train was in the middle of a lot of crevasses and had to be gotten back the way it had come, and turned around. It was too dangerous to drive these tractors here, so we got out the rope and tied it to the controls. Then we started the tractor up, put it in low gear and walked about fifty feet behind the tractor sled and a little to one side. We drove it kind of like you'd drive a team of plow horses. In this way, we were able to make a circle and get the tractor out of the crevasse area. We did this carefully and safely with each tractor and sled, but with a lot of worrying. I stayed at the location and slept in Max Kiel's bed so that I could be available to help in any way I could.

We searched for a way to get across the crevasse area; there were dozens of crevasses. A helicopter came out from the base. Commander Robert Graham was the pilot. He had a lot of trail markers aboard. He asked me if I would go with him in the helicopter and throw out trail markers. The bamboo pole and red flag on the end would go straight like an arrow, as the flag acted like a feather on an arrow.

We started out to mark a trail through the crevasse area. The pilot told me to sit with my legs out the door. There was a strap with a snap on it, which he snapped around my waist, and we started out turning around and around trying to find a trail that looked best.

When he wanted me to throw a trail marker down, he would tip the helicopter over so I could throw the trail marker straight down. Each time I thought I was about to slide out, but I didn't. We kept on all day marking a trail, about five markers to the mile.

We kept on marking trail until we had to land to refuel the helicopter. When we did get on the ground, I discovered that I didn't have my safety strap on. I didn't know that it had come off. We fueled up and kept on throwing down the trail markers. I watched my safety belt this time.

The helicopter went back to base, and I stayed with the tractor sled train. There was one sled that had a bunkhouse on it. There were three beds high, one above the other, for the crew; I had Max's bed.

We were weeks getting through that crevasse area. We dynamited our way through, and when the top of the crevasse fell in, it was filled with snow,

Lloyd and camera equipment in Antarctica

Lloyd and Seabee members with snow weasels

and we went on to another. The largest crevasse of them all took one hundred five thousand cubic yards to fill it, and still left twelve-foot high walls on each side of the road bed.

Here is another letter I wrote February 23, 1956:

Dear Family,

Hi! It has been four months since I left you folks in Seattle. It sure does seem a lot longer than that. But I guess that is about one-fourth of my sentence already served. I will be glad when half of the time has passed; then it will seem like going downhill from then on, I hope. One more year and I will be getting close to the U.S. Then there is a chance that the ships will be going home early next year, as the building at L.A. and McMurdo will be done this year. The Byrd and Pole Stations will have to be built, but are smaller, and there may be another crew come down for that. I will probably have to catch the last ship home, though.

The Edisto and the Wyandot finally came and took all the non-wintering-over personnel with them. It sure is good to have a little room to ourselves. The ships were here for two days before they could get into the ice on account of the storm we had at the time they got here. Since they left, we have cleaned our house up a lot, put in partitions and now have electric lights. We have tunnels between the buildings, and yesterday the Chaplain and I made a tunnel at the back door. The tunnels are made of a wood frame covered with chicken wire and then burlap over the wire. The snow is supposed to fill up the holes in the burlap and make it wind-proof. Yesterday, they installed a loud speaker system in all buildings, and this morning they woke us up with reveille.

Chet and I have our room in pretty good shape now. I will try to draw you a diagram of our house. There is a hall the full length of the building down the center with a door on each end. As you go in the door, there is a little closed-in part of the hall as a vestibule, then another door and you are in the hall. The first room to the left is ours. It is about fourteen feet long and not quite eight feet wide. My bed is on the left going in and Chet's on the right. I have elevated my bed about a foot to give more space to put my things underneath.

I have my locker alongside the foot of my bed and facing the head of the bed. Alongside of the head of the bed is a small stand fourteen inches wide with a drawer for writing paper, etc. The typewriter fits nicely on this stand. I have a folding chair handy to use when I want to type or just sit down, which I have had no time for so far. Everyone is expected to work here. There is so much to do yet.

The weather has been good this year, I guess. The last few days have been windy, though. Great chunks of the barrier ice have been breaking off and going out to sea the last few days. I guess the water is rough out on the bay. I can see one chunk at least two miles square that just broke off in the bay.

Today is laundry day for the officers, so I will gather all my dirty clothes, of which there are many, and try out the new washing machines. Wouldn't you like to be a mouse in the corner while I am doing that?

We have had a lot of trouble with the snow melters and have barely had enough water for cooking. I think they are doing a lot better with it now, though. The snow is hauled in on big sleds and shoveled into the snow melter, and, all in all, it is a big job. The jet heaters are not installed yet, but when they are, we will have a heat outlet in our room, so that we can regulate the heat.

The tractor train will be leaving in a day or so to cache for next year's tractor train that hauls the Byrd Station material in to Byrd Land. I was going, but they are so late getting started that I maybe shouldn't go away from L.A. at this time. I would be able to get the same pictures next year anyway. I will be on that train for sure.

One of the fellows wants me to do some work for them, so I will say goodbye for now. Lots of love. I sure miss you. Tell everyone hello for me.

Rear Admiral George Dufek had said goodbye to seventy-three Americans at Little America, and left on the Glacier.

It was March, 1956 when wintering-over began. There was so much work to do at Little America. Interiors of buildings had to be completed, supplies had to be retrieved from the snow, tired tractors needed maintenance after a strenuous unloading schedule. Routine had to be set and responsibilities assigned for the long winter night, which was fast approaching.

Ships had unloaded five hundred tons of supplies at Little America to be used in building Byrd Station in Marie Byrd Land. Long, hard, cold man hours were spent sorting and packaging these mountains of supplies. Each piece must be loaded on sleds that tractors would drag six hundred forty-seven miles over the ice to 80 degrees South, 120 degrees West.

It required great energy to find and pack the items, and mental strain of attention to details. Planners knew by experience that there are no nail kegs, no corner stores, no means of makeshift once the builders had arrived in Antarctic's barren heartland to erect their bases. If they didn't carry their materials with them, they would have to do without.

Camp on the way to Marie Byrd Land

Between February and October, Little America recorded one hundred fifty-six inches of snowfall. The lowest temperature was recorded at Little America on August 9, 1956 - minus seventy-eight degrees Fahrenheit.

Meteorologists have worked out a rule of thumb which estimates that one degree of cooling results from one knot of wind, so a temperature of minus seventy-eight degrees fanned by forty knots of nearly constant duration of wind at Little America was tantamount to one hundred twenty-eight below.

At Little America, unloading operations had been rushed when the bay ice unloading platform began to break up in January, 1956. As a result, sleds were loaded at shipside, rushed to the barrier and unloaded pell-mell in an effort to avoid losing cargo through breaking bay ice.

While no cargo was lost through the ice, the jumbled cargo at the offloading site was to cause grief through the 'long night.' Electronic tubes were mixed with potatoes and panels, and electric wire was mixed with lumber and hair tonic. Byrd Station materials were blended with Little America's operating supplies - supplies needed for the wintering-over men. Some will never be found.

The winter night is here for the next four months. Our things are packed away in our rooms. Captain Whitney has decided to distribute all the beer and pop to everyone here at Little America. He says to drink it up or save it; there isn't any more. Each of us got our share.

I didn't drink beer, but I got my share, and I was able to put it under the bed. I knew almost everyone would drink theirs up quickly, so later in the winter I would be able to make a deal for help if I needed it.

Dynamiting the roofs of crevasses

We had nineteen buildings. There were twelve people in ours, including Chet and me, Jack Bursey and a pilot, Commander Graham.

They were all easy to get along with. The men were chosen so that they would get along. I don't remember any trouble or bad arguments between any of the people at Little America. Captain Whitney had all the houses wired so he could switch to each room and hear what everyone said.

Our group disconnected the wires in our room and filled the speakers full of paper. We never heard any repercussions from headquarters about that. We had a nice room where we sat around a table and talked or played cards.

By walking down the alleyway a short distance, there was a recreation room with a ping-pong table, and we could see a movie sometimes. Across the alleyway was the cook house and mess hall and their cold room. All the boxes in there were always frozen. They would take a box of steaks or whatever and put it into the thawing-out room. There was no complaining about the food, as we had the best.

Antarctic crevasse with broken roof

One time after we had been in the houses a month or so, the cook announced that on a certain date they would have pizza for dinner. It was funny how those men acted. They yelled and hollered, and they just couldn't wait. I had never seen a pizza, so I was thinking that it must be going to be a big day. When the time came and we had the pizza, I liked it, but I wondered if their excitement could have been because they hadn't seen a pizza for so long.

I had my camera and took pictures on pizza night, as well as at Christmas and New Year. I tried to keep up picture-taking on everything that happened at Little America; one session

Antarctic wind

80

on each subject seemed adequate.

The Intern doctor that spent the winter with us was Dr. Ehrlich. One night he came to my room and wanted to talk to me. We went out where no one could hear. He didn't want anyone in camp to hear. He said that one of the Seabees had to have an appendix operation, and he didn't want anyone to know about it until after the operation. He wanted to know if I would help him with it. I said that I sure would. About an hour later, I was there with my camera and took pictures of getting ready for the operation. I don't remember if Doc used ether or something else, but he had just opened the incision and had the appendix on the outside when the lights went out. The light plant had to be fixed. We waited for quite a while, but finally Doc decided we would have to do something. By this time, the fellow was coming out from under the anesthetic and wouldn't lie still. Doc was afraid to use more anesthetic for fear that when the power came back on a fire might start. We were in a small area and the ether smell was awfully strong. The patient was straining, and Doc couldn't get all the parts back inside the incision so it wouldn't dry out. "Can you hold him still?" Doc asked me. So I held him down and held the flashlight so the doctor could finish the operation. It must have hurt the patient quite a bit, for he was wiggling and groaning, and his muscles near the incision were tight. Doc had a hard time stuffing everything back into the incision. At last, he managed to do it and sewed him up. We stayed with the patient until he came to.

It must have been time for the cooks to get up by the time I went to bed. I didn't tell anyone what had happened. I wondered how the man would do after his ordeal. A week or so later, I could see him out in the room once in a while. I guess he got well right on schedule.

I liked to watch the fellows playing ping-pong. I never had played ping-pong. Doctor Ehrlich and two other Seabees seemed to be the best players. There was always a waiting line for the one table. Sometimes they would ask me to play, but I didn't want to waste their time learning. My roommate, Chet Twombly, came one day, and he too had played and was good at it, so Chet and I would come down when everyone had gone to bed. Sometimes we just listened to good music.

At other times, Navy photographer Chet Stevens and I would spend time developing some of our still pictures. I would clean my camera equipment if I needed to keep busy.

"Little America" before the snows covered the roofs.

EXPLORING IN THE ANTARCTIC CREVASSES

I talked to one of the Seabees about making a light cable ladder with aluminum rungs for going down into crevasses. He said that he'd get the cable and aluminum pipes and bring them to my room. In no time, I had the materials in my room.

I started in cutting the pipes about a foot long. I wanted the ladder two hundred feet long, so I made it in two sections in order to fasten the ends together. I don't believe a crevasse can be over one hundred eighty feet deep, because the weight of ice causes it to squeeze together at the bottom.

I knew two hundred feet was okay. I didn't want to climb down and find out I had run out of ladder. When I finished the ladders, I rolled up each section in one roll. The rolls were very light, and I hoped they would hold me.

I planned to take my camera, tripod and film and let myself into some crevasses that I knew about, and get inside pictures. I had a good flashlight, so I walked in the dark about a mile to a crevasse I knew about and dug a hole big enough to let my ladder and myself down there. The roof of the crevasse was only about three feet thick.

I could see the bottom of the crevasse about one hundred twenty-five feet down. It looked like a smooth bottom. Next, I put my ice ax in the snow as solidly as I could and tied my ladder to the ice ax as an anchor. I let my ladder down.

The ladder more than reached the bottom of the crevasse, so I started down the ladder. It wasn't very easy going down the swinging ladder and holding the flashlight. I put the light in my pocket and kept going on down by feeling my way. Once in a while, I looked with the flashlight, then put it back in my pocket.

When I got to the bottom, I could see that it was about twenty feet wide and like a skating rink on the floor. Water had come in from the ocean. I was standing at about the water level of the bay. It was beautiful. The flashlight didn't light up a very wide area, though.

From the bottom looking up at the roof of the crevasse, it was beautiful. The roof looked like the bottom of a big round-bottomed boat with diamonds all over it. I realized I would have to take a lot of pictures here, so after walking up and down the crevasse, I decided to go back to base and see if I could use a light generator and fix a sled to pull it with, and then come back better prepared.

I wondered if I would be able to get through the snow hole at the top of the ladder. I was afraid my ladder might cut into the snow and ice and I might not be able to get my hands on the ladder at the top. I made it okay, and went back to Little America V.

I had no trouble getting a light plant, a sled and extension cords to reach down to the bottom of the

Lloyd with ARRIFLEX camera

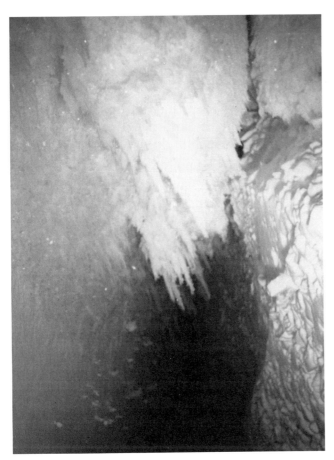

Crevasse with crack in the roof

crevasse. I then talked to my roommate, Chet. At the beginning of the four month winter night, the word was passed that anyone going outside should get permission from the Officer of the Day.

Chet and I had an arrangement between us. When I would go out, I would explain to him where I was going, sometimes taking pictures of the Aurora or looking for a crevasse to get into. I would leave my snowshoes sticking upright in the snow where I entered a crevasse. He would know when I got back.

Everyone was aware of our arrangement and let us do it that way. I never went out in bad weather, just in quiet times.

The next day after I had my outfit together, I pulled my sled and equipment back to the crevasse. Putting my ladder in place, I started the generator and let down the lights and cords, then took my camera and went down.

Now I had plenty of light. This much light made it many times more beautiful. The walls were straight up and down, and at the bottom as it joined the floor, there was a windrow of pure salt on each side. The salt averaged six inches deep.

It is very quiet and there's never any wind in the crevasses. When there is a big storm out toward New Zealand, the big swells move the ice up and down. The walls creak and groan as they move up, and new water can come into the crevasses at that time and sometimes put on a shiny new floor.

It would be a great place for ice skates. I knew I had filmed some very nice scenes in the crevasse tonight, so I climbed back out, loaded up my things and went back to my room. Chet always felt relieved when I got back.

When I returned, I wondered if the Commander might want to talk with me about wandering around in the dark without permission, but it never happened. One of the Seabees told me that the Commander had decided that I was able to take care of myself. I found out next spring that Commander Whitney had had some conversations with my bosses at the studio.

When the first mail came, the studio had rigged up nylon ropes

Lloyd on the bottom of a crevasse

83

Lloyd standing close to crevasse roof

with a harness for me. This was sent to me with warnings to be careful and not take any more chances in the crevasses than were necessary.

Commander Whitney asked Erwin Verity the question, "Where did you ever find a man like Lloyd Beebe? He seems to be able to do all the work that our Seabees can and some things we wouldn't dare to."

There was nothing more at Little America to film, so I spent much more time in the crevasses. Some of them I could walk a mile or more in. Sometimes, the crevasse may almost close up at the bottom, and it is necessary to crawl through a ways and then it may open up wide. It is very pretty. If there are great swells on the ocean from storms, it can be a little frightening.

This makes you wonder if a big piece of the Ross ice shelf might be floating away. There is about eight hundred feet of ice under where I am walking at the bottom of the crevasse, and it is all floating on the sea water.

The time came when I needed more lights and wires, and to pull the sled farther from base. None of the Seabees ever expressed any interest in going with me. I decided the time had come to use the ten full cases of beer under my bed. Everyone in camp was out of beer and hadn't had any for two months.

I let the Seabees know I was going into a crevasse and needed help pulling my equipment; also, that I was ready to give a full case of beer for each person that helped me this day. Three people of the trail party said they would go for a case of beer each. We got the light plant to the crevasse I had discovered. I had already made a hole in the top of the crevasse. We started the light plant. One fellow didn't want to go down the ladder, so he was left to keep the lights going. The rest of us had flashlights and plenty of extra batteries.

After the camera gear was down and the lights were on, I started filming. We had a lot of light cable, so I could move around to some beautiful places. Everywhere there were diamonds. When I had filmed everything possible, we decided to walk on up the crevasse.

The two fellows with me were enjoying it now. It was so quiet that it seemed safe. We each had flashlights. After telling the man who was up at our entrance hole what we were going to do, we started up the crevasse. After traveling about a mile, we came to a problem.

When the crevasse walls, over a long period of time, had spread out, they split like a snarly piece of wood with slivers from one wall to the other. The floor was forty feet wide. There was a sliver of ice from the bottom right-hand wall that was twenty feet wide and eighteen inches thick: a perfectly formed ribbon of ice. This ice ribbon crossed in front of us two feet off the floor, and then went one hundred feet to the opposite top wall of the crevasse.

I told my helpers to stay back, and that I would step on the ice ribbon easy and hurry across. I did that, and was most of the way across when there was an awful noise, and I just got out from under the ice ribbon. I and everyone else had their flashlights on and were waving them around to try and see what was happening.

That ice ribbon had all crashed in a mountain of ice between my friends and me. They started calling me and were sure I was under the pile of ice. I called back and said that I was all right, but they didn't see how I could be. After a few minutes, I climbed back over the ice to where we were all together.

We agreed it was time to call it a day, and we did, taking all our things back to the base. I gave the guys the agreed on case of beer each and some extra. They told me not to call on them any more, that there wasn't enough beer anywhere to get them in a crevasse again. Back at the base, they were glad to have been there, the way it turned out.

I knew how lucky I was and was glad to start something new. I did get down into more crevasses on the tractor trip to <u>Byrd Station</u> when, during the building of the road, they needed to know the nature of the crevasse: size and shape and depth. This road to <u>Byrd Station</u> was six hundred forty miles from <u>Little America</u>. <u>Little America</u> was closer to the South Pole than any other human settlement.

Another letter, September 28, 1956:

Dear Family,

The winter is almost over here now, and I am starting on my first letter. Most of the fellows here haven't written any letters and are just beginning to worry about getting some ready to go out if the chance to send some should come. We may get home as soon as our mail.

The planes should be going back in January, though. They are to get here by November. Of course, we are looking forward to getting our mail more than anything else. I think that will make us more anxious than ever to get started for home.

I have had a lot of sleepless nights just because I started to think of home and couldn't quit. You remember how I couldn't sleep just before coming down here. It has been like that ever since winter started. I guess it will be that way until I get home with my family again. If I start thinking of home, I might as well give up going to sleep for the night.

At the beginning of winter, I loaned my typewriter to Commander Jack Bursey to write a book, and he is still using it. I am using Chet's now. Jack always has the page he is working on in the typewriter, so I don't like to take it out when I want to use it a while.

The first part of winter I kept busy trying to get some movies of Auroras, or Southern Lights. Erwin said it has never been done, but I think I must have gotten some. Sure hope so anyway. I must have spent at least a hundred cold, clear nights out there trying. The coldest night I was out was seventy-eight below. I say nights, but it was whenever the sky was clear, then I stayed out until I got too sleepy or it would get cloudy. Then go

The winter night

to bed, and miss most of the meals.

We have a store that is open an hour each day, so I kept a good stock of candy bars to eat while I was outside. The last two months the Aurora seems to have disappeared. Sometimes we see some very faint ones. It is getting so light now that I have given up getting any more and can only hope the ones I have will be good enough.

It took me at least an hour to get ready each night to take pictures. First, I had to get an armload of hand warmers and chemical heating pads started to keep camera and batteries warm for long periods. I was always having trouble with my electric timer, too. Now I can think of other things.

Bob Graham tells me that I have a schedule to talk with Erwin tonight at eight. Erwin sent a message a week ago and said it was important that Roger Broggie and Winston Hibler talk to me, so last night a California station made arrangements with this station for tonight. I hope it will be a good patch and I can answer all the questions that they want answers to.

They are sending two photographers to the Antarctic for <u>Deep Freeze Two</u>. One is to go to <u>Knox Coast</u> and the other to <u>Weddell Sea</u> and stay the winter. The studio wants to know about winterizing camera equipment. They have already talked to Elmo, I think. It is nice to think of those fellows on their way down here and us on our way home. I have only talked to Elmo one time since coming down here, and that by radio, but he must be ready to go home by now, too.

We have been nice and comfortable this winter. The weeks seemed to pass quite quickly, but there are so many of them. I guess it is just a long time. The first of the winter I studied Spanish, then as time went by I felt that I needed more exercise. Ping-pong being about the only game played here that has exercise connected to it, I started playing. I had been watching for some time, and the fellows kept trying to get me to play. All Navy recreation halls have ping-pong tables, so there are a lot of good players here.

I had never seen a game played before, but soon got the hang of it. The last month I have gotten to where only one player here can beat me, and he doesn't beat me any more than I beat him. A little more practice and I could win regularly from him, but since the sun came up I haven't much time to play. It has been a week since I played. The ping-pong balls are about gone anyway. I think there are two left, and they only last a day or two each.

Two weeks from now the recreation hall will have to be filled with beds and be gotten ready for the fellows who are coming in on the planes. That may be the end of the movies, too, as the only place left with enough room to show them would be the mess hall, and that is a busy place and will be a lot busier when the Navy planes start coming and going at all hours from New Zealand.

I am thankful that we have our rooms and it won't be a madhouse like it was last year with sleeping bags all over the floor when the ships get here. Of course, it may be that when we go to <u>Byrd Station</u> we will lose our beds. I intend to fly back here once in a while if it is possible to keep up with the pictures on this end. In that way, I may be able to save my room to keep things in.

I may not be able to send letters too often, but I will send radio messages the same as I have been. The planes may be flying to New Zealand regularly with our mail. I will be glad when I can call you up from New Zealand, or wherever our first stop will be.

It seems we may go back on the aircraft tender <u>Curtiss</u>. That ship is from the west coast, so some of the men here think there is a good chance that we may come into San Francisco. If that happens, you and the boys can meet me there. The Navy will want all the publicity it can get, so we are pretty sure to stop at one or two other countries on our way home.

I don't know if I ever told you the names of the people in our building, so I will now: Chaplain Peter Bol, Jack Bursey, Don Mehaffey, George Purinton, Vic Young, Bob Graham, Wes Seay, Paul Streich, Chet Twombly and his roommate Lloyd Beebe, who I hope you still remember. They are a good bunch, and I think I have the best one for my roommate.

Chet has a radio in our room, and we each have earphones to listen with. We get the news every day if we want it. I don't seem to care much about world news, though, and listen only once in a while.

September 29. It was bedtime when we finished talking on the radio last night, so I didn't want to start up the typewriter. We had a real good phone patch and talked for an hour. I guess I managed to answer all their questions okay. Erwin said he would call you today, so you probably know more than I do, as I spent most of my time answering questions.

Roger was on one phone and Erwin on another. Roger gave me a couple of pats on the back about my photography that I couldn't hear. I asked him to repeat, and Erwin spoke up that Roger had complimented me on my pictures and that should make me feel good. I said I needed something like that to cheer me up.

Then Erwin said, "Here is something else to cheer you up." He said I had gotten a raise, and that I would be surprised when the next check came. He is sending a letter to explain. I told him thanks, and I guess he knew that had something to do with my coming down here. Now I will have to get busy and earn it.

He said the showing of <u>Arctic Wilderness</u> had been postponed until about this time next year because they had completed <u>Secrets of Life</u> this year. I will be home to see it that way. I expect to be on the ship and headed for home late in February at the latest. The ice will be getting too heavy for regular ships at that time of the year.

October. I don't know why I left this letter so suddenly, but here I am again. Seems like there should be a lot of things to write about after being gone for almost a year. Can't think of too much, though. I haven't had my clothes off for two days now. We have just about had all the night that we will this winter, so I have been taking pictures outside with lights at the darkest time of the night. The next thing will be to get pictures of the inside of the tunnel. There isn't enough light in it for color pictures, and it is hard to put more lights in it. I think I had better try to make a sled and put lights on it, then mount the camera on the sled too. I might be able to push the sled and camera smoothly enough along the tunnel.

Yesterday I went out to the airfield and took a few rolls. The Seabees are starting to smooth the field and get ready for the planes to come. I have been down to the bay three times already. There is about seven or more feet of ice as far as you can see. So far, we haven't seen any penguins or seals. One day, we did see a skua gull fly over camp. I guess he didn't like what he saw, as he hasn't been back.

You know those photography magazines that I brought down here to read? That's right, I still have them to read. I probably won't have much time from now on. I guess I had better bring them home with me, huh? Maybe I can read them on the way home and throw them overboard as I finish them.

Got yours and the folks' messages. It is nice to get them. Erwin must have told you that I might be flying home. That is in the contract, remember? If we want to, we can. Probably I will come by ship unless Erwin should ask me to fly. Of course, there is plenty of time to think of that. You might think of what you would want to do about meeting me if we should come in at San Francisco or anywhere else. You might like to take a trip by that time. If not, I could be home in one day anyway. I will have to go so close to the studio that they may want me to stop a day or two.

We have just heard that a plane will be taking our mail back to New Zealand by the first of November. Probably it will come back with more mail for us.

It is a beautiful day here, but forty-seven below, so you see the summer is not quite here yet. October 24 the sun will be up twenty-four hours; that will really start the summer, I guess. That will also be over a year since I left home. I bet I will see a big change in Melvin and Kenny when I get back home. They have grown so much that I won't know them. We will spend a lot of time together.

October 13. Today has been declared cleanup day. The Admiral will soon be here, and everything has to look its best. I guess there will be cleanup days every day or two until he gets here. We have inspection twice a week. One is sanitary inspection and the other is to see how clean the rooms are. Two fellows come around and write down what is wrong with your room, and it is published in the plan of the day, which is a sheet of paper with the day's schedule on it. So far ours has always been okay.

They are due to come any minute. We really cleaned up this morning, so I am sure we will pass this time.

They just came in, and guess what? They didn't even look in, just walked by, after all our work too. Chet and I are the only civilians in camp. I think they let us get away with things.

We are going to have a party tonight in the recreation hall as it will be turned into a barracks building as soon as the Navy planes get in. No more parties from now on. That doesn't matter to me, as all it amounts to is a beer party, and I usually don't go anyway. Tonight it will be a little different, and there are to be some eats to go with

Seal on Antarctic ice

the drinks. Also, a couple of the fellows are going to play some music. That will give me a chance to take a few pictures. I have taken six hundred fifty-six rolls of film so far. With the film I have on hand and what they are sending me (four hundred rolls), I will have six hundred rolls of color film to shoot up. When I ordered it, I expected to go on around the continent on the last ship to go home, but now that they are sending two photographers to the new bases, there will be no reason for me to go that way home, and I may not need it all. I will try to use it all, though.

I will say goodbye now and start another letter. Sure miss you.

A LONG WINTER NIGHT, BUT THE SUN CAME BACK

Through the winter, the Seabee mechanics had worked on the tractors and other equipment in order to be ready to resume the trail and building of <u>Byrd Base</u> six hundred forty-four miles from base. The time came when the weeks of twilight began after the four months of darkness. It would gradually become lighter until the edge of the sun would show on the horizon. The sun would show that way the full three hundred sixty degree circle, and each day show a little more of the sun.

As soon as we could see to walk outside, everyone was anxious to go out and do something. At breakfast one morning, the men were talking about what we should do. One fellow spoke up and said, "Let's go out on the ice and build snowwomen." Everyone had a big laugh, and thought it was a good idea. It was almost a year since anyone there had seen a woman.

<u>Little America</u> was now snowed in; only the

The sun came back

roofs showed. You could walk right up on the roofs. The snow was at roof level and was swept off the roofs by the wind.

Through the winter night is a time for everyone to think of home. Most of the Seabees seemed to be single men. Most of them had been in the Seabees for several years and were a chosen group of men. The Navy might have picked out men who were, for the most part, without worries of wives and children. I only remember that they talked mostly of girl friends.

Everyone had put a circle on the calendar at January 21st, the date we could expect to go home. To make it as easy as possible in the long time since leaving home, I had kept busy and tried not to think of home too much.

Memories of home and faces were a little like a misty dream. By now we felt like we were on the downhill. We would only be here for one more spring and summer, then the trip home. We still had a lot of crevasses to cross. Some of the men were not anxious to go on any more long trips.

Commander Whitney made a ruling that if you had served on one tractor train trip, you didn't have to go on another. That didn't apply to me, so I went on all four trips from <u>Little America</u>. As long as I was there, I wanted to go on the trips and complete the film coverage I was there for.

It was hard work, but very interesting. The <u>Little America</u> base would be overflowing with newspapermen and scientists after the ships came back for the summer. They would get off the ships and ride over to the base, then go back to the ships and write their stories. A few may be lucky and get a ride on a plane over the tractor train.

The trail-blazing party and the tractor train were getting ready to go to locate and build <u>Byrd Station</u>

Only roof tops showing at "Little America"

six hundred forty-four miles from base. I filmed and helped out any other way that I could. It took a lot of work to dig all the material out of the snow and load all the big sleds. They had already built two wanagans, which are cabins on sleds, and used for cooking and eating. These occupied two of the twelve sleds that would be on the trip.

Sled loads averaged twenty ton payloads, and each followed rumbling tractors over the soft snow at three miles per hour. Meanwhile, the advance party refueled and headed deeper into Marie Byrd Land, planting trail flags five to the mile along a straight trail which, on completion, would be named Army-Navy Drive.

Another letter, October 23, 1956

Dearest Family,

Well, the planes didn't get in yesterday as they were supposed to. You can bet the fellows here were disappointed. They hate all 'airdales' now for a few days. That is the nickname of anyone connected with aviation.

We were all set to go out to the field and meet the two planes at 1900 last night. Finally word came that they were not coming. Only a few of us were allowed to go. No word has come to this base as to whether the Admiral is coming on this plane. I think it has Commander Whitney a little worried, but he doesn't want to show it.

While I am thinking of it, those envelopes with the first letter and the ones to Melvin and Kenny are marked on the 4th of July. The only ones stamped on that date were for those of us who wintered over. Most of the men sent one or two. I had the postman here cancel a few for me to send later. When I get those addresses you are sending, I will try to send a Christmas card to each. We have plenty of cards here. Hope I get it done.

It is funny, but there just doesn't seem to be anything to write about. All I can think of is to get finished and go home to my family. Nothing else seems important anymore. It has been over a year now since I left you in Seattle. Really not so awfully long until we will be together again. My guess would be about five months.

Things are getting behind schedule here every day that the planes put off coming. Most ships would have to get out of here by the end of February, as the ice is pretty thick at that time of the year.

The sun is up twenty-four hours a day now starting today. The sun set and rose last night for the last time for six months, so we should have a lot better weather ahead of us. Today it is cloudy and the wind is beginning to blow. We may be in for a storm for a day or so. I hope not; I am anxious to get my mail and send out the mail that is to go home and get rid of the exposed film. Some of the planes have gone back to New Zealand from McMurdo, so I expect that Elmo has sent his film back already.

It was nice to talk to you by radio. The ham radio got to be a plaything of the four fellows that are allowed to operate it. They talked to their families every few days. No one else is supposed to go in with the ham radio. I know I could have talked more, but I didn't feel like asking all the time when it was their job to call us when they could make a phone patch. I guess we were lucky at that.

They are liable to shut down the ham radio soon anyway. It will probably interfere with communications with the planes and trail party. You will be able to send messages to me as often as you want. I think I can send them to you except when I'm at Byrd Station.

When I get your letter, I will have some questions to answer, and it will be easier to write. I will try to write often. I guess I should write a note to those people in New Zealand. Goodbye for now. I love you very much and miss you. I will write again soon.

October 25th - Another letter:

Dear Family,

Well here it is the 25th, and no mail. Almost every day we get word from McMurdo that the mail is on the way. It is about time, as the fellows here are getting pretty anxious. They are starting to draw cartoons about the mail service, the airdales and everything connected with the delay in the mail. The bulletin board in the mess hall is where they hang them. I think everyone is getting a kick out of them. There is always a crowd standing there seeing if there are any new ones. The whole wall is almost covered with them now. The cartoons are about everything from trail parties of Seabees and tractors with airmail and planes loaded on sleds headed for L.A. and the pilots telling after arrival what a tough flight it was, to a newcomer taking a shower and a lot of fellows who wintered over, with just their heads and beards sticking over the top of the shower stall, just watching them soaping themselves.

For several days now the planes have been supposed to be coming, but always after we wait a few hours, we get word that, due to this or that, they are unable to come. The truth is, I think, that the Pole Station is where most of the publicity will come from, and the correspondents are all over there, so they want to get started on that first.

I think they should have planned on flying out to Byrd Station too. It is a good bet that they will never get Byrd Station out as far as they would like to, but they will at least take it as far as the time will permit and set it up. The bosses wouldn't want to admit that they failed. The plan was for six hundred miles. I hope they get all the way.

Some of the fellows want me to go out and play volleyball with them, so I will go out and play a few games, then it will be time for the show. We have seen all of the shows, but they are running them over, and some of them are good enough to enjoy the second showing.

Well, back again. We had a few good games. The snow is so slippery that you are falling down all the time. I wish Melvin and Kenny were here to help win. We played three games and won two of them. One of the games we had only three on our side, and the other team had four, and we still won. It looks funny to see the fellows playing outside with frost on their beards.

While we were outside, word came that the mail was coming on a plane tonight. By now the fellows are all betting that it doesn't arrive. It is sure to come one of these times, though. Could be tonight.

I am going out to get pictures of the plane bringing in the mail, and after that the sorting of it and fellows reading it. Probably won't be able to read mine until midnight. Sure am anxious. Now I wish I had written more.

I had better go out with my cameras and be ready when the plane gets here. I think the plane will go right back, and this letter will probably not go. I will try to mail it, though. I sure love all of you and miss you. It won't be very long till we will be together again, so lots of love for now.

Another, dated October 28, 1956:

Dearest Sweethearts,

Well, the mail really came in the night of the 25th. We stood out on the runway for about an hour waiting, and finally saw a speck in the sky, and it turned out to be the plane.

It was thirty below and a little breeze was blowing. I took pictures of the landing and unloading of the plane, and then came back to L.A. and shot some more of the sorting and reading of the mail. When that was over, I got my letters and read them. Just finished at 0300. It sure was nice to get the mail.

The pictures you sent arrived, too. The pilot of the plane gave them to me as I was taking pictures at the plane. Not a word from the studio, though. No film or equipment either. I was hoping to get the film, as I am behind on the indoor pictures and would like to catch up while I have time to do it.

The next day, we were allowed to sleep until 0800, as everyone had lost a lot of sleep reading their mail. I am my own boss, but I like to keep their hours as much as possible. I don't want them to think that I am a privileged character. I have gotten along real well with the men. Haven't had any trouble at all. In fact, I guess they think of me as another Seabee. I did have trouble refusing to drink with them. They couldn't see why I didn't drink with them. They gave up long ago trying to get me to drink.

Another plane came in today and went back already, at least started. No mail came, though. I guess we will be getting mail in quite regularly this summer. I will try to write often.

The Glacier arrived in McMurdo today and it is expected that she will be coming here as soon as she is unloaded. I hope that my equipment from the studio is on board. It will be nice to go down and see if the same fellows are running the ship; also to go to the store and get things that we haven't seen here, like hair oil. That is one thing that was not ordered for here, and everyone's hair is dry.

We also kind of hate to see so many new people coming, as it makes a lot of work, and it is a madhouse when all the correspondents get here. They think they deserve the best of everything. If they don't get all they think they are entitled to, they threaten to send in bad press reports and all that kind of stuff.

The men wouldn't care, because they don't get much anyway. With the officers, it is much different. I get along good with them, but I do get tired of their search for publicity. If the reporters are here, that is where they will be, and if I start the camera they usually head for it, just as if they didn't know. It is a big joke with the men.

I like it really, as it makes it easy for me. Sometimes, I just pretend to take their picture to make them feel good. It makes it easier to get help from them when I need it. Taps has just sounded, and I had better quit typing so I will say goodbye for now. Lots of love to all of you.

October 29, 1956

Dearest Family,

Today the weather is clear with a wind of ten knots, some blowing snow in the air, thirty below. Really a nice day, but nothing new to take pictures of. The trouble is that I have taken all the everyday pictures, and unless something new takes place, I can't keep very busy.

The Army people are here now and are getting the crevasse detector ready, so that will be something different. It sure is a contraption. The trail party will be going soon, and I think I will go with them if they will let me. That should be one of the most interesting trips.

I have already taken a lot of pictures of the tractor train party's trip last year, so won't take too many this year. The trail party is scheduled to leave soon after the Glacier gets here. Two weasels, one Snow Cat and two D8s will go with them. One of the weasels will have the crevasse detector on it. The D8s will fill the crevasses as we come to them.

There will be a lot of them in that one spot before coming to the plateau. I think they will take much longer in filling them than they expect. Anyway, if I go with them, I may not be able to get my pictures and send them in before the army of T.V. men at McMurdo gets over.

Commander Frazier who is at the head of the trail party told me that he had promised the CBS and NBC men at McMurdo that they would fly them out to the trail party when they got out to the most interesting part. Also, all of the correspondents.

Those fellows have been giving parties and wining and dining the officers like Frazier in New Zealand and the U.S. before leaving. It is kind of disappointing to me, and I guess to Elmo, too, to have expected to be the only outside photographers here, only to find all of these newcomers turned loose.

Erwin doesn't like it, I bet. In a letter from Eleanor written last February, she said that Erwin had written the proper authorities in Washington and protested. Apparently, it didn't do any good. I just hope I can get a few good sequences that they don't have, like a good one on crevasses and possibly something on wildlife. It is going to be hard to get a lot of new pictures this year. Mostly the same things will happen again.

We used to get a newspaper, but haven't had one for several weeks now. The news just isn't coming in, I guess. They are plenty busy with the communications, as all the messages from McMurdo are sent here and then on to the states or wherever else they are sent. I sent Erwin a message telling him that the film had been sent. Now I have to send another one for parts for one of my Arriflexes. Yesterday I took both of them all apart and cleaned the old grease and oil out, checked over the parts and oiled and greased them again. One of the gears was broken and will soon have to be replaced, and one camera motor went bad, so I will order another while I am at it.

I'm sure these are dull letters, but I can't seem to think of anything except that I love you and want to be home again. The news here is that twenty-seven days after leaving the Antarctic, we will be in San Diego, and we might leave here around the 20th of February, with a week's stop in New Zealand. Of course, the work will have to be done. Lots of love to all of you. I might see you in San Diego.

The heavy tractor trail averaged forty-five miles per day on good going. The new crevasses were blasted and filled with snow and packed. The blasts were set off with electric caps. Whenever I was close, the blasters would want to take a short cut instead of running long wire out, in order to stay safe if the roof of a crevasse fell in. They would touch their blasting wires on my camera battery, and the blast would go off. This was much faster, and I spent a lot of time helping them this way, although I knew there was a chance of being too close to a crevasse when the top fell in. I went along with it until some of the officers who were watching told the blasting crew not to do that any more, and I knew they had the right idea.

Safely on the Rockefeller Plateau, the train formed up for the remaining four hundred fifty-seven mile trek to 80 degrees South, 120 degrees West. The trail ran almost constantly uphill until, at base site, the elevation was five thousand one hundred fifty feet. This trip had mechanical problems and miserable weather.

Fleet in the ice

On arrival at <u>Byrd Station</u>, parts were delivered for the station at 2 pm, December 23rd. The first load was taken from the sled cargo. A meteorology building was set up in nine hours after the train's arrival.

Burning eleven thousand gallons of fuel provided almost exclusively by airlift, the train had accomplished successfully the longest and largest tractor swing in Antarctic history.

When the tractor sleds were all unloaded and the buildings up, we turned around and headed for <u>Little America</u>.

OUR LAST DAY, THE BIG TRACTOR TRIP IS OVER

When we got back to Little America, there were a lot of strange people wandering around who had come on the ships. There were some Army ice experts and scientists from the ship who wanted to go out to the big crevasse area and get down in the crevasses to do some studying of ice under pressure and other things. They sent some Seabees with them, and also asked me to come.

We went out in weasels and Snow Cats. We were to stay a few days until the Army could get the information it wanted. We stayed in makeshift tents made out of parachutes. You could see through them.

The next morning, we started looking for the deepest crevasses. The army fellows had a cable ladder like the one I had made. They put the ladder in place, and two of them climbed down. They had an ice ax let down to them. I filmed all this, then decided to go down with my camera and take a few pictures of what they were doing down there. I tied my camera and tripod on top of my packsack, and started to go down the ladder. One of the Army men objected. He said that I wouldn't be able to climb out one hundred seventy-five feet of swinging cable ladder with a heavy load. Some of the others agreed.

It was bright light now. I had been doing this in the dark all winter. The Seabees were getting a kick out of this, too. They said that I could get out, so I went down to the bottom and filmed their work.

When it was time to go back up the ladder, the Army men went up first, while I steadied the ladder so it wouldn't swing so much. They were stopping to rest once in a while. I put my pack on and started. I knew with my pack it would be better to keep going, and I did. As I got close to the top, I could see the Seabees smiling.

When I climbed out of the hole, one Seabee whispered to me, "You made it up the ladder a lot easier and quicker than the Army did." One of the Army men said to the Seabees that he would pay the bet when we got back to base. After about a week's stay around the crevasses, we went back to Little America.

A letter, November 5, 1956

Dearest Family,

We haven't had much news here lately, but today the Little American newspaper came out, and there doesn't seem to be anything except bad news. The world seems to be getting all mixed up again.

Maybe we all should volunteer to come back down here for Deep Freeze 2. I think I will take a chance and come back to the U.S., though.

I keep wondering what you folks are doing at home this time of the year. Melvin must be duck hunting or getting ready to. Kenny is shooting the bow and arrows and helping Grandpa with the chores around the farm. You are piling the wood, scrubbing the muddy footprints from the floors caused by the fall rains outside, and I hope, as I am, hoping that I will be home soon.

The new rumor that is going on here is that the Curtiss will leave here for Auckland, New Zealand, then to Sidney, Australia and from there nonstop to San Diego. Sounds like a nice way to come home, doesn't it?

I would rather stop in Australia than anywhere else on the way home. I think we may have a choice of flying home from New Zealand. The Curtiss is a pretty fast ship, so I will probably come home on it to San Diego. There will be a few pictures to take on the way.

San Diego is going to look awfully good to all of us. If I don't go to the studio, then I wonder if Erwin will meet me there. He will probably want you to meet me and then have us come to the studio for a few days. That would be fine with me. Lots of time to think of that, and I no doubt will think of it a lot.

I have a calendar here in my room that a British Commander on the Glacier gave me last year. It has a pretty girl on it. She is sitting on a rail fence. I have been marking off the days as they come along. I haven't got a 1957 calendar, so I will use May over again for January and June for February as far as the 28th. By that time, we will be on our way home.

I always mark the day off the first thing every morning. Jack Bursey says I do it wrong, and should wait until the day is gone to mark it off like he does. Everyone has a different way of enjoying marking the days off or turning over another month.

One of the fellows here can hardly wait till the end of the month, and when it comes, he rips the page off the calendar and tears it in as small pieces as possible. Then he throws them all over and seems to let off a lot of steam.

While I am thinking of Jack Bursey, he was telling me he made up a little story about me being stuck under the bed and the boxes falling on me. He got a kick out of it, though, and you probably did too when you received his letter.

I guess you haven't sold the farm yet. I think that if Dad ever wanted to sell the farm, the best way would be to let us have the last bid. Then we could either buy it or sell if it was too much for us. I wouldn't bring up the subject, though. I think if it didn't cost too much, we would be better off to keep it.

It would surprise me if it would sell readily at the price Dad would want anyway, so it would be better to act willing to sell if it came up, but keep the right to the last bid. It is a good place for the kids to grow up and will always be worth as much as now.

November 6

Just received your message late last night. Was glad to hear that you are getting some ducks, Melvin. When I get home, you and I and Kenny will go out together. Maybe Mama will go with us too.

I got most of the letters up to September. There seems to be about ten missing; could be on the Glacier. She should be in sometime today. I don't think that we will be able to go aboard, as they are low on fuel and are going right to New Zealand as soon as unloading here is complete.

I guess they will unload with the helicopter and not break any ice in Kainan Bay. I intend to walk out to get a few pictures. It will be at least ten miles out from the barrier. I am hoping that my film is on board, but don't believe that it will be. Seems if I remember right, the Glacier left before that equipment left the studio.

I almost forgot. I received the fruit cake. I am afraid I have been a little selfish with this one. It sure is good; almost gone, too. I ate quite a bit of it while I was reading the letters. Seemed like I was home for a little while there.

November 10

The Glacier came and is gone again. We could just see her from L.A. I walked out almost to the Glacier one day. In fact, she was only here one day. Before I got quite out there, I became interested in getting some pictures of the helicopter crossing back and forth over the barrier as it unloaded the ship. As a result, I never did get all the way out there and decided that I would go the next day. I had been down there on the ice since 2 am.

They were to be unloading for two or three days. The next morning at 0400, the <u>Glacier</u> sent a message that it was underway for New Zealand. They had even forgotten to pick up the mail and two fellows who were to go back with them. They finally sent a

Lloyd on snowshoes with camera equipment

helicopter in to pick them up. I did manage to send my film with one of the fellows who went home. I told him to give it to one of the officers on the <u>Glacier</u> that I know, and am sure he will take care of it.

I didn't have time to write to Erwin to explain the film, though. It seems I make a habit of that, but I was trying to get enough film to fill up a case before writing about it. I wanted to send as much as possible before the mob from <u>McMurdo</u> got here.

Well honey, I will say goodbye for now and write to the studio, and try to write you another letter before the plane leaves. I sure miss you and will be glad to be on the way home. Lots of love.

Following is the letter written by Jack Bursey to Catherine:

My Dear Mrs. Beebe,

I am sure you are not expecting a letter from me, because you have never heard of me, or know that I exist. But I am taking the liberty of writing to you in behalf of your husband, Lloyd, who I have known now for almost a year. I am sure, you no doubt will want to hear the story of his life here in the Antarctic and how he behaved while sojourning on this most desolate continent that we call Antarctica. So I told Lloyd I intended to write you and tell you all about his escapades here.

First, let me say, I became acquainted with your husband while traveling on the <u>U.S.S. Glacier</u> from the United States to the great White Continent, as we call it. After talking to him on the icebreaker and living with him here in this isolated place, I got to know him pretty well. In traveling over the snow and ice, I had great respect for him, and knew that I had met a real man.

The load he used to carry on his back and the way he walked on his snowshoes and the steady gait he kept up reminded me of the things I used to do during my boyhood days. It always gladdens my eyes to see and know a man who could take it, and not stumble and crawl, as I have seen many of the so-called explorers do. I could tell immediately that it wasn't the first time that he had walked over the snow with a pair of snowshoes.

As I came to know him better and found out some of his past history, it was similar to the life I had led in far off Newfoundland. He told me of his trips to Canada, working with the Indians and driving a dog team. This is the kind of work I have been used to a good part of my life. In fact it was this training that prepared me for a place on the first Byrd Antarctic expedition to the South Pole in 1938.

I am writing this letter about Lloyd and, therefore, I'd better not get carried away with my own experiences, which I am sure you are not interested in. At <u>Little America V</u> we lived in the same hut together called the BOQ (Bachelors Officers Quarters), but not in the same cubicle. Lloyd and Mr. Twombly were bunkmates.

I lived across the deck from them. This put me in very close contact with him, and I visited on numerous occasions. We had many conversations about home, the things we did and life in general, and of course, the common gossip that spread through the camp like wild fire. You might be sure there was plenty of that.

Where there were listening boxes in every building and tunnel here, one only needed to open his mouth without saying anything before the word had been caught by many ears and broadcast from one person to another, with much more added to it. So, consequently, we had to watch our words for fear of the meaning being taken wrongly.

Lloyd has told me about his cougar and mountain lion hunting many a time, and the way he had to wrestle with that untamed cat, tied it up, threw it on his back and carried him out of the thick woods. That takes nerve, and I am afraid Lloyd got one on me there, as far as hunting the mountain lion is concerned. To grab hold of a fighting cat, with claws spread like a wild eagle, would be too much for me, and I would be tempted to shoot him on sight instead of waiting for him to climb a tree. Now on the other hand, if it was to catch the slow moving seal, that would be more up my alley.

Only a day or two ago, I was talking to Lloyd and bawling him out about the condition of his bunk and the space in which he lives and has lived ever since we became stranded on the barrier.

To begin with, let's you and I pay a visit to him in his place of rest and see how he occupies himself. To get in his room at first would be difficult. We would push the curtain to one side to pass through. It is yellow in color and hangs down from the top above. It hangs loosely from an iron rod which the curtain is fastened to. Lloyd sewed a hem in it at the beginning. Just picture him sitting by the table trying to thread that small-eyed needle with his big fingers and doing the sewing. Of course, I was on the other side of the table trying to put a hem in mine. However, Lloyd did a pretty good job, and it serves the purpose very well.

Once inside of the curtain was almost as far as you could go without tripping over some gear that was roughly thrown down on the floor. The little desk was a litter of supplies, odds and ends of every description, and clothing lying around. When I say clothing, he hardly ever hung it up (laugh!). As far as boxes were concerned, there were too many to count, all packed and thrown around and piled on top of each other, underneath his bed and extending out from the side, and other places where he could squeeze one.

It seems as long as there was room enough for Lloyd to put one foot forward with enough open space between the boxes, so that he could swing his body in his bunk, he was satisfied. On the wall back of his bed he hung some of his clothes on nails that he had driven into the plywood. Many times I would visit him and find all of his clothes down on the floor. It seems they had a way of working off the nails and falling down. Lloyd would knock and throw them all down trying to find the one piece of clothing that he wished to wear on going outside.

I remember one time I looked in to say hello. Oh yes, I was going to ask him to have a root beer with me. I did not dare ask him to have a beer with foam on it. How he hated that nasty, foul tasting liquid. When to my surprise I could only see a pair of legs sticking out from underneath his bed, which was just high enough for him to crawl under and among his boxes. On further investigation, which I took it upon myself to do, and knowing Lloyd was a good sport, I found him wedged in between the numerous boxes.

It seems that Lloyd was trying to find a certain box, and he had pushed them apart from one another until he got so far in he could not get out. Just then, the boxes crashed down on top of him, and he was jammed in between the debris. I used to call it that, because there were no heads or tails to it.

Seeing the predicament he had forced himself into, I grabbed him by the feet and yanked and yanked until I suddenly broke him loose, and he came out a much disgusted man. The box he was looking for was the last one inside and underneath all of the others. I broke out two cans of soft beer and we laughed over it.

You know that wasn't all. That man had another cache just outside the hut where he used to keep a lot of the extra boxes that contained his spare parts that would require a small ship to carry. I would hear the lids slamming and a lot of noise going on as if someone was wrecking the building. This was Lloyd feeling his way around in the dark, trying to locate some one item that he had laid away someplace in the box. Inquiring as to what he was doing, he would say, "I am trying to find something and I don't know where I put it."

Lloyd told me many stories of his life and the home in which you live. It must be an ideal spot, and one which most men would enjoy with such surroundings. The flocks of ducks and bird life sitting down in the back yard, the fish and trout in the river running through your property must be a man's paradise.

He told me of the trip that you and he made up the mountain hunting cougar, remember? Both of you with packs on your backs that would load a horse, and you carrying the biggest load. When he mentioned that, I couldn't help from calling him all the nasty names I could think of. To let a woman carry a load like that on her second honeymoon was too much for me. Please forgive me. I told him he was a downright rascal and didn't deserve such a woman.

However, he later smoothed it over by saying that you enjoyed the trip and felt no after effects from your pleasant trip. I felt better. He is a hard man, and I would suggest that you trim him down to your size when he returns home. However, he did say that if he put things away neatly you would not know him, for by now you are used to his ways.

One thing about him, Mrs. Beebe, he is doing a good job down here for Disney, and you can well be proud of him. By the time he returns, he will have a remarkable movie that will create a lot of laughs for the American public.

He is out in all kinds of weather at night as well as day. Night after night he stood out in the cold all alone to get the pictures of the Aurora Australis, and I am sure he will have a record and as good a collection of this phenomenon, which we know so little about, that has ever been taken.

You have a fine man and one to rely on to do the work that he is called upon to do faithfully. We have had a good time together, and I hope that we will be friends for a long time. We sail and leave home on great adventures, but the homecoming is the best part of the trip. I would like to say in closing, Mrs. Beebe, I wish you and Lloyd a wonderful time and a happy reunion when he returns.

Sincerely yours, Jack Bursey,

LCDR, USCGR

Jack Bursey and the six other members of the trail-blazing crews to Byrd Land sent for me to come to the recreation room, and Jack said, "We have decided we want you to have the trail-blazing flag that rode on the front of the snow weasel all the way to Byrd Land and back to Little America, thirteen hundred miles." I was surprised and glad they thought enough of me to give their flag to me. We had spent a lot of time together. We still have the flag here at Olympic Game Farm.

Lt. Commander Jack Bursey lived in the room next to Chet Twombly and me. Jack had been to the Antarctic much more than anyone in our building at Little America, first on Byrd's Antarctic Expedition of 1928 - 1930, again on the U.S. Antarctic Service Expedition of 1939, and finally on Operation Deep Freeze of 1955 - 1957.

Some of the Seabees were young men, and Jack Bursey seemed twice as old to them. They seemed to think he should have stayed home. After Jack led the trail-blazing tractor train through the crevasses to Byrd Land, the ones who had their doubts about Jack Bursey changed their minds.

When they returned, they were saying that Jack Bursey was one tough man; he stood on the front of the lead vehicle all the way and back, and planted each trail marker. With that wind cutting into his face, they didn't know how he could have done it.

From that time on, they thought differently about Jack. He might have been only fifteen years older than the rest of the fellows, and he had a lot more experience, which they found out. Soon after I got home, Jack sent me a copy of his new book, Antarctic Night.

I tried to catch up on the changes at Little America, and before long the calendar pointed out that we were up to the red circle around the date of January 21st, and the ship Curtiss had not come yet. The Curtiss came on January 29th. They had a load of new Seabees and scientists.

This was our only wood fire in 18 months in the Antarctic

100

23

GOODBYE TO THE ANTARCTIC

They offloaded the passengers with a helicopter, and immediately I and all the people who had wintered over were taken aboard the <u>Curtiss</u> with the helicopter, and we were off the ice and headed for Sidney, Australia.

The sea plane tender <u>U.S.S. Curtiss</u> was the ship we were to ride all the way to San Diego, California with a short stop at Sidney, Australia.

Chet Twombly and I spent quite a bit of time playing ping-pong. This was a nice steady ship to ride on, not at all like the rolling ice breakers.

What a relief to be aboard and getting closer and closer to home. When we came into the bay at Sidney, it was a very beautiful sight. I don't believe I have ever seen a prettier harbor.

As we came to the dock, I could see a crowd of people there to welcome us, and I recognized Jack Couffer, a photographer that I would later work with for Disney Studio. He was waving and calling to me as we came in.

I got off as soon as I could, and Jack was there as well as the head of the Disney office in Australia. The studio had asked him to be there to meet me. The three of us went to the Disney office to plan our stay in Sidney.

When we found out that we didn't need to go back to the ship for three days, Jack and I decided to go see Al and Elma Milotte, who were working on a film for Disney, so without delay, we got on a plane for Tasmania. We had a fun visit with Al and Elma, and I returned to the <u>Curtiss</u> in time to start for San Diego.

While at the Disney office in Sidney, they told me that Erwin wanted me to call the studio when I got in. I did that, and called Catherine and family in Sequim, Washington.

It was a nice relaxing trip home. At San Diego, there were Catherine, Melvin and Kenny on the dock waving. Quite a few were there from the Disney studio. It was great to be with my family again. Catherine and the boys had driven down to the studio, and Erwin and his wife brought them to meet me in San Diego.

When I looked at Mel and

Our family is together again on the U.S.S.Curtiss

Ken, I could see from the way they had grown that I had missed a year and a half of their growing up.

We went to a motel that they had reserved. The next day, we went to the studio. We all went on a free trip to Disneyland, as usual. That night there was a welcoming back party at Erwin's house. Erwin invited the people that knew us the longest. He had let some other bosses at the studio know about the party, not dreaming they would come.

But they all did come, and Erwin, who is a worrier, didn't know what to do, especially when Bill Anderson, who was head of the studio, came in with his wife. There wasn't room for everyone. When Bill Anderson said, "Come on, Lloyd, and sit on the floor with me," we did. Then some more did the same thing.

There wasn't much room to move around, but everyone had a great time. We had all we could eat. It was the best party we could have imagined. We enjoyed ourselves, but were in a hurry to get back to our home. There were, however, several friends' places to stop at along the way. One was Archie Pierce's house. He was the owner of the Snow Cat factory in Medford, Oregon. We also stopped at the Cummings in Medford.

When we got to our farm, we had a reunion with my mother and father. They seemed about as well as when we left.

Mel, Ken and my father showed me all around the farm. Dad had quit milking cows and just raised calves now.

We had one more place to visit. That was Catherine's father, mother and three brothers at Nooksack, Washington. We arrived in Nooksack about three days later to find them all healthy.

I had been lucky with my in-laws. I always felt like one of the family. Catherine's mother used to say that I was her favorite son-in-law. Catherine was the only girl, so she only had one son-in-law.

After a couple of days we got back to Sequim and relaxed. We would have two weeks to rest, and then go to the studio and get ready for Brazil.

After two weeks at our farm in Sequim, we were ready to go to Brazil. Erwin called from Disney Studio and wanted to buy our car and send it with us to Brazil. We were going to film a jungle show that would be called Jungle Cat. Cars at this time were almost impossible to buy in Brazil.

When we arrived at the studio in Burbank, California, we found that the Customs in Brazil had changed their minds, and said that the permits to take the car would take a week or two longer. Winston Hibler said he knew just the place for us to spend some time.

Hib had spent some time at the San Carlos Ranch close to Carmel, California. Hib called and made arrangements for us to spend all the time on the ranch that we wanted, as well as making reservations for us at a motel in Carmel. Jim Bacchus, Eve Arden and other actors were staying there. It was twenty dollars a night. That doesn't sound like much, but in 1958, it seemed like a lot of money. The next morning we went to the San Carlos Ranch.

There was a metal gate at the entrance to the San Carlos Ranch. The gatekeeper had been informed of our coming, and he gave us a pass which also permitted us to go through to other areas of the ranch.

It was ten miles from the gate to the ranch house. We discovered that the Prince of Wales and other famous people used to come there for polo games and vacations. There were large horse barns, dance halls and a theater. There were many deer and wild pigs to see from the road.

We met the foreman of the ranch, George King, and he invited us to a barbecue that night to be cooked in a Chinese brick barbecue pit that stood in the yard. They were going to cook a wild pig that roamed the ranch.

There were people from Standard Oil Company as well as some of the townspeople at the party, and we all had a wonderful time. We learned more about the glory days of the ranch.

Catherine, the boys and I had enjoyed a great first day on this ranch. Some of the roads went through redwood forests with very large trees, just all types of beautiful country. We spent a few days traveling around the roads.

Catherine had asked around and found a little house next door to the motel we were in for twenty-five dollars a week. We moved out of the twenty dollars a day motel, and into the nice little house. We felt better that we were not wasting the studio's money.

The California deer season was on, and the foreman said that they could use a little venison to eat, and suggested that I go out and try to get a buck deer. I didn't want to go with a rifle, but I did have my bow and arrows that I was taking to Brazil. The next day, I went deer hunting. I got a nice buck deer and bobcat with the bow. The foreman was glad to get the deer.

They were starting to bring in the hay to the barn on the ranch, so I said, "Melvin and I will come and help get the hay in," and a few days later it was all in the barn. Our whole family enjoyed looking over the ranch.

The Customs in Brazil kept putting off the permits. Altogether, we waited three weeks for the word to go to Brazil. We finally got a call from the studio to get ready and come back to the studio. We checked out and then got another call from the studio that it was a false alarm. The Customs had put off the permits again for one more week.

The lady that rented the house to us felt bad, for she had already rented the place to others. She said that this is what we should do: her family would move to another house that they had to fix up, and our family could move into their house until we went to Brazil. We didn't want to take their nice house, but Mr. & Mrs. Charles Stoops insisted that they wanted to do this for us.

After another week, we came home from a last day at the San Carlos Ranch to find a big cake and a going-away party ready to start. It was a very nice thing for them to do.

When the time came, we got on an airplane from Los Angeles to Panama with a stop in Guatemala, and on to Rio de Janeiro for one night.

24

HELLO TO BRAZIL

The next day, we arrived at Recife, Brazil, and the airplane just kept flying around and around. They eventually announced over the loud speaker that they were emptying the gas tanks before they could land. We landed safely, and were met by Jim Simon and family. Jim is another Disney photographer.

They took us to our apartment. The Simon family lived in the apartment across the hall from ours. Disney photographer Hugh Wilmar and his wife, Mary, had lived in our apartment. Hugh had moved to Manaus on the Amazon River to film for our show.

The Wilmars had a maid who worked for them, and she sort of came with the apartment. Catherine didn't need one, but we felt she would help us learn to speak Portuguese. We found out a good maid could buy better bananas and other food that salesmen came to sell door to door.

We enjoyed our maid, Ducy. The maids come from the poor people, and in their homes there would be people sleeping all through the day taking turns. The ones with jobs could sleep when they needed to; the others whenever they could. There would only be one room, made of mud and sticks.

Having someone to talk Portuguese with did help us to learn. I am sure we were learning a poor grade of Portuguese. None of the fellows we had working for us on this film could speak English. Everyone speaks Portuguese in Brazil. I had been trying to learn a little Portuguese after finding out that we were to come here. I got some books to study and records in Portuguese to listen to. It was fun to tell these Brazilians who lived in small villages about the world. They knew nothing about where Brazil was. They thought all the land in the world was connected in one big land mass, and the water encircled the land. These people were sure Portugal was next to Brazil and that is why they spoke the same language.

The people here are good at figuring out what you are trying to tell them. Because they know so little, I could have long talks with them about the world, the sun and moon, the Russian Sputnik that was sailing around the world at that time and people going to the moon and back. There would be five or six fellows listening to me. When one of them would understand something I was trying to make them see, they would explain it to the rest. The look of surprise and understanding was great to see, and they would keep getting closer to me. I didn't have to know much about a subject to be very interesting to them.

After a few weeks of talking, I was learning a little Portuguese. Clementino, who was one of our helpers, started looking at a piece of newspaper whenever he had time. He would ask what this or that word meant. Clementino had never been to school, but before we left he got us all together and showed us he could now read the newspaper. It was a big and proud day for Clementino to show us he could read. Then when Catherine came in, he showed her how he could read, and he had a big smile on his face most of the time from then on. He was proud, and we were all happy for him.

For a while, we kept traveling out from Recife filming animals and birds in the jungle. We had several fellows that would help us when we needed it.

Native Brazilian houses on the Amazon River

When traveling through the jungle, we took notice of all blazes, creeks and trees as we moved along. It was a good idea to look back once in a while so it would be easier to return the way we had come.

When we had a guide, we asked questions about the names of trees and plants. It was difficult because we could not speak the Portuguese language very well. It did help us to learn the language, and the guide could understand us better as time passed.

Each day we felt a little more at home in the jungle. I knew I could find my way if the guide was to leave me for some reason.

People who traveled with us through the jungle carried a machete to cut limbs and bushes as we moved along.

At night we would keep a small fire burning. This would give light and also smoke to keep the mosquitos from getting too thick. Most of the night we would sleep sitting by the fire, sometimes moving closer to the smoke to chase the bugs and mosquitos away. When awake, we would listen to the sounds of the jungle: the sounds made by the night birds and animals.

One day we went to a lake in the jungle. There was a slender tree that bent over to the water. There was a sloth at the end of the tree that was touching the water. The sloth was hanging upside down as they usually do on limbs. This sloth was hanging there and drinking out of the lake. Sloths are usually high in trees and eat only leaves, and they get enough water from the leaves they eat. They don't often come down to the ground. Other animals would get them if they did, as they move very slowly. Eagles catch a lot of them. Everyone we talked to had never seen one drink water in the jungle.

We also saw and took pictures of a tapir swimming in the lake. Tapirs are related to a rhinoceros. They can weigh up to six hundred pounds. They are also related to horses. They have a short movable trunk like an elephant. We spent a lot of time taking pictures of the tapir. He would go under lily pads and come up with a lily pad on his head or back. We were wading around to our shoulders in the lake following him.

After we became acquainted with an area, we could go on trips alone with our cameras. We always remembered the things and sounds that worried the natives. I always watched for animal tracks as I moved through the jungle and along streams.

Most of the jungle was too dark for us to take pictures with our color film. We soon discovered that we must find areas where the light from the sky could get to the ground. Along streams, ponds, lakes and swamps there was light for filming

Jaguar in tree in Amazon forest

105

scenes of wildlife and scenery. This meant spending a lot of time wading in the swamps and creeks and along the shores of the water and open area.

We saw many new animals in Brazil. There were several kinds of monkeys and marmosets, sloths and snakes, tapirs and jaguars. There were also many kinds of terrain, but I will always like our forest, mountains and animals at home the best.

Euclides was the rough carpenter. Euclides had a white stripe in his hair. He had ten kids, and all had a white stripe of hair. He was proud that all of his children had this stripe of white hair.

All of these fellows were poor. Before they had a job with us, they wouldn't know where they could get a few beans for a meal. Euclides said he could always take a chair on the sidewalk and charge two cents for a haircut. Clementino talked so fast that even the workers couldn't always understand him.

Marinho was our favorite. He was very helpful and would want to beat us to any work he thought we were going to do. Marinho could also understand us better than the others.

We had to hire a man, Ben Gerjoi, who was in the black market. He was needed to deal with the

A hunting jaguar

Brazilian Customs. You couldn't get anything through Customs unless you put a certain amount of money in between the papers. If the money wasn't there, they would put your papers on a pile of other papers until you put money in with your application papers. Ben knew how much it would take. When that office was satisfied, they would take the papers to the next office, and it would start all over again.

We never could get our car off the dock, and when we left the next year, we still didn't have the car. We bought an old pickup.

Drivers in Brazil use their horns all the time and seldom turn on the lights. If the car broke down, they would do a complete overhaul in the middle of the street.

If you got run over, it was your own fault for getting in the way. Often you could see dead people lying on the sidewalk. If you stopped to help someone, you were responsible for paying the hospital bill, which was usually pretty cheap.

One day, we could see some of the maids from our apartment looking at a man lying by our front steps. Catherine sent our maid out to see what was the matter with him. When she came back, she told us that this man was from the interior of Brazil. He had come to town for an appendix operation, which took all the money he had, so he was kicked out of the hospital. The man started walking home, the incision came open, and he was lying down to die. We asked the girls how much it would cost to send him to the hospital to get him fixed up and a ticket back to his home. They came back and said that it would cost fifteen dollars. We gave the woman who owned the apartment the money, and she said that she would take him and see that he got on the train to his home, which she did.

The animals and birds were all new to us. We kept taking pictures of the monkeys, sloths, jaguars, giant anteaters, tapirs and many others. There were plenty of snakes and beautiful birds. The jungles were

TELEGRAMAS PARA TODAS AS PARTES DO MUNDO

RR154/JR1600/BNA204

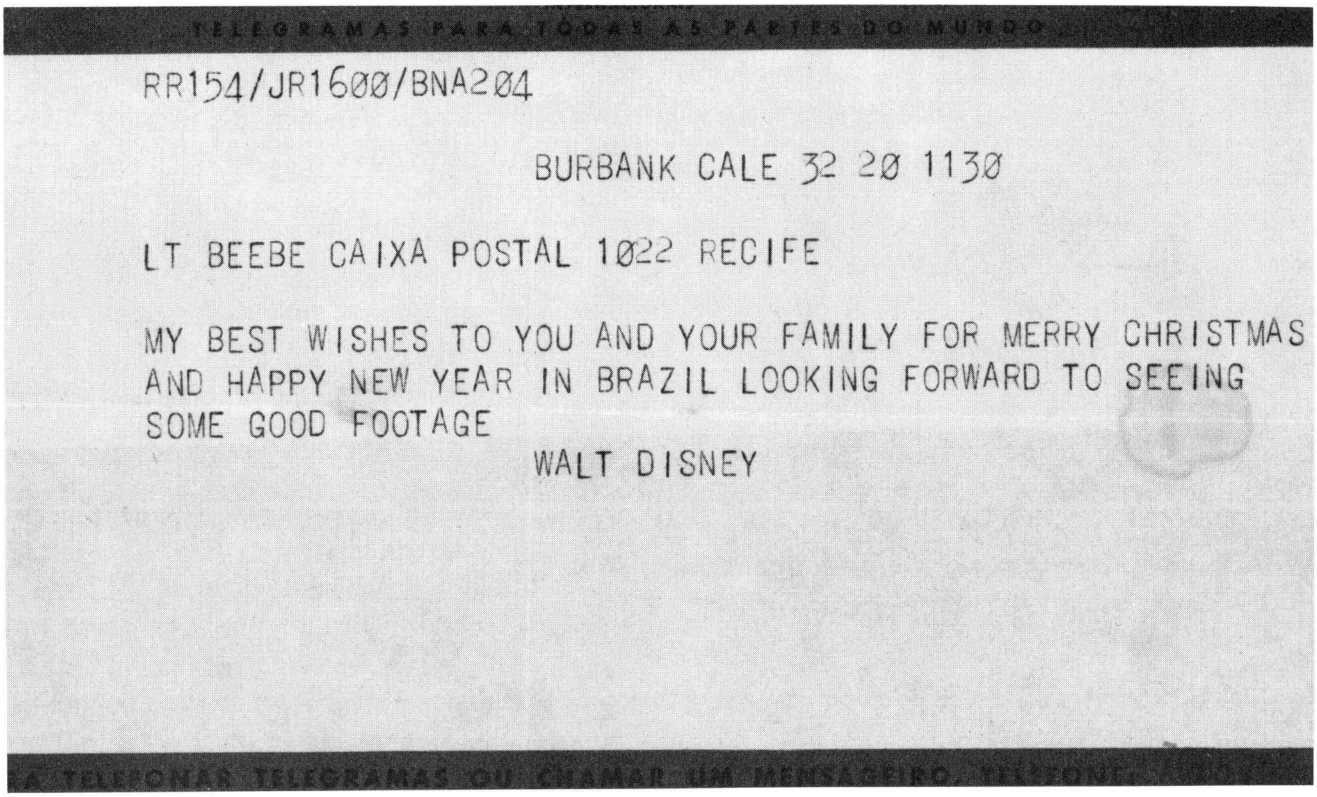

BURBANK CALE 32 20 1130

LT BEEBE CAIXA POSTAL 1022 RECIFE

MY BEST WISHES TO YOU AND YOUR FAMILY FOR MERRY CHRISTMAS
AND HAPPY NEW YEAR IN BRAZIL LOOKING FORWARD TO SEEING
SOME GOOD FOOTAGE

WALT DISNEY

A TELEFONAR TELEGRAMAS OU CHAMAR UM MENSAGEIRO, TELEFONE:

Telegram from Walt Disney

great and had all kinds of trees that were also new to us.

We lived only a half mile from a beautiful beach. Melvin especially spent a lot of time swimming and fishing in the surf. It was warm water. It rained hard for an hour every afternoon. He gave the fish he caught to the maids to take to their families.

Mel had a correspondence school course as his schooling. Ken started school in a church that the Air Force wives taught for their children. The American Consul sent a driver in a long black car to pick Ken up every day for school. Ken was the first one to get in each day, and he looked pretty small in that big car.

Sometimes we would go to the show at the U.S. Naval Base. If kids or someone else was laughing or noisy, the lights would come on, the picture come to a stop and a formation of cadets would march down the aisles. They would gather up the culprits and escort them out of the theater, the lights would go out and the picture would come back on, and the film continued.

After a lot of trips to film animals, birds and jungles, we were just about finished with this show, Jungle Cat.

Months ago I had told Marinho that if they wanted to go to the United States, I would pay all expenses for him and his wife, Cecilia. He talked it over with his wife, and they agreed that they wanted to go. A few days later, Marinho came to work and said that Cecilia was up on the hill crying, saying that she couldn't leave her mother, who lived in another town. She hadn't seen her mother for years. Marinho said he was going anyway. I told him that I wouldn't do anything to separate them; either they could both go, or both stay. Marinho and Cecilia didn't have any children, so they could get permits to enter the United States. It is hard to get permits for people who can't read or write. Marinho could read and write a little, but Cecilia not at all. We had her practice signing her name.

They must pass health tests and fix their teeth and be in all around good health. We had all this taken care of in case they wanted to go. Cecilia didn't want to leave the home that we'd built for Marinho and

Catherine and Ken on the Black River in Brazil

her. We'd hired Euclides to buy ground and build a house for them. This house was like all the other houses in that area. It had a good view, but was made of mud and sticks and painted yellow. It had one room, open windows and a tile roof. The cost for this was one hundred dollars.

All these poor people look at Americans as millionaires. Euclides had been asking us to come up to his house. I could see he felt it would help his prestige if we would go to his house. We promised to go one Sunday.

Euclides lived up on a hillside below Marinho's house. Our family started up the dirt road between rows of yellow houses all built the same. As we walked up the road, we could hear people saying that the Americans were coming. Every house had people looking out the windows or from behind the houses, and kids were playing in the street. When we got near Euclides' house, his family was in front of the house. Everyone knew that the Americans were to come to Euclides' house, and he was so proud. We were glad we came, as all the people living there were proud that we came, and Euclides was the center of it all. We stayed about half an hour, and then went home. I think those people will always remember the day the Americans came to see them.

When Euclides first worked for us, his little boy of about six was there, and he wanted to be near me, so I gave him a piece of gum. He took the wrapper off and broke off a little. I asked him why he didn't put the whole stick in his mouth, and he said that there were other kids in the family, and he must save the rest for them. This little boy told people that he was going home with Señor Lloyd, and Euclides wanted him to go. Almost any family would want their kids to go to the United States.

One night Marinho and Cecilia were over at our apartment to visit us. While listening to us talk, she realized that we would be going back on the plane, too. She asked in Portuguese, "Are you going on the plane if we go?" We said yes, that we would be going too. Cecilia then said that she would go. We asked about her mother, and discovered that had been just an excuse. She had really been afraid to go on the plane, but if we were going with them, she wanted to go.

One morning we read an article in a newspaper that reported some officials as saying that the butter company was putting too much vaseline in the butter, and there was more sand in the sugar than was allowed.

In the meantime, Hugh Wilmar had finished the filming at Manaus, and started for home via Lima, Peru, where he had always said he wanted to retire and live out his life.

Ken with pet snake

BACK TO THE FORESTS

We were getting ready to fly back to the States when Erwin Verity called and said that Hugh Wilmar had been killed in a train wreck in Peru. He wanted us to come back by way of Peru to pick up Hugh's cameras and equipment. We were to film our way up the Amazon River, and then to Lima, Peru, where the equipment was.

This changed everything for Marinho and Cecilia. When we got to Panama, we would call Jim Simon, and he would put Marinho and Cecilia on the airplane for Panama, where we would wait for them. I promised if they didn't get there, I would come back after them.

After filming along the Amazon, we came to Lima. The studio had a man waiting there to help us. The papers said that Hugh had been killed in a spectacular train wreck in the mountains of Machu Picchu.

We stayed in Lima, Peru for two days, then got on a plane for Panama. When we got settled in the hotel, we called Jim and told him to send Marinho and Cecilia; that we would be waiting for them in Panama. Jim called back and told us Marinho's scheduled arrival. There would be an overnight stop at Caracas, Venezuela, then on to Panama the next day on Pan American Airline.

The day Marinho and Cecilia were to be in Panama, we stayed at the hotel. We kept on the telephone to the airport to make sure they would be there. We didn't want to give up our room, as they were impossible to get unless reserved. We finally got word that they wouldn't be on the airplane. The officials in Caracas had taken Marinho and Cecilia's papers along with their passports, which they had no right to do. They wouldn't let them on the plane. Pan American tried to help, but didn't succeed. Maybe tomorrow, they said. Marinho and Cecilia were alone in Caracas and scared to death. The language was Spanish in Caracas, and they couldn't understand what was going on. Two days went by, and we were in our hotel in Panama and on the telephone all the time. We were told that an airplane was on the way. Pan American people thought Marinho and Cecilia might be on the plane, and they would call us as soon as they found out. Marinho and Cecilia didn't have a visa for Panama, so we knew we had to get on that plane and fly with them on to the United States.

The call came from Pan American officials saying that Marinho and Cecilia were on board, but they were very frightened. I told them to just say, "Lloyd Beebe." They called back and said that when they had said "Lloyd Beebe," Marinho and Cecilia were all smiles from then on.

We checked out of our hotel room, met the plane and went on board. Marinho and Cecilia were relieved and very happy to see us. It was funny the way things turned out. Marinho, who always said that the plane ride wouldn't scare him, was afraid on the plane, and Cecilia had a ball all the way to Los Angeles.

A studio car met us at the plane and took us to the Disney Studio. We took Marinho around the studio, then visited with Erwin and others before going to our motel, where we stayed three more days.

I went to the studio for a couple of days, and we took Marinho, Cecilia and the kids to Disneyland. I heard Marinho talking about the cars. They said it must be true. I asked what was true, and they said all the cars on the streets. They had been to a show and saw all the cars, and someone told them they just gathered up all the cars in town to shoot a film, and they could see that the movie had told the truth.

We had fun showing them supermarkets. I would say, "Cecilia, would you please open that door for us?" She hurried to open the door, but it opened before she could get there. After that, she just laughed and kept going back and forth, letting the door open itself.

The next day we went home to Sequim. Marinho and Cecilia were to stay at our house. My mother and dad were fine, and we enjoyed our reunion. Dad was still raising calves to keep himself busy.

Catherine and I decided that it was time we bought Dad's share of the farm. When we bought the place in 1940, it cost seventeen thousand five hundred dollars. Now it was 1958, and Dad's half was worth forty thousand dollars. We also bought his house, so we owned everything. Dad and Mom would live there as long as they wanted to. They were free to retire if they wanted, or use the farm and sell hay. We planned on more filming. Dad could use Marinho to help him. We paid Marinho so much a month until we got back from the next film.

It was like going home to arrive in Alberta. I don't know of a more beautiful spot than around Banff, Alberta. We had spent two or three years in this area. We stopped to see our friends Art and Rita Krowchuck at Canmore. It was good to see them again. We had a lot of nice times together.

We went on to the Kananasksis Ranger Station houses, where we were to make our headquarters. Bill and Ginny Bacon had been there for a short time waiting for us to get back from Brazil. Bill and Ginny had a wolf and a husky dog, Smokey. The Bacons would be helping on the show.

There were to be actors in this show, and a husky dog named Nikki, who was to grow up with a bear as a friend. We met Bill and Ginny. Both were very friendly, and we were to become very good friends.

Nikki, Wild Dog of the North

There were several nice log cabin homes. We moved into one. This was a great place for the boys to live. There were lots of woods all around and the Kananasksis River was close by for fishing.

Bill and I looked the place over and started to plan where to begin. We needed two husky pups that would grow up with bear cubs, so that they would be friends.

Making movies is usually hard work. With wildlife films, it is always in beautiful country, and work can be fun. That is how it has always been for me. The camera work is much the same each time, but the interesting things that people do while working and after hours are always different in each location.

While we were filming this show, the name was Nomads of the North. Its name was later changed to Nikki, Wild Dog of the North. After it was finished, it was changed to just Nikki.

We had to get two very nice husky puppies, and that was easy, as Bill and Ginny had been looking for them. We picked out two puppies that looked the same.

Now for the bear cubs. The Park Rangers had promised to catch some black bear cubs. They were busy, and we began to worry that our huskies would grow too big for bear cubs. They needed to live together while they were little.

Bill and I decided to get our own. The Rangers would be glad to have it taken care of. We drove around the roads until we saw a female bear. We found one with four little cubs. We jumped out and caught one little cub. We put it in a cage in the back of the truck. Then we decided to chase the bears to see if the mother bear would send the cubs up a tree. We were running and yelling, and up the tree the cubs went.

The mother stopped about two hundred feet away and watched us. I had a gunny sack. I said, "Come on, Bill, you keep the bear away while I climb up the tree and try to get one more cub." The tree was a tall spruce. I hurried up the tree and heard Bill say, "I can't keep her back. She is going up the tree!"

I knew I'd better keep going up, and those little cubs would go all the way up. I chased up to the very

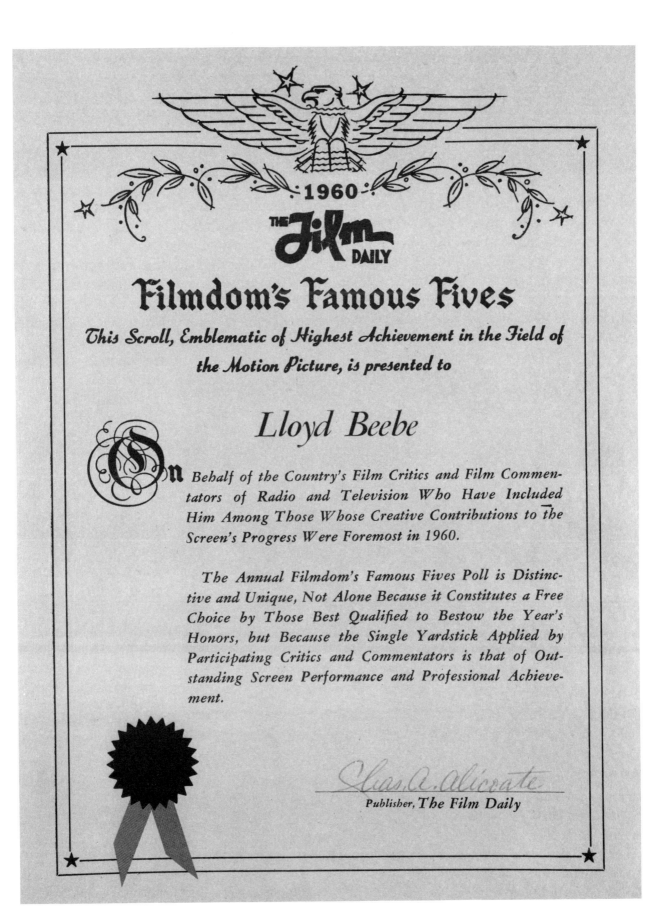

1960

THE Film DAILY

Filmdom's Famous Fives

This Scroll, Emblematic of Highest Achievement in the Field of the Motion Picture, is presented to

Lloyd Beebe

On *Behalf of the Country's Film Critics and Film Commentators of Radio and Television Who Have Included Him Among Those Whose Creative Contributions to the Screen's Progress Were Foremost in 1960.*

The Annual Filmdom's Famous Fives Poll is Distinctive and Unique, Not Alone Because it Constitutes a Free Choice by Those Best Qualified to Bestow the Year's Honors, but Because the Single Yardstick Applied by Participating Critics and Commentators is that of Outstanding Screen Performance and Professional Achievement.

Chas. A. Alicoate

Publisher, *The Film Daily*

Filmdom's Famous Five award given to Lloyd Beebe in 1960

top, and the mother bear was right behind me. I reached one cub and handed it right back below me to the mother. I handed her the other two, and she started down the tree. I watched her and slowly came part way down. She took the cubs a little way, and then she checked the cubs over. The cub we had in the back of the pickup was crying for his mother. She must have heard this other cub and thought it was still up the tree. She ran to the tree and started up. I decided I wouldn't climb any farther up the tree. If she was to push me off the tree, I didn't want to fall seventy-five feet! She came right up to where I was. I started kicking the tree by her feet and yelled at her. I was making as much noise as I could. She was so nice about the whole thing. She was just even with me and looked me all over and smelled my legs and hands, then decided that I didn't have her cub, so she started down the tree and I followed close behind her. When she hit the ground, I was right behind her. I had gotten a little tired trying to scare her away, so I walked back to the truck. Bill was as close to the tree as he dared to be.

We were both of the opinion that we should quit for the day. After resting a little, we thought we would drive down the road a little farther. We finally saw a bear with two cubs. I think we forgot about quitting for the day. We jumped out and gave chase. The two cubs went up the tree. I went up the tree and followed them all the way to the top. We were near a lake, and an outboard motor was whining out on the lake. I was a little gun shy, I think. I asked Bill if the bear was making that noise out in the brush.

He didn't know, so I grabbed a cub. This cub was huskier than the first, and it was hard to keep him quiet and climb down with one hand. I finally got down and went to the truck. By this time, Bill had figured out that the noise must have been an outboard motor.

When we were safe at the truck, Bill had a big laugh. I said, "Okay, you hold this cub until we get home," and he did. I knew he would be tired by the time we got back to camp. A bear cub stays quiet for a minute and then explodes every little while, and you have to keep a tight grip all

Ray Jewel, Jack Couffer, Erwin Verity, Winston Hibler and Lloyd Beebe pointing

the time. Before we got home, Bill said, "This guy is sure strong. I don't know if I can keep this up much longer," but he made it, and we now had our husky pups and the two bear cubs.

Art Krowchuck had worked with us on White Wilderness, so I called him and told him we had a job for him taking care of the bear cubs and helping Ginny with the dogs. Art came out that same day.

Photographer Jack Couffer and his wife, Joan, came from Los Angeles to work on the film. They soon moved into one of the other houses.

Erwin sent six birch bark canoes that Indians in Quebec, Canada built for us. We spent the next day trying them out in the Kananasksis River. We found out that real bad rapids could break them, but they were great to use.

My old friend, Dell Ray, came from Sequim to work for us. Now we had our crew for a while.

We needed a black bear that was tame for a sequence in this show. There was a fellow in Calgary who had a wrestling bear. This man said that he had never let this bear loose in the woods before, but he would do it.

Scene from "Nikki, Wild Dog of the North", filmed in Alberta, Canada

BLACK BEAR CAUGHT WITH A STRING

We were filming in a rocky area along the Kananasksis River. There was a clear little lake about seventy-five feet wide set in the rocky terrain. The bear wanted to chase everyone who came close. I guess it was a lot of fun for the bear.

We all had our turn, and the only way to stop him was to jump off the rocks into the lake. We were filming him, and everyone had a lot of laughs. It was a big male bear, and even though he was declawed and his fangs were pulled in front, no one wanted to get caught.

We had our camera tripods standing on the level rocks, and Bill Bacon teased him and the bear came for him. Bill stumbled backwards over our camera tripods and broke three of them.

That was enough for the bear, so he went over the rocks and jumped off into the deep, fast river. Art and my son, Mel, were good swimmers, and they jumped in and went downriver with the bear. We all started to run downriver. After about four hundred yards, the bear got out on the other side of the river.

We got across the river, and I ran to where the bear had gone into the woods and up a steep mountain. I was ahead of the rest and got up the hill out of sight of the others on the river. Once in a while, I caught a glimpse of the bear. I didn't know what I was going to do if I caught up with him.

Wrestling bear which had to be recaptured after jumping into the Kananasksis River during filming

I felt in my pockets for anything to help. There was a piece of parachute cord for leading a dog. It was about six feet long. I made a loop in one end like a lasso as I was trying to get close to the bear. He was a little tired, too, as he had kept going straight up the hill.

The bear stopped, and didn't want to go any more, so I tried to use my string to throw the loop over his head. By the time I had a two foot loop, it wouldn't reach more than three feet. Each time I tossed my string, he would run at me, and when I ran he would stop.

I tried several times, but the cord wouldn't reach until the loop fell off his face and onto his foot, and he stepped in it. I pulled it tight. I ran and kept hold of the cord. The bear was pulling on the cord, so I found I could pull and he would pull back. I could stop him from chasing me by pulling the cord.

When I heard people on the river calling each other, I called for someone to bring some rope, and

114

someone passed the word. I kept on pulling the string when we moved forward.

Art and Bill came with two ropes. We got them on the bear, one leading him from each side. We started down the mountain. There was a dam about half a mile above where we were, so I yelled to have the man at the dam shut the river off for a few minutes, and he did.

About the time we got to the river, the river was dry. There was a man on a rock who had been fishing; he still had his fish pole in hand, and the line still in a puddle. As soon as we crossed with the bear, Catherine called the dam, and the Calgary Power Company turned the water back down the river. That fisherman surely was amazed at what had happened. He folded up his fish pole and left.

The man who owned the wrestling bear thought he had lost his bear when it ran away. We could hear him saying over and over, "I have lost my bear. Now what will I do?"

We got the bear back to the truck and returned him to the owner. He had never thought that we might try to get the bear back. We didn't try to do any more filming, as we had the pictures that we wanted. We were a little surprised at the way it turned out.

This show starts with an old mother bear and her one cub, Neewa. They see the camp of Challoner on the beach by the river. The canoe is by the camp, and a husky pup plays around camp.

Neewa's mother is killed by a male bear, and Neewa is later found by the man and Nikki. The man finds the dead mother bear and eventually has to tie the bear cub and Nikki together as they travel down the river. The canoe tips over at a bad rapids, and Neewa and Nikki are swept over a falls and down the river. The man searches, but cannot find them. The two young animals still tied together travel on land for months. They become friends. Eventually, they get untied and grow up together. In the end, Nikki and his owner, Challoner, get together again.

At the studio, there was a problem, as Nikki had no mark that Challoner could recognize. When Walt Disney heard about it, he simply said, "Let Nikki recognize his master," and it was solved. Walt usually had the right answer.

We had a lot of fun on this show. Jack and Joan Couffer and all the rest of the crew were happy together.

One day, we were told that the train had hit an elk, so we went there to get some meat for our animals. Some animal had eaten the belly out of the elk, and the flies had laid eggs all over the meat, and maggots were all over the exposed meat, but we could cut that part out. We were doing this when Art Krowchuck coughed, and his false teeth came out of his mouth and dropped right into the pile of maggots. Art picked up the teeth, wiped off the maggots and put his teeth in his shirt pocket. Knowing Art, we wondered if he was going to put them back into his mouth just to show us. We teased him from time to time about this.

We were out one day and took some pictures of a bull elk chasing Bill Bacon's dog, Smokey. Smokey was fighting back. That gave us an idea to finish this sequence, if we only had an elk.

The Ranger, Frank Jones, has been a good friend ever since we were here filming White Wilderness, and he said, "I will get you a bull elk." It was winter, and the elk were hungry, so Frank started feeding them in his corral, and when they got used to going in, he shut the gate.

In the meantime, we had built a pen in which we could take a few pictures. We took our flatbed truck down to the Ranger Station and had a rodeo. We got the elk all tied up and lying on our truck, drove the fifteen miles to our elk pen, put him inside and untied him. It was a success, and we had a good sequence of Nikki and the elk.

We had a lot of snowball fights, as it was winter, and these fights were easy for someone to start. We were always ready. When they charged me, I never ran. I kept my eyes open and made them pay more as they charged in close. When they got in close, I would pretend to throw, and they would duck. Then when they peeked out again, they usually got a snowball in the face.

One day I had my snowshoes on and was standing about six feet up on a log. Art, Bill and Jack were by the truck with one hundred feet of snow between me and them. They didn't have snowshoes on. Art yelled, "We got him now," and they started wading through the snow toward me. I knew they intended to reach up and grab the tips of my snowshoes and pull me off that log. My log had snow on it, too.

When Art got about thirty feet away, I told him not to come any closer, as I would jump right on top of him. Art was ahead of the others, because he thought it was going to be fun. When he got close and leaned over a little, I landed on his back with my snowshoes and pushed him down into the deep snow. I jumped up and down a few times, just enough to tamp him into the snow some more, and then went back to the truck.

By that time, he had gotten out, and we all had a big laugh. Art said in a joking way, "Beebe, some day I will get even with you for that." I said, "Art, you have to learn. I told you I would jump on you. It was your choice."

Art Krowchuck was a very good hockey player. He spent every winter playing on a hockey team, and was usually the best. He would come to work with his arm in a sling all week and work with one hand, then on hockey nights take off the bandages and go play hockey.

He had all his teeth knocked out playing hockey. We would go to the games sometimes to watch. They get really rough. If we were not giving him a job, he would join a hockey team for the season, and his family wouldn't see him much until the hockey season was over.

I decided to make our big lawn into a skating rink so that Mel and Ken and everybody could learn to

Lloyd Beebe, Tom Buchan, Bill Bacon, Jack Couffer playing broom ball on the ice

116

skate. I piled the snow in a wall around the yard, then got a hose long enough to reach all over the yard. The temperature was at least twenty below.

I set the water at a fine spray and pointed it in there, and it froze. I started by putting a lot of water on the ground, and then just spraying the fine mist. I kept it up all night. It took several nights to finish it.

After, there was a heavy coat of ice all over. I could let the water on the ice for a few minutes, go to bed and get up two or three times a night and put on another layer of water. I had to do this at night, because we were filming every day.

The ice rink was finished, so we all went to town and bought ice skates. Mel and Ken spent all their time skating in the daytime, and we had lights for skating at night.

I had skated on ice when I was a kid, and that helped, but I fell as much as anyone, because we were all trying to do more than we were able to. Then someone introduced us to broom ball. In this game, everything was like hockey, except that skates weren't worn, and we used a broom instead of a hockey stick. Without skates, we fell as much as if we had them on. Everyone would push and shove trying to get the puck in the net. After playing for two or three weeks among ourselves, someone said that we ought to challenge Art's hockey team to a game of broom ball. Art thought that was a good idea, so he arranged everything for a certain day. We fellows were in good shape. There was a small crowd to watch the game. I doubt that anyone thought we had a chance, unless it was Art. He knew we were as tough as he was, and we knew that without their skates, it would be a little more even. They had played broom ball many times. The game was an upset, and our crew won. It was a lot of fun. Art and his team said that we were just lucky and could never beat them again, so we set a date, and we did it again. Everyone had a good time, and we went into the house and had a party. Some stayed to skate.

Frank Jones, the Ranger of that area, knew I had hunted cougars, and he was having problems with cougars. He asked about my helping him, so one weekend I went back to Sequim and got two of my dogs and came back to the Kananasksis. Every weekend and some mornings I would hunt, and finally caught seventeen cougars, which Frank bountied. I told him that I was just paying him back for all the things he had done for us, but he wouldn't hear of that. We would all go to town for a big dinner in Banff every so often and use the bounty money.

Then, the Calgary Zoo called and wanted to know if I could catch a male cougar for them, as their male had died. I caught one and took it to the Zoo.

In my travels looking for filming locations, I had located a wolverine den. I was hoping that it held a female and that she would have a litter of young. Every week I would carry one quarter of horse meat up to the mountains and throw it over a rock ledge, and after falling straight down, it would land close to the wolverine den. I could look around and see the wolverine was still there. If she would let the little ones out to play, if she had any, I might get some great pictures. I did this every week until the snow was gone. I began to think that she wasn't going to have little ones.

Bill and I carried a live trap up there and put it at the den site. When I was gone, Bill kept going back, and finally the wolverine was caught. We used that wolverine on other shows. We named him Joe. We had him until he died of old age.

One day Erwin Verity called up. He said that Walt Disney, his wife Lillian, Walt's brother, Roy Disney, and his wife Edna were coming to see us on a certain date. When it got near the time for them to come, Erwin would call up and be worried that someone might say things to the Disneys that would upset them. Also, the insurance company was worried about them all riding in the same plane, in case of an accident. We knew they would be at our place around noon. We went to work as usual that morning, and planned to take the afternoon off. When we got home, the Disneys were just arriving. We went in and ate dinner which the girls had prepared, then showed them around our operation and the surrounding country. I think they had a very nice time. They would be staying at the Banff Springs Hotel. After visiting with us, they left to go to their hotel. As soon as they left, I called Erwin, as he had requested. Erwin had been worried, as others at the studio were. He felt relieved that they had come and gone without having any problems.

The Disneys came back the next day, and we spent much of the time with them, then we all had dinner and they returned to Calgary and on to Los Angeles the next day, and once again the studio returned to normal.

Lloyd explaining the next sequence to Walt Disney, Joan Couffer and Edna and Roy Disney on the set of show, "Nikki"
Photo credit: Bill Bacon

THE BIG CLAM FEED

We had a lot of friends in this area, so we thought it would be nice to have a big party and invite everyone. We talked Dell Ray into going back to Sequim and digging enough clams for a big party. These people seldom have a chance to eat clams. We knew we could depend on Dell; he lives on the beach with clams at his door. Dell got back on the date agreed on; he had driven all night. He had several garbage cans full of clams, lots of crabs and other things. Catherine and other people got busy cleaning clams, then boiling and grinding clams for fried clam patties, saving clam nectar and getting many other things ready to eat, and putting up tables. Dell had put on many meals for crowds in his mountain packing business. Everyone was helping. By 5 pm, we had the greatest clam feed anyone had heard of. Everyone ate as many clams as they could swallow. To this day, whenever we meet anyone from there or go back, they always talk of the great clam party. We had Forestry, Park, Guest Ranch, College and Calgary Power people there.

When fall came, we were on our way to Sedona, Arizona to film the show <u>Lobo</u>. Erwin had rented a place four miles from Sedona. It had quite a few acres of red rocks and locations for filming part of the show, and room for wolf pens. We got busy and built the pens.

I went to Sequim to get Marinho and Cecilia to come to work with us on this picture. I knew they would be perfect to take care of and help train the wolves. They had never done this, but they learned quickly and listened to me when I helped them.

There was an unfinished small house that Catherine and I fixed up to stay in. There was another small building we fixed up for Marinho and Cecilia. It wasn't very good, but it was much better than the house they had stayed in when in Brazil.

This was the first time we had ever spent any time in the desert. It was a nice change. It was cold at night. This winter, it was colder than ever before. All the pipes in Sedona froze, and the wash basin pipes froze, raised up and fell off the walls and toilets broke in the motels. No one here was prepared for cold weather.

Every morning was cold, but after the sun came out, it was warm. We could look for and find arrowheads and tools the Indians who lived here thirteen hundred years ago had left. After each wind or rain, we would find new treasures.

Ken was going to school in Sedona, and liked everything except rattlesnakes. The fishing was good in Oak Creek. There was a big creek wash that was dry near the house. Once in a while, it would rain hard in the mountains, and then all of a sudden water would come in a wall and transform the creek into a big river. If you were on the other side when the water arrived, you had to walk a mile and a half to the highway bridge and back down the highway to our place. The water would even wipe out trailers and campers that stopped too close to the dry bed.

We now had wolves in our pens and were working with the wolves so we could handle them. We had already started to film the picture. Al and Ingrid Niemela came to help with the wolves. Al had trained dogs and was very good at it.

Marinho and I spent a lot of time with the wolves. I wanted him to take it slow, so he depended on me to tell him what to do. There was one very big wolf shipped to us, and he looked mean. We took his shipping crate into one of the empty pens and sat down by it and talked to the wolf. I even had Marinho talk to him in Portuguese. We fed him bites until he relaxed, and finally he wanted us to let him out. We still let him smell us as we sat by the cage. When he started to tell us we were his friends, we let him out, and he was thankful. No one but Marinho and I ever got to be friendly with him.

Dell Ray came with the trailer we had bought on <u>White Wilderness</u>. He opened the door, and out jumped Billy, the young elk we had at Kananasksis. It was nice to have Dell with us; he could do about anything and could take care of the place if I was to be gone. Dell started back to get two of his horses to use in the show, and he would also be one of the actors.

I had seen advertisements in <u>Wildlife Magazine</u> of a man near Cottonwood, Arizona who took sportsmen out on cougar hunts. One evening, Catherine, myself and the boys were going to Cottonwood. This hunter lived right on the highway. We stopped and were surprised to see big semi trailers and trucks with pictures of cougars and hounds painted on the sides. We knocked on the door, and an old man came to the door. He came out on the porch and sat on the steps while we talked. He told about his business. He took parties out for a week or two at a time cougar hunting. He took his dogs, horses and equipment up a trail that led to the top of Mogollon Rim. They would stay at his hunting cabin up there. They rode horses around until they found a cougar track, and if the dogs tracked it, the client could shoot it. I couldn't see how he could get any place without a horse.

Catherine and I had to take our car to the Ford garage in Flagstaff. The mechanic was Dick Marshall. I soon found out he was the best cougar hunter in that area. There were several young men talking to Dick about his hounds and cougar hunting. It was all interesting to me, so I listened while he was working on my car. These young men would say someone had traded his truck for a lion dog. Everyone called a cougar a lion in Arizona. Dick Marshall had told one of the boys that he had one hound he would sell to him for seven hundred dollars. I could see this kid couldn't pay that much, and knowing hunters, I figured this was his worst dog. I finally said that I wouldn't mind buying a good dog. I got the idea it was not unusual to pay two thousand dollars for a lion dog.

When our car was ready to go, Dick asked me if I wanted to look at his dogs. I told him no, that I had to go to Pennsylvania. I might stop on the way to try and buy a good coon dog. Dick said that I would never get a lion with coon dogs. He said that he used to have the best coon dog in the country and he couldn't ever get a lion, and that you just can't catch a lion with a coon dog. The boys were very interested in our talk, and I said that I knew I could catch cougars and lions with a coon dog. We had to come to the garage several times for a variety of things. The garage was part of Babbit's Store, the biggest and best store in Flagstaff. The boys were there each time, just to talk hounds. Dick would ask if I had my coon dog yet, and I always had to tell him not yet.

Erwin called from the studio. He wanted me to go to Kane, Pennsylvania to look at a bunch of wolves for this picture. There was also a pack of hounds in this show, so I decided to see the wolves and come back on the train to Neosho, Missouri and buy a few coon hounds to use in the picture, and I might want to keep some of them. It didn't seem that I would ever need to hunt for bounties on cougars, but I wasn't one to take chances.

I flew to Pittsburgh, then took a bus to Kane, Pennsylvania. I looked at the wolves. I didn't think they would ever work out. I talked to the owner, a Dr. McLeary. He was about ninety years old and not well. He said he had a young couple that was interested in caring for the wolves.

I got on a train for Arizona and got off in Neosho, Missouri. I chose this place because I looked in the outdoor magazines for ads to sell dogs. Almost all of the ads were from one of these three states that came together near here. I found a taxi man. He didn't seem to be busy. I gave him one hundred dollars to take me around to all the coon hunters. He knew quite a few. I knew about hound men. You can't believe most of them when they tell you about their own dogs. All of them would say that they had the best dogs in the country. I didn't try to make a deal with any of them the first visit. We talked about other peoples' dogs, too. Some would say that so and so had a good dog, but my dog is better.

Soon I knew the names of the dogs each had. I never took anyone's word about his dog, but I listened carefully when a hunter said another hunter had a good dog, but you couldn't buy him, or he might be about as good as his own dog.

I finally decided on four dogs. I went to each place and asked if they would sell the dog I knew was his best dog. Each man would say the same thing, "I would sell my wife before I would sell that dog."

I learned if I stood around they would always decide to sell for a good price from one hundred to two hundred fifty dollars each.

I got the dogs I wanted. It was late. We stopped in town for something, and a truck drove up and parked. Three dogs were tied on an open truck. I got out and started talking to the dogs. A fellow came up, so I told him I had been looking for good coon dogs. He said, "These are for sale; I have to sell them. I just hate myself for even thinking about it."

He had trouble with family, or he was moving; I don't remember what was his problem. I felt like he was telling me the truth about the dogs, and they were worth it. I didn't need seven dogs, but I paid him. I kept thinking of one of those kids who hung around the Ford garage talking to that cougar hunter. If there was a good one I didn't need, I might give him a hound dog.

The next day, I hired a man at the lumber yard to make dog crates. I got on the train that night and started for Arizona. I just sat in my seat and tried to see as much of the country as possible. I had to keep the dogs watered and fed.

We arrived at Flagstaff, and Catherine was there with a truck. In about an hour we were back at home with a bunch of hounds.

We had gotten acquainted with Mr. and Mrs. Hancock. They lived at the mouth of a beautiful canyon under the Mogollon Rim. Catherine and I visited Mr. and Mrs. Hancock quite often. They had a cattle ranch.

Mr. Hancock and another rancher neighbor of his came over and said, "We heard you had some hounds. We wanted to ask you if you would come over and try to catch the cougars that are getting our calves." I told them that these were coon hounds and it would take a few days to get them switched from coons to cougars. I would only have weekends and a morning once in a while to hunt them. They said that they belonged to the Cattlemens' Association, and they paid a bounty on each cougar killed, but they would personally appreciate it if I would give it a try. I asked about the hunter with the big outfit down the road. They said that he still took out clients, but they knew it had been over three years since that hunter had caught a cougar. The dogs ran anything, and he told his customers that they almost caught a cougar today.

My next day off, I went up to Red Rock Canyon with two of my dogs. I led the dogs so I could talk to them and keep them from running deer or other unwanted animals. I had to find out what kind of dogs I had. I found a cougar track, and the dogs could smell it. I encouraged each dog and petted them to let them know I was following the track, too. They kept on getting more interested as we went along. At last we came to where the cougar had been lying down. Disturbed by us, he had moved. The track now was a hot track. As we followed the track, the dogs were pulling me ahead, and I was trying to make them excited, and they would bark and I could see that they knew I wanted them to chase that cougar. I let one go, and he started on the run. Then I let the other hound go, and they started to run and bark. I ran after them and tried to find cougar tracks and dog tracks together, and I did see them several times. After a mile, the dogs quit barking. I knew the cougar was in a tree. When I got to the pine tree where the dogs were looking up the tree, I petted the dogs and pounded on the tree with my hand as high on the tree as I could reach. The dogs started to bark more and more, as I let them know it was all right with me. I knelt down with my arms around them and encouraged them as much as I could. After a few minutes, I tied the dogs in a safe place, shot the cougar and encouraged the dogs as I turned them loose. They rushed in and smelled and worried the dead cougar. I had picked out the two dogs I thought were best, and it turned out that way.

We were just up the canyon from Mr. Hancock's house, and he had been listening to the barking. He soon came riding on his horse. He was happy we had caught a cougar, and said, "Let's put him on behind my saddle and I will take him back so the women can see it."

THOSE BEAUTIFUL ARIZONA RED ROCK CANYONS

It was good to have an excuse to hike up and down these beautiful canyons. The red walls went straight up for a thousand feet on both sides in some canyons, usually with a creek and tall pine trees in the bottoms. I went up every canyon that I could find.

Dell and I went out cougar hunting every day off we had for a while, and I took Marinho out once and caught three cougars that day. Altogether, we caught twenty-one cougars around those canyons. I had to pull a lot of porcupine quills out of the dogs before we were through. We used the hounds as a pack in the film, and they did a great job.

One day the young fellow that I liked, the one I had felt sorry for at Dick Marshall's garage, came to visit. His name was Bill Sanders. He still hadn't had any luck hunting. I knew he felt the same as I had when I wanted to start hunting. He hadn't caught anything, as his dog wouldn't tree bark. He wondered if I might be able to loan him a dog that would help train his dog. Ordinarily, I would not loan a dog, but I did have more dogs than I could use. I picked out a dog I knew was a good tree dog and told Bill he could use her. It was worth it to see how happy that made him. About two weeks later, Bill came back all smiles. He had caught a few coons and his dog was learning a lot from the dog I loaned him. The thing that tickled him was that Dick Marshall had asked him if I had one more of them coon hounds that I would sell him.

He said Dick wasn't having any luck hunting lions. I knew part of why he wasn't having much luck. Dick had a big Army truck with huge tires to go over the snow. He carried horses in the back of the trucks and his dogs in boxes on the sides. He traveled on the roads that were up on the rim above the head of the canyons. I had known he would be there, so I went up a canyon and crossed below the rim to another canyon each time I went hunting. I was catching them before they went up to the rim. It was steeper and less snow where the deer were staying.

Lloyd, Mel, Ken and dogs with cougar

There was a hunter in Prescott, Arizona who had written an article in a magazine called Full Cry. It was a hound magazine that I didn't know about. This man came over from Prescott to visit us and see our animals. He said he had written an article for the Full Cry magazine about a fellow who came to Arizona and thought he could catch lions with coon hounds. In it he expressed a lot of doubt that this could be done. Now that he found out he was wrong, he wrote another article for the magazine, and he brought the new story and gave the magazine to me. He told of the article he had written in the Full Cry magazine, and said that when he had made a mistake he was always ready to eat crow, so he wrote about this guy, Lloyd Beebe, who had gotten coon hounds and started right in to catch lions and how many he'd gotten in a short time. But he had something in his

Billy the elk with dead cougar aboard and Dell Ray with Lloyd and dogs

defense. When he arrived at our location, he found that we were working for Walt Disney Studio, and were training twenty wolves to be in the show. He then realized that this man he'd been writing about wasn't an ordinary hunter. He felt a lot better now that he could see what was happening here. He knew he wasn't the only one who thought the way he did. This man ran a butcher shop in Prescott, Arizona, and we stopped to see him on our next trip through Prescott.

About three weeks later, Bill Sanders came back one evening and told me he had been hunting with the dog I loaned him. There were two young fellows hunting with him. They had a coon in a tree, and a boy went up the tree to shoot the raccoon. One of the boys in the tree was going to shoot, but dropped the gun, and when it hit the ground, the gun went off and shot my dog. He had taken the dog to a veterinarian, and the dog was fixed up and getting well. He had paid the seventy-five dollars for the operation on the dog, and he really felt bad. I wanted to reimburse him for it, but Bill said no. I never asked for the dog back when we left Arizona. I was sure the dog had a good home.

In the show, Lobo was chased by a pack of hounds and another time by hunters on horses. We needed a place where Lobo could get away from them. We found a perfect place in Sycamore Canyon. If we could find a tree long enough to span the chasm from one side to the other, it would be great. First, we had a logging truck bring a tree up, but it didn't look as dangerous as we wanted it to. We had the truck come back and bring us a skinny log and take the first log back. This second log was just right. After a lot of work, we got the log winched into place. Now we would have to train wolves to walk across. Al Niemela had a wolf that liked to walk logs; that had given us the idea. We trained some of the wolves to walk logs about that size, only not nearly so high or long. Al said that Shadow would walk the log across the canyon. The canyon was one hundred fifty feet deep under the log, and there were rocks below. I went across two times and cut the knots and a few limbs off, so that the wolf or anyone would not trip and fall off. Mel also walked across when I wasn't there one day. If I had been there, I wouldn't have let him do it.

"Lloyd walked the log to make sure it was safe for the wolf. He walked it twice," recalled Catherine, who had the anxious time of watching her husband perform the perilous feat. "He walked it a second time with an ax to chop off any rough spots that might hinder Shadow's walk. The worst part was that Lloyd woke up that morning feeling a little dizzy - dizzy even before he went over the chasm!"

When the time came to film the scene, we had eight cameras set up. The signal was given, and the cameras began to roll. Shadow, the wolf, started on this dangerous trip over the canyon. Everything was going well when Shadow suddenly saw how high above the canyon he was, and how far it was to the rocks below. He froze, crouched and turned crosswise to the log. The log was so small that his four feet were together, and he was tipping back and forth. It looked like he would fall and be killed on the rocks below. Shadow was teetering on the log, and we were all, except Al, helpless to do anything to help. As Shadow was teetering halfway turned around, Al said, "Shadow, come" and walked straight away like he was leaving. Not wanting to be left alone, Shadow straightened up and hurried off the log. Everyone took a deep breath and wondered what we would do next.

Now a new kind of training had to be done. We had to prepare Shadow for the depth of the canyon. We built decks with boards extending on each side of the log, and a wire mesh tunnel was constructed to allow Shadow to see the depth, but to keep him from falling. In this way, the wolf could get accustomed to the void and gain the confidence he needed to overcome the dizziness brought on by heights. With the construction on the sides and around the log, Shadow became used to the emptiness below. Little by little parts of the walkway and tunnel were removed. In time, Shadow lost all fear of heights, but at the same time he lost all respect for the log crossing. He was trotting across the log with total disregard for his safety. Something had to be done to reinstate his respect for the danger involved. We took Shadow back to the practice log once again. This time, when Shadow was part way across, the crew shook the log, causing a sudden slight movement of the log. Shadow lost some of his overconfidence. He slowed down and placed each foot with studied care. This time when the cameras rolled, we recorded Lobo crossing an abyss where no human was likely to follow. In performing this feat, Shadow produced a rare act in motion picture suspense.

Lobo and his pack of wolves got away from dogs and hunters on horses by walking across this dangerous log

We eventually had to train other wolves to cross. It was easier when Shadow would go first and other wolves followed him. The pack of dogs chased Lobo and he lost them at the log, and some horsemen had to quit following at the log.

When we first tried to get pictures of Shadow crossing the log, we had brought a chicken in a cage in case of emergency to show Lobo from the other end of the log. The chicken got out of the cage and was out on the log before we saw it. The chicken walked back and forth on the log for about an hour before it got off at one end, and we continued. Everyone got a big laugh out of that.

When we were almost finished with the show <u>Lobo</u>, we made sure that we took the log down from the canyon and cleaned up all the parts of the project near the log.

From 1960 to 1961, we all learned to love Arizona, but still we were glad to go back to Sequim and the Olympic Peninsula in 1961.

Walt and Roy Disney visited us to talk about making animal films for them.

GOING BACK HOME TO SEQUIM AND AN OCEAN FISHING TRIP

The following article appeared in the <u>Port Angeles Evening News</u>, July 28, 1961:

BEEBE FAMILY BACK FROM MOVIE FILMING LOCATION

Lloyd Beebe, wildlife photographer for Walt Disney, and his family are at home in Dungeness, on two or three months leave between assignments.

The Beebe family returned recently from Sedona, Ariz., where for the past year and a half he has been working on <u>Lobo</u>, a wolf story.

They lived on a 120 acre farm, leased while the picture was in the making. It had a partly finished house, and they fixed it up and moved in.

Working with Beebe was Jack Couffer from Los Angeles, and the two families were left pretty much on their own until the picture was finished. Contracts with the company were made by mail or phone, and maybe once a year someone came out to see how they were getting along.

When they needed people in the pictures, Beebe said, they used local cowboys, or some of their family. Their son, Melvin, who just recently graduated from high school by a correspondence course, worked with the animals, around the buildings, and took still pictures. Mrs. Beebe bought supplies, paid bills and helped wherever she was needed along with taking care of her family. Their younger son, Kenny, attended school seven miles away in a 'ghost town'. The need for more schools brought into use again the schoolhouse in a deserted mining town.

With the Beebes in Arizona was the couple they brought back from Brazil, Mr. and Mrs. Marinho Correia. They are expected to arrive next week. Also returning from Sedona is Dell Ray, who worked with the animals on location.

Beebe started working for Disney in 1951, and his assignments over the past 10 years read like an adventure series. Going backward, before Sedona he was in Alberta, Canada for a year and a half working on <u>Nikki, Wild Dog of the North</u>, now showing at the Lincoln Theater in Port Angeles.

Prior to that, he was in Recife, Brazil, working on <u>Jungle Cat</u>. He spent 18 months in <u>Little America</u> in the Antarctic working on <u>The Seven Cities of Antarctic</u>. He made four different trips of 1200 miles each across the ice, and says 'that was the place I was gladdest to get out of.' It was also the only assignment where the family couldn't go with him.

Before that he was in Canada for another 18 months, this time working on <u>White Wilderness</u>, and his first work was on <u>Vanishing Prairie</u>, parts of it done here at home.

When asked what place or incident stood out in his memory of photographic adventures, Lloyd Beebe, raised on the peninsula, told not of animals of the Amazon jungle, dangers on the ice floe, or heat of the Arizona desert, but of a fishing trip in Canada.

While working on <u>White Wilderness</u>, he and John Tenner of the Canadian Wildlife Service were flown in with canoes to two arctic rivers looking for Canada musk ox. It was the first time for 100 years men had been in that part of the country.

'The fishing was wonderful...(the musk ox were interesting and a little dangerous, one just about ran us down one day)... but you never saw such fish!' he said.

Beebe likes this job. He likes being outdoors and working with animals. When he decided he wanted to take pictures of them he had never seen a movie camera. He used to do a lot of cougar hunting and had hunted with a bow and arrow, and knew he could get close enough to wild animals to take pictures. He said he didn't dare tell people what he meant to do, because he knew nothing of photography. He bought a camera, and started taking wildlife pictures and reading books on the subject.

Melvin was four years old when Beebe made The Little Archer, a short of the boy going out to hunt with bow and arrow and returning home with the animals trailing behind him. Warner Brothers bought it.

It was hard getting started and they just barely got along, Beebe said. Money borrowed on their old car brought money to buy more film more than once. Then he got to the point where he had so much footage and money invested he had to do something or quit, so he bundled up some film and sent it to Walt Disney.

There just happened to be some cougar pictures, and Disney, then making Vanishing Prairie, was looking for pictures of cougars that weren't tied up or being shot. Beebe got a phone call from Hollywood the day after the film arrived with an offer to buy it, and they wanted more. He went to see them, came back and worked for six months keeping track of his time, and then went on a salary.

He has worked for Disney longer than any of the wildlife photographers who started with the series, and is the only one left of the original dozen or so. He says knowing animals is the most important part of his job, and never has trouble with his film.

The Beebes like Dungeness better than any place they have been and look forward to the time when they can retire and build, much as they have enjoyed most of their assignments. Melvin is at a point where he must decide if he wants to go to college or into the service and won't be at home, but Kenny is going into the fourth grade and wants to stay here, so he can ride the school bus like the other kids.

Hollum Hunley had a fifty-five foot fishing boat. Hollum had tried to get me to go fishing with him for years, and I never had time. This year, it was about the first of September, and I could get away for a few days. The salmon fishing season was over. Hollum wanted to go out from LaPush to where the tuna fleet was, one hundred miles out into the ocean. I thought it would be a good chance for Mel to go, too. I told Hollum we would go. On the day we were to meet him at his boat at LaPush, it was very foggy, so we stayed on the boat for two days, hoping the fog would go away. It did not happen, and Hollum finally said he would take the boat down the river to the fish buyers and fill up the hold with ice. Next morning, Hollum thought we'd better go downriver and out into the ocean in the fog and hope we got into clear weather. It is a dangerous place at the mouth of the Quileute River, with lots of rocks. We kept going on through the fog and skirting high pinnacle rocks all the way out into the Pacific Ocean. We finally got out to the tuna boats and started fishing for tuna. It was late and the weather was getting very windy. It was the beginning of the worst storm of the year. Hollum put out the sea anchor and let the wind blow us all night. The next day, it was rough on the water. At daylight, we could see none of the tuna fleet, and we spent the day trying to find them, but with no luck. The automatic pilot quit working, as well as all other radio equipment. The only instrument still working was the compass. The weather now was terrible; the seas were like mountains as we climbed over them. Mel was in the bunk, and the waves were throwing the boat around so much that Mel was thrown out of the bunk and landed on Hollum's legs, and Hollum could no longer stand up. The boat was left for me to get it back to LaPush or somewhere else. I knew I had a bad problem and a lot of responsibility. I had never run a boat like that. I just had to do the best I could. Mel and Hollum were in bed. It was hard to stand up. I held on to the wheel with my legs braced wide apart. We didn't know how far it was or where we were. I tried to think what direction I should be heading. I sure was glad the compass was working, if it was. Everything was soaking wet. All evening and through the night I held on to the wheel and kept on the heading that I had decided on. The moon came out, and I could see the reflections on the tops of the mountain peaks of water as we kept climbing up and up to the tops and then down on the other side to the bottom, and start climbing back up again. All the time I tried to keep on the right direction; hour by hour I was learning a little more about the controls. It was hard to stand and keep my balance with the terrible rocking and rolling of the boat. All the time I was wondering what part of the coast I would be coming to. I worried because there were rocks all along close to the shore. Finally when I was on top of a mountainous wave, I thought I could see a light reflecting from the top of a wave. I just kept going in the same direction. The time came when I could see the light every time I was up high on a wave. Then, in a little while, I could see the light blink on and off. I knew it was a buoy light. Each buoy light is set to blink every so often. I thought I remembered how far apart the lights blinked on and off at LaPush. The timing seemed right for LaPush. Later when I could see all the tall rocks in the moonlight, I was sure this had to be LaPush.

We still had four or five hours until daylight. I would have to keep the boat going back and forth along the coast and all those rocks until after daylight. I knew I should never try getting into the river past the rocky sides even in daylight. If I could use up five hours and then wake Hollum, I could let him pilot the boat into the river to quieter water. We were a mile or two off shore but very close to large rocks all along. After I piloted the boat for fifteen or so minutes one way, I would turn and go the opposite direction. I was so sleepy that I would almost fall asleep standing spraddle-legged and hanging on to the wheel. Several times when I got to the next turn around, I couldn't think of the compass heading I had been running back and forth on. I felt a little panic, because I couldn't remember the heading. The moon was gone and there was fog, so that I couldn't see the rocks. Each time this happened, I figured it out again, but for a moment I may have been heading for the rocks. I made it through to daylight, and then I called to Hollum. He said that this boat had to have high tide to get into the river. He knew when the tide would be high. I had three more hours to go. Now it was light enough to see the rocks and the mouth of the river. That even helped my legs, which had gotten pretty tired as I tried to keep standing up. It wasn't so rough close to shore, and the rocks probably broke up the waves a little.

Hollum finally got out of bed and made it over to the wheel and said he could get into the river now. We got into the dock and tied up. We didn't take long loading up our pickup and heading for Sequim.

Hollum had told me he would have to buy a Loran before he could go back out fishing. It would cost two thousand dollars, and the banks would not loan him the money. I told him to come to Sequim and I would sign for his loan. Hollum said he would be there. The next day, Hollum came to Sequim to borrow money at the bank. He was late, so we hurried to the bank. They closed at 5 pm. The Bank Manager said that there really wasn't time to make out the papers, so why didn't I just loan him the money? We had been spending our money fixing up the farm, but we had a little money in the bank. I said, "Okay, give me the two thousand dollars from our account." I said to Hollum as I handed him the money, "Take this money and if you can't pay it back, just forget it, and don't worry about it." I think I was glad I wouldn't be going with him.

INCREDIBLE JOURNEY AND DISNEY'S WILD ANIMAL FARM

Walt Disney Studio put lights in our barn for indoor photography, as well as a sound stage. Now we could keep filming even in the rain or bad weather. We have our own crew that does all the directing and camera work. We send the film to the Disney Studio for editing and for finishing the movie.

In the next few years we shot many films here at the ranch. We didn't let people come in to watch, and no cameras were allowed on the ranch except Disney's equipment. This was the only Disney film crew besides Disney's studio in Burbank, California. We worked steadily on one film after another.

The Incredible Journey was the first film shot at the farm after it was named The Disney Wild Animal Ranch. It was called this by everyone until it became the Olympic Game Farm in 1972.

The Incredible Journey took place in a part of Canada which is in a deeply wooded wilderness. It is a vast area of lonely lakes lying in endless chains, a land of unnamed streams and torrential rushing rivers.

The movie starts out with John Longridge, a bachelor who is spending a quiet evening in the company of some old friends, a Siamese cat in his lap named Tao, a white Bull Terrier, Bodger, asleep at his feet and a Golden Retriever lying on the hearth. John Longridge is not their real master. The Hunter family had left the animals in his keeping while on a trip to England.

The telephone rings. It is a typical party line telephone common to rural areas. He picks up the receiver and says, "Hello, hello, sorry, I can't hear you very well." Then Mr. Longridge's housekeeper Mrs. Oakes' voice says, "What time are you leaving in the morning?" He answers, "About seven." Mrs. Oakes' voice, "Oh, well I can't." Her voice drifts off in static. Then she says that she can't get there till 9 am tomorrow. He says, "That is quite all right, Mrs. Oakes." She says, "Are you sure 9 am is all

Bodger, Luath, and Tao of the movie "The Incredible Journey"

right?" Longridge says, "Perfectly all right, and before you get here, I'll take" 'POP', the phone is cut off. He says to himself, "Oh well, it wasn't important, anyway."

Mr. Longridge writes a note for Mrs. Oakes, "Dear Mrs. Oakes, We are out of coffee. Please order some more. I'll be taking the dogs and Tao, too, of course." Reaching the bottom of the page, he tears it off and begins another, "Out for a run before I leave, and will give them something to eat. I know they will be fine." He signs the note J.R.L., and tucks it under a glass paperweight. During the night, Tao, the cat, knocks the paperweight off the table, and the last half of the note floats down into the fireplace and burns up.

In the morning, Longridge lets the animals out to play until Mrs. Oakes arrives to clean the house. She reads the note that says he is taking the animals with him. By that time, the animals had started to go back to their real home. Luath knows it is west of here, but two hundred miles west through wild country. Now the incredible journey has begun, with many exciting and dangerous events to come. They arrive on Peter Hunter's birthday long after they are given up for lost.

This was a great picture, and it was fun for us to have done most of it. We did the first two-thirds of the picture, and then we had to go to Quebec, Canada to finish the picture. The show was supposed to be made in Canada, but we did all of the traveling of Tao the Siamese cat, Luath the Golden Retriever and Bodger the Bull Terrier right here at Sequim, Washington.

In 1962, we worked on Those Calloways as well as several other shows at the same time. While we were filming for Disney, we hired a crew to build an eight-foot high fence with an overhang on the top so no animals could get out. Catherine and I hired this crew and bought wire posts and built other pens and tried to think ahead and be ready. The pictures we made here were always the best that Disney put out in the animal line.

We were working on other pictures when Wild Goose Calling was started. We put in a field of corn along a pond and took pictures of geese in the corn field. We also sent geese and corn stalks to the studio for shooting on the back lot of Disney.

Later, we went with Disney to Vermont to work on Those Calloways. There was snow and the weather was cold. There was a film crew from New York on the job. It was hard to work in the snow. Every time you do a scene, you must fix all the tracks so it looks like new snow again.

Part of "Those Calloways" was filmed in Vermont

Dell Ray and I were there. We had brought a wolverine and other animals. Filming was going very slowly, with days passing and not much to show for it. I wasn't doing any filming here because of the New York crew; they were all union, and probably wouldn't want me to work unless I joined the union.

Winston Hibler was the producer in this film, and I could see he was getting upset with the progress on this show. Hib always got a string out of his pocket when he was getting irritated, and tied it in knots. That was what he was doing now. Pretty soon he beckoned to me to come over by him. He said, "We are not getting anywhere. Lloyd, you could do this up in Washington, couldn't you?" I said, "Sure, we could." There was a big log jam set in the picture. Hib said, "You could build another log jam exactly like this one, couldn't you?" I said, "Yes." He said, "Look over the log jam and take any measurements you might need. We can't go on like this, and here is what I am going to do. I will go back to Los Angeles and leave you in charge. You will be the director and everything. Just try to get what you can for a week. Then, tell the crew that we have finished and go back to Sequim and finish the picture except for a few parts we can do in the studio." So Hib and all the people from the studio went back to Los Angeles. Hib had told the crew that I was the boss before he left.

We started filming, and I said that I needed all the help from the crew I could get. The head of the film crew said he didn't believe that Winston Hibler would turn over this operation to me unless he knew I could do it. It surprised me that he knew I could do it. I guess I knew it too.

We spent a week at it, and the whole crew was happy and did real well. The studio called back and said that we had gotten a lot more and better film after Hib had gone home. Hib said he should have gone home sooner.

I tried to get finished with the parts we couldn't do at home, like a sequence of old cars. Also, Brandon DeWilde was the main actor in the movie and couldn't walk on snowshoes without falling down in the scene. So, I took Brandon for a walk on snowshoes and showed him how to get along without falling. After that, he did all right.

At the end of the week, I told the crew that we were finished, and they were all glad to get out of the snow and believe that they had finished the show. They even had a party after work.

Dell and I gathered up everything of ours and went back to Sequim.

The first thing was to get a log jam built to match the one they had built in Vermont. Bill Koehler was the trainer of Brandon DeWilde's dog in the show. We spent three weeks in the Cascade Mountains and a few days in the Olympics finishing Those Calloways. We had Brandon DeWilde's clothing to use for a double when we needed it.

We filmed several sequences of the dog and other wild animals. Now we only needed to go back to our barn and finish the sequences of the log jam pile.

Brandon DeWilde had crawled into the log jam in Vermont. We had to finish shooting a wolverine and Brandon fighting and wrestling in the log jam. I put on Brandon's clothes, and the wolverine and I had a big fight, and we were finished with the show.

Then Hib called and wanted me to bring the wolverine and come to the Burbank studio. They had a few new things they wanted to do. They had built a log jam in their studio also to use with Brandon DeWilde, Brian Keith and Walter Brennan.

Dell Ray and I got to Los Angeles and were to be at the studio for a week. We kept the wolverine close to the sound stage where we were to use him. The first two days, we let the wolverine get used to his surroundings. When people thinned out, we let the wolverine, Joe by name, walk around the log jam and walk all the logs so he would be ready when called on. Walt Disney and the other bosses came to look at Joe. Walter Brennan spent a lot of time talking to us.

On the third day, the wolverine was to be the star. Dell and I didn't belong to the Hollywood union, so the studio had to pay a union animal trainer to be there, even though he didn't want to do anything. He was there to watch.

Winston Hibler came to me and said that there were several animal trainers who wanted to come in to watch, that they had heard we trained our animals with a buzzer, and they wanted to see how we did it. I told Hib that it was all right with me. It had never occurred to me that everybody didn't know about this by now.

The director told us before each shot which log the wolverine was to travel on and the route he was to take. We put our buzzers in place and were ready before the cameras. All day this happened, and the wolverine never missed a shot. We would buzz the buzzer one time only before Joe was out of the cage, and just before he had reached the first buzzer, we would buzz the next buzzer, and he would change logs to the next buzzer, exactly where they wanted him to be. No matter where they wanted the wolverine to go he did it without one mistake. In the afternoon I dressed up in Brandon DeWilde's clothing and fought with the wolverine. We rolled around inside of the log jam in a wrestling match. Joe didn't want to do this, so I had to grab him to start, and it was up to me to hang onto him and roll around under the logs with him. The director said, "We got it."

Bill Bacon as the trapper in Minado

The cameramen had to change their cameras to new positions before the next shot, which was the wolverine standing on the end of a high log that stuck out from the log jam. It took so long for the cameras to get ready that the director came over and told me that there were only five minutes left to get the shot.

The wolverine was to jump off the end of the high log and land on my shoulders. He asked if I thought we had time to get the shot, that they would have to pay overtime to everyone and gave other reasons why they would have to stop. He wondered if there was any chance of getting the shot in five minutes. I said, "I think we can, if the cameras are ready."

I was to stand in front of a camera looking over my back at the wolverine as he jumps on me, and we go down and start a fight. The cameras checked over, and they said, "Roll camera." They wanted me as far from the wolverine as possible. I tried, but Joe didn't want to jump that far, so I said, "I have to let him jump a little shorter first."

I moved up two feet closer, and Joe jumped and we got that. Then we buzzed the buzzer and Joe ran back through the log jam, got on the end of the log and I stood back further and said, "Ready." The cameras rolled. I called Joe, and he made a great jump, and the director said, "Beautiful. This is a wrap." We still had a few seconds left.

With a buzz of the buzzer, Joe was in his cage. I had been so busy that I couldn't enjoy how the people reacted to the wolverine doing everything without wasting any time. The Hollywood trainers were amazed that we had been working with buzzers since 1952 in animal training, and wanted to ask a lot of questions. From that time on, all animal trainers used our method and they still do today.

Dell and I stayed two more days until they had developed the film. Everything was okay, so we loaded up and went back to Sequim.

Shows came one after another, some of them with actors as often as with animals.

In 1963, we did a wolverine show called <u>Minado</u>. We had to get some wolverines somewhere. The studio came up with two wolverines that some Indians captured in northern Canada. They were about half grown.

Marinho, Ken and I spent a lot of time in the pen with them. We had them in cages eight feet long, four feet wide and four feet high. Ken and I spent the most time with them, as we kept them in our yard. Our crew was always small. Usually we only had five or six people on our crew, including me.

Bill Bacon came and joined us. It was good to have our old friend with us again. We decided that Bill could be the trapper in this show. Bill had to grow a beard. By the time the wolverines were ready, Bill's beard was in good shape.

We moved a cabin that we had here up into the mountains. This was a log cabin with all logs numbered and color-coded, no nails in it, so it wasn't too hard to move. We enjoyed the work on this show because it was all animals except the trapper, Bill. We were in the woods every day of filming.

While we were working on this show, I got a call from Erwin Verity. He called to tell me that Walt Disney had died. That hit us pretty hard. We were good friends with him. Every time Catherine and I had gone to the studio, Walt would take us to dinner. He also came to see us in Sequim once in a while.

Erwin had spoken about it several times, that we were the only ones that Walt and Roy ever went to visit. When they came to see us, we never let others know they were here, so they could relax and enjoy themselves.

We knew it would hurt the studio. Without Walt, the Disney Studio did go downhill for a while. When Walt was there, he didn't want his good name on the picture if it wasn't good. He would tell the producers to go back and work on a few things again. Without Walt, the producers could stop work on a picture before it was as good as they could make it.

Our son, Mel, left for the U.S. Army in 1964, and went to Air Traffic Control School in Oklahoma. When he graduated, he went to Germany for three years, and then worked in air traffic control in the United States in 1968. At that time, he and Charlotte Renhard were married; they later divorced.

Catherine and I became grandparents when Robert Lloyd Beebe was born, February 13, 1969. Then on May 4, 1975, James Lee Beebe was born, and we now have two grandsons.

While we were working on pictures at home in Sequim, Catherine and I had talked about building a house here. We decided we had traveled enough. We could stay here in Sequim and keep busy on films. We were working on the new house. It was on a hill above all the animals and fields. It had a great view of the fields and Olympic Mountains. We could see everything that went on at our place.

One day, we were sitting down eating our noon meal, when we heard my mother screaming, "Lloyd, Lloyd, come here!" We knew what had happened. I jumped up and ran down a steep trail and through the barn to my folks' house. My mother was standing by the wood pile, where she had found my father lying where he had been cutting kindling. I could see he had been dead for some time. Some of the men came as I gathered my father up in my arms and started for the house. Some of the men wanted to help, but I said, "No, I will carry him to the house." I laid him down on his bed. My mother hugged and kissed him, and wanted us to do something, but we knew it was too late and my dad was gone. We called his doctor. He came right out and said that there was nothing we could have done for Dad.

I had never had a real argument with my father, but I still thought I should have spent a lot more time with him lately. I guess that's the way it always is.

We had my mother come and stay with us for a few days, and then she wanted to go back to her house to stay. We tried to keep her wood cut and piled, but she did a lot of it herself to keep busy.

WE BUILT OUR NEW HOUSE ON THE FARM

For months, Catherine and I had been working on the basement of our new house. We sometimes hired the Hennessey brothers to help us. Winston Hibler was having his new house built in Los Angeles at the same time. Hib had taken us up to see his house when it was just started and again after it was finished.

Our new home overlooking the farm

Winston Hibler and Erwin Verity came up to talk pictures with us and to look at our house. Catherine and I worked in all our spare time. Dell Ray worked some days.

Erwin Verity said, "Lloyd, why don't you hire some more help and have them work on the house? We would rather pay for the help. You can just keep thinking of the shows we are working on now and the ones we might do in the future."

We hired the Hennessey brothers; there were four of them. Joe was the oldest, and he stayed home and did the housework and cooking. Bob, Fred and Tom Hennessey came down, and once in a while they would help with the house. The rest of the time, I had them work on the outside fence around the eighty-nine acres of our farm. The fence would be eight feet high and have an overhang so animals wouldn't get over it. I bought the wire, and the crew cut our own posts. When that was finished, we didn't worry about animals getting us into trouble.

We trained animals every day. Without a good outside fence, we weren't quite as relaxed as we are now. The Hennesseys were a lot of fun for everyone. Joe would have an extra pie in their lunch every day, so we all got pie when we were around. Some of our workers were always there, and they said you've got to eat it because Joe always throws it out every day and makes new ones.

We made about sixty-five shows for Disney and helped on more than one hundred others. Now that I am writing this story, I wonder if it was in any way boring to film them all. The next show was always new and different to work on, and I don't think we were ever bored.

The next one that I really wouldn't have wanted to miss was Charlie The Lonesome Cougar. I always loved cougars. I was anxious to get started on this, as I was always into the training of animals that we used. It helped to know all about them and what they could do. This was in 1965, and we had some great cougars. After the screen tests were over, Ron Brown, an actor from California, was chosen as the actor in <u>Charlie The Lonesome Cougar</u>. Ron was a good-looking young man and easy to work with. Everyone liked Ron and his wife, Sue, and the children, Randy, Rhonda and Jan. They all moved up to Sequim.

Charlie had every kind of excitement that we could think of as he was going up around a logging camp. When he was grown, Charlie even entered the log rolling contest; he had everyone cheering for him. Near the end, Charlie was chased by a pack of cougar dogs and had to jump on a log going by in a log flume. This log flume came from a mountain and was seven miles long. It went around hills and cliffs, and was more exciting than any amusement rides you could find.

Charlie stayed with the log until just before it went into a sawmill. There was a bushy tree that had fallen across the flume, and Charlie got brushed off. Next, Charlie got in a lot of trouble in the mill.

We had a lot of rides in that flume, too. It was ours to use on weekends, as the mills only ran five days a week. We had to take a lot of trips on the logs, because there was no way to get off or get Charlie off after he started down the seven-mile trip until he got to the slow waters.

We had a boat that the son of the mill owner had made to go down the flume in. The son had gotten married, and now had children, and he didn't want to use it any more. We used the boat some to help with the camera work. It was a good film and I enjoyed the cougars very much.

We used several cougars on this show because we had to have them in all sizes. The male cougar that we used the most we called Charlie. He was a great cougar. Some of the crew started to play with him in between filming and spoiled him a little. Playing with a cougar is the worst possible thing to do. If you keep it up, the cougar gets so it doesn't want to quit when you do.

Everyone here knew they should not play with the cougar, but some of the crew couldn't resist the temptation when we were not

Charlie the lonesome cougar

looking. Although Charlie was not a threat to them, he didn't know when play time was over. It got so that Charlie, after filming a scene, wouldn't come when we called. We all knew he was hiding in the trees and brush watching and waiting for us.

I said to my crew, "You fellows have been spoiling Charlie by playing with him, and we have to finish this picture before correcting him, so we will all take turns bringing him back from his hiding place." Whenever Charlie didn't come back, the person whose turn it was had to go out through the brush and shake bushes and make noises. Suddenly, Charlie would run out of the brush, take a flying leap and land

Big Ted, king of the grizzlies, has just chased the camp cook up a tree

on his shoulders so they would both go down.

It was all in fun. Charlie wouldn't have his claws out. Some of the crew liked it, but some didn't. Everyone had to take his turn, and it wasn't long before they had enough and agreed that they shouldn't have started playing with Charlie in the first place.

Cougars are stubborn, and it took a lot of work to make Charlie stop jumping on people. We were careful to see that it didn't happen any more.

One day, we were going out to work with a big friendly bear named Como. Terry Rowland was putting a rope on him. Terry started showing how funny it was to put his finger in Como's ear. Como would shake his head, and Terry and others would laugh about it. Terry put his finger in Como's ear one too many times. The bear caught Terry's finger in his mouth and wouldn't let go. If Como thought Terry was pulling his finger out of his mouth, he would tighten his grip. Como didn't bite hard. He just wanted to keep the finger so Terry wouldn't put it in his ear. Everyone could see what was happening; even Terry knew Como was being reasonable about it.

After everyone had enough laughs about it, we talked Como into letting Terry go. I think Como knew he had taught Terry a lesson, and Terry didn't play that game any more.

Another day we were working with Como. Marinho had just started to work with us with the animals. We were taking pictures of Como in a thick grassy area with canary grass about three feet high with a creek running through the flat ground. We gave Marinho a sack of doughnuts so he could give one to Como when he called him. When Como found out Marinho had the doughnuts, he kept getting closer, and Marinho started to move away, and Como kept coming. Marinho hadn't worked with any bears, so he moved faster and faster, and Como stayed right behind him. Marinho was scared by now and started running from Como. Como stayed right with Marinho. Marinho was sure Como was after him and ran full speed. Marinho was very quick and had to run in circles to keep ahead. The circles got smaller and faster. We were shouting for Marinho to give him the doughnuts, but Marinho couldn't understand. Como finally caught Marinho and sat on him while he ate the sack of doughnuts. Marinho now knew it was the doughnuts the bear wanted. All through this sequence, everyone had laughed and cheered. We all knew Como wouldn't hurt Marinho. It had been very serious for Marinho. When the bear finished the doughnuts, he got up and let Marinho know the chase was over, and Marinho started to laugh with everyone else.

136

The next show that was new and different to me was in 1968, <u>The King of The Grizzlies</u>. Winston Hibler called from the Disney Studio to ask if I thought we could do a show about grizzly bears. There would be people in the show, and they would be as close as possible to the grizzlies. I said that I didn't know much about grizzlies. Hib knew we didn't have any grizzlies. He said that if we did this show, at least we would have some grizzly shots to use in other films later on. The studio had been thinking of this show for a year or two, but hadn't found anyone who would give it a try. They said they had just waited for a time when I would be free to talk about it with them.

The Alaska Game Department sent us two wild Alaska brown bears about seven months old. They were mean rascals. We started in training them, and they responded. We would never be able to pet them, as we had to move right ahead with the picture.

We bought a family of bears from Woodland Park Zoo in Seattle. The cubs were too old to handle, but we started in training them. The adults, female and male, had never been handled before.

As we worked with the bears, the studio had us filming parts of other shows that they worked on at the studio. Whenever we thought we could get a few scenes for the grizzly picture, we would do it. We had to find a way to handle wild-type bears. We had used electric fence on cattle, and I knew that worked. When we were milking cows on the farm, one thing I always remembered was that the bull we had on the farm was kind of mean, and the fence by the barn where the bull spent his time had a single wire across as a gate, but it was electric. The cattle fences just went on and off and gave you short shocks if you touched them. We all got shocks regularly, and it didn't hurt. It was like a bee sting, but you were scared of it.

This bull we had always stood with his head over the fence wire when the cattle came by him, and then again after milking. He would check the cows in and out of the barn. One morning, we noticed the cows had come in and out and the bull was standing in the same spot. We had forgotten to hook up the gate, but he wouldn't step across where he knew the wire was every day.

I thought we might make the electric fence work for the bears. We started the bears' education. Because of the bears' long hair, I knew they would have to touch the wire with their noses, feet or ears. We started out with a cattle electric fence, then went to a Model T Ford coil, which is a harder shock and the spark would jump an inch or so. It also made a pop when they got a shock, and that scared them.

I knew if an animal went through an electric fence the first time, he might keep running through the fence. I had seen a pig we once had that ran through the fence and got a shock. After that he would never stay in. He would see the electric fence, and he would start to squeal and run as hard as he could through the fence, squealing all the time, then he would stop and eat the grass or whatever it was he wanted to get to. I didn't want to have that happen to a bear, so I had our training fence close to the wall of the barn so the bears would know they couldn't go through and would get in the habit of jumping back to get away from the fence. In that way, they would always stay inside. It worked. We soon had the bears trained so that we could take them out in strange places, and they would stay inside the fence. We later had the bears so they would stay inside with a string or wire around through the woods. We could lay the string or wire on the ground if we showed it to them. Even the big male bear got so we worked him close to horses and people as though there was no fence. We worried a lot at first. We knew, however, that if we didn't make mistakes and watched the actors closely we would be all right.

We filmed half of <u>The King of the Grizzlies</u> here in Sequim, and the other half in the Canadian Rockies near Banff, Alberta, Canada.

KING OF THE GRIZZLIES

The story was about a rancher, Colonel Pierson, and his ranch foreman, Moki, an Absaroka Indian who had been to school in Pennsylvania. When he came back as a man less than a year later, he found that his people had moved north to live on the reservation, and in this land of his youth, he also found an unexpected return to his boyhood memories.

One day, the Colonel and Moki came upon a grizzly fighting in the brush. "Grizzly!" shouted Moki, "and one of our bulls." The Colonel whipped out his rifle and shot three times, and a mother grizzly and at least one cub were dead.

One cub, a male, had run and fallen off the bluff into the river, and went down the river rapids and out of sight. Moki said, "Too bad." The Colonel looked up sharply and said, "Too bad about the bull or the bear?" "About the cub," said Moki. Rising, the Colonel faced Moki squarely. "You've got a new totem, Moki - cattle. Remember." "Yes, sir." The Indian's eyes held the Colonel's for a moment.

The bear cub reached the other side of the river, almost drowned and exhausted. It climbed a tree and tried to sleep.

The next morning, Moki rode his horse across the river looking for stray cattle. He finally saw unexpected marks on the soft ground - bear tracks. Dismounting, he knelt and saw the imprint of a four-toed bear cub - a perfect enlargement of the tribal totem mark his grandfather had burned into the back of his hand so long ago.

Slightly bewildered by the coincidence, but strongly impressed, Moki remounted and followed the cub's trail away from the river bank. It was plain that this was the same cub that had fallen in the river. As a cattleman, he thought it a good idea to keep tabs on this young grizzly. When the trail reached the tree, the cub was still clinging to his perch. It peered at the man on horseback. Moki tapped the pommel of his saddle, thinking what action to take. He had two choices: he could shoot him or he could ride off and leave the bear alone, but he'd grow up to be an adult grizzly in cattle country, and that wouldn't do at all. Presently, a grin replaced Moki's thoughtful frown, and he dismounted. It occurred to him that there was a third choice, and that was the one he decided to take. He would capture the cub, tie him up and turn him loose in the high country, far from the Colonel's ranch.

Moki pulled the cub out of the tree with his horse and tied him up. It was hard to get the seventy-five pound cub on an unwilling horse, but he finally succeeded. Moki didn't know for sure just why he was about to set a grizzly bear free, but as he rode to the high country, he recalled the legend of the bear clan, as his grandfather had told it long ago.

Hours later, Moki dismounted at the base of a high waterfall and loosened the slip knot that held the cub lashed to the saddle. Nimbly dodging the flashing teeth and claws, he cut off the rope that hog-tied the bear's legs.

The bear started to wobble away making disgruntled sounds. This cub bear would grow up to be <u>Wahb, King of the Grizzlies</u>. Moki watched him go and shouted after him, "Now you stay up here where you belong, you hear? Come back to my country and we will both be in trouble."

Grinning he raised his right hand in the Indians' gesture of peace and called out in the Indian language, "Go in peace, oh my brother." Then Moki said with a chuckle, "Don't thank me - thank my grandfather."

Now began Wahb's experiences as he grew to a tremendous size and was the king of the grizzlies.

We filmed Wahb all the way until he weighed fifteen hundred pounds in a lot of exciting sequences. The bears were working better than we had ever dreamed they would when we first started the picture. I guess that had a lot to do with the great satisfaction and enjoyment we felt when making this show.

It is always so nice to do a job whenever other people expect it to be impossible, and it turns out easy with thought and hard work. As we filmed, we had to use bigger grizzlies. Now we are using Big Ted.

He is so big and beautiful.

Moki was working on a new horseshoe when the Colonel joined him. Moki said, "But take a look at these three wolf brushes I brought in. That's the last of the pack." The Colonel said, "Good work. I'm glad we got rid of that bunch of cattle killers." Moki said, "Yes, sir, but just the same, I'm going to have the boys fence off that timberline."

The Colonel said, "Oh, how is that?" Moki said, "It's pretty wild back there. I saw a grizzly." The Colonel raised his eyebrows and said, "Too bad you couldn't get a shot at him." "I might have," Moki said, "but I wanted to get the wolves. Anyway the bear was hightailing it for the mountains."

"Good," said the Colonel, "let's hope he keeps right on going." Moki grunted, "If he doesn't, I'm going to be real disappointed in my grandfather."

"Your grandfather? What do you mean?"

"Remember the cub we knocked into the river a few years back?"

"Sure, we got his mother and sister."

"Right. The cub had four toes on his right-hand foot. The grizzly I saw today left a four-toed track. Could be the same bear."

The Colonel pushed his hat back. "How could you know how many toes that cub had? We lost him in the river."

"Yes, sir, but I found him the next day alive and up a tree. Then I got to thinking about my grandfather, about totems and Indian legends. First thing I knew, I had that cub hog-tied and was headed for the high country; turned him loose up there."

Colonel Pierson shook his head and said, "Moki, sometimes I wonder if you are not more medicine man that cattleman."

Moki nodded, "Yes, sir, sometimes I wonder the same thing."

Several days later, three of Pierson's ranch hands were setting up a fence across the mouth of a small canyon that cut through the rim rocks. The man called Shorty began to sink the posts in the ground, while the other two drove off in the spring wagon to get another load. Shorty had planted a half dozen posts when he decided to sneak a nap in the shade of a small tree. He covered his face with his hat and was soon dreaming of fried chicken.

Shorty was asleep when Wahb ambled into the canyon, digging beetles, grubs and roots. Spotting the line of newly planted posts, he toppled them over one by one, finding a feast of beetles in the soft soil around each one of them. As he tipped over the last post, the sound woke Shorty, who jackknifed to a sitting position and found himself face to face with a grizzly bear.

Almost as startled as Shorty, Wahb gave a surprised "Woof" and froze staring at him. Having heard that people have escaped the attack of grizzlies by playing dead, Shorty fell flat and lay still. Luckily for him, the trick worked. Wahb sniffed and nudged the terrified cowhand. He even licked Shorty's bald head. Wahb then moved into a stand of small pines.

Presently the men in the spring wagon returned and called out to Shorty. Shorty jumped up, leaves and dirt falling off of him as he ran toward the wagon yelling, "Grizzly, grizzly!" At the same time, Wahb raised up to full height to see what was happening. The noise and the sight of the grizzly scared the horses, and Shorty had a hard time getting in the wagon before it raced down the trail at high speed. We filmed Wahb as he went up the canyon.

Back at the ranch, Shorty blurted out his story to the other hands as many times as they would listen. "There he was just as close as you to me, mean little red eyes, big mouth loaded with teeth about this long. I tell you boys, if I hadn't rolled over and played dead, I would be wearing a live bearskin coat right now. Yes, sir, I'm lucky to be here all in one piece."

His listeners were still showering him with questions when Colonel Pierson joined the group. "All right. You and the others had better break it up and get back to that fencing."

139

Moki saw the group dispersing as he drove back into the yard area with a wagon load of barbed wire. "What're those men doing here; they're supposed to be setting fence."

"They were setting fence, but they ran into trouble"

"What kind?"

"Grizzly trouble, Moki."

Moki's eyes clouded. "Oh, what happened?"

"Your grizzly friend came back, the one that was hightailing it for the mountains. Shorty could have been killed."

"Was he hurt?"

"No, but only because he had sense enough to play dead."

"That's good."

"But it could have been bad, Moki, so I've a job for you. They have a load of bear traps at the KayCee Ranch. You borrow them and spread them all over the area. That grizzly of yours has got to be caught."

Moki scowled. "I'd rather get him with the rifle, sir."

"Maybe so, but we have a ranch to run. We don't have time to waste or men to risk." Then the Colonel spoke more gently, "You going to be a cattleman or a blood brother to a bear?"

"Right now, I'm a cattleman. I will get the traps."

"Very good. Get started."

Moki tried, but did not catch Wahb. During the four years that followed, Colonel Pierson's empire developed and expanded at a tremendous rate. Now there were logging, sawmills and mining activity.

Moki had little time, but during one slack period before spring roundups, Moki took an Indian vacation alone among the crags and peaks. One evening as he sat before the campfire in a forest glade, a small sound caught his attention, and he glanced over his shoulder toward a slight ridge.

Presently, Wahb loomed up out of the darkness, rose to his full height and stood motionless in the flickering fire light. Moki remained frozen, gazing at the grizzly towering above him. Without moving his head, his eyes moved to search for his rifle. It was leaning on a tree between him and Wahb, but beyond his reach. With his eyes on Wahb, Moki came slowly to his feet and turned so they faced each other silently. On his face was no hint of a cattleman; it was pure Indian that confronted the grizzly. His expression was one of awe, perhaps at the size of the bear, or perhaps because of his silent, unexpected appearance, as though he had materialized from somewhere out of the past.

Wahb's expression was intent, as if things long forgotten were on the verge of being remembered. Moki weighed his chances of getting the rifle, but it was plainly impossible. While his eyes held steadily on the grizzly, slowly and almost without his willing it his right hand rose upward in the Indians' gesture of peace. Then in a soft, low voice he spoke the half forgotten words of the past in the Indian language, "Go in peace, oh my brother."

After a long moment, Wahb dropped to all four, and Moki tensed himself for a leap to his rifle. Wahb turned away, and his huge form soon blended into the darkness beyond the glade.

Moki's arm dropped with puzzled disbelief. He had said, "Go in peace, oh my brother." With a shake of his head, Moki returned to the present. Taking his rifle, he walked to the place where Wahb had stood, and knelt to examine the ground. In the light of the fire, he saw what he had expected to see: the track of the four-toed grizzly. With his arm extended, he measured the track with his open hand, and found it to be a span-and-a-half in length. His eyes shifted to the mark of the grizzly that had been burned into his hand. Was there somehow a bond between him and this grizzly? His path and that of the four-toed grizzly seemed destined to cross and recross.

Rising, Moki stared into the darkness. One thing for certain, never before had there been such a grizzly as this one, except in his grandfather's legends.

One day during the filming of <u>Wahb, King of the Grizzlies</u>, we were working on the Bow River and

140

the Toronto union crew was working on one of the sequences of the show. The crew was set up on the high rocks along the river. There was a very rough rapid under the banks of the rocky sides of the river. You could not walk along the river. The rock walls went straight up for twenty-five to fifty feet. There were three of us there to assist the crew if they needed our help. As I looked up the river, I caught sight of a rubber boat with two men in it coming around the bend. I hoped they wouldn't come on down the rapids.

While working on different pictures, we have seen several boats in trouble on this riffle. The rubber boat pulled over to shore for a minute or so to look before they came on through the riffle. I hoped they would know enough to go back. But, instead, the boat pushed out into the current and began the ride. I called for Terry Rowland to run to the truck and bring the long rope that was there. Terry started out running, while I tried to think of what we could do. The film crew from Toronto all stopped to watch. There was one bad curl riffle near the upper part of the riffle that was the worst part, but it was all bad. I had checked all the possible places I could get down to the river. The boat reached the riffle with the bad curl and turned over immediately. It stayed right below the curl for a little while, and then came on down. It was upside down, and we could see only one passenger hanging onto the rope at the side of the boat.

Terry got back with the rope. As I climbed down through the rocks to the river, I was tying a loop in the end. I had a lasso ready as I got there. I got as far into the water as I could and called to the man hanging onto the boat to catch the rope. I threw the rope over the boat as he went by. The man got a good hold on the rope. I intended to let out the rope as the boat swung to shore. One of my helpers, thinking I needed help, grabbed the rope and pulled the rope out of the man's hand. What a disappointment.

There was one more spot I could get to the river if I could get there before the boat went past. I ran up over the rocks and tried to get the loop ready for one more try. I ran along the bench and through the rocks. Here I could wade out to my waist. I called the man and told him that this is the last try, and for him to be sure to hang on, and we wouldn't pull hard on the rope. I carefully threw the rope again, and it went perfect, and the man got his hands on it. I let him get a little below, but held enough to let the boat swing in to shore as I walked downriver. When the boat came to shore, the man sat in the water. I turned the boat over, and there was the other fellow. He had plenty of air under the boat, and was hanging on tight. Both the fellows sat in the water for about twenty minutes until they felt rested enough to be able to stand up. The men were working in the Banff Springs Hotel, and had just decided to take a ride. It turned out lucky.

The other film crew had watched. Some of them didn't even get out of their chairs. They kept saying, "I hope they don't drown right here in front of us." None of the three of us ever thought of not trying to help. We had the advantage of knowing what the boat was getting into.

S eeta the Mountain Lion was a very tough show for any animals to work in.
We had to use about eight great cougars to do this show on time. It was very hot in Moab, Utah. They really wanted to go to a shady spot at the hottest time of the day. The rocks and dirt were so hot that it cooked the animals' feet.

My hounds had a sequence in this show with hot ground and cacti scattered around the ground. The pads on the bottoms of the dogs' feet came off, it was so hot. The sand was hot several inches into the ground.

Mr. White was the man in charge of getting film crews to come to Utah. He told us that it does rain here, but it never reaches the ground. I could see how it might evaporate before it reached the ground. It sure didn't rain while we were there.

Most of the filming was done at the Arches National Park, which is located just out of Moab, Utah. There were a lot of interesting sequences in this show. One I will never forget.

When the hounds were chasing Seeta, the mountain lion, she had to jump from one rock to another. If she missed the jump, she would fall one thousand feet straight down onto the rocks below. I get a chill in my body when I think of this. Sam the cougar had so much confidence in us, himself and his ability. I will never stop loving that cougar.

This jump took place at Dead

Seeta the mountain lion leaps from one rock to another across a 500 foot deep canyon

Seeta and her kittens

Horse Point, twenty-five miles from Moab, Utah. It meant jumping from a scary rock overlooking the Green River which runs into the Colorado River Canyon. It may have been thirty feet from this rock to another rock with a flat top. Sam was a great jumper, but he let us know it was a little too long and high to start right in and jump it, so we built a bridge and pushed it out from the first rock until there was about twenty feet to jump, and Sam jumped it several times; it was easy for him. We then kept pulling the bridge in until he would make the full jump. Sam knew what he was landing on was good and solid.

If we were going to film this jump, we had to do it on Monday, as the movie was about finished. I worried about this jump until Monday. The union film crew were coming to shoot it. When they got here, they were all frightened at the sight they saw when they looked down. Most everyone said that the cougar would never try to jump that.

When the Director said, "Roll camera," Sam ran and made that terrible jump. Everyone watching just couldn't

Lefty the dingaling lynx

praise Sam enough. The Director said, "Perfect!" Directors, however, never want to stop with only one take. There are many reasons why something could be wrong with a scene. We let Sam do one more and it was also perfect. I told the Director that if they got the shot, we didn't want Sam to try it any more. He had a conference with his crew. They checked their cameras and said, "We got it." No one really wanted to let Sam take that chance again. By now, Sam was the only one not worried.

The next show was <u>Dingaling Lynx</u>. Ron Brown was to be the actor in this show, as he had been in <u>Charlie the Lonesome Cougar</u>. This was another fun show. It is now 1967, and we will stay in Sequim, Washington.

Erwin called and told me about some Rocky Mountain bighorn sheep on Wild Horse Island in Flathead Lake in Montana. The studio was thinking about making a show called <u>Rocky the Bighorn Sheep</u>.

Erwin wanted me to go over to the island and check out the sheep that were there. He gave me the name of Robert McDonald and his phone number in Missoula, Montana. I called Mr. McDonald and made an appointment to meet him at the Polson Hotel in Polson Friday afternoon.

I flew to Polson and Mr. McDonald was there. He was going to take me to the island right away. We went in his car a few miles along the lake to a place where he had a small twelve-foot aluminum boat. We started out to the island. The weather was calm and we had no trouble. We reached the island, where he owned a guest house. In fact, Mr. McDonald owned the whole island. It was about five miles long and three miles wide.

Flathead Lake is a very large lake. I went for a walk on the island and saw a few bighorn sheep. I was impressed with this as a film location.

I returned to the house, and we talked until bedtime. I was going to get up early and hike around the island until 8 am. Mr. McDonald said he would have breakfast ready, and after breakfast, we could both look over the sheep and the island. He asked me to have a drink before we went to bed. I said, "No thank you." He had a drink or two, and then went down a long hall to his room. There were quite a few rooms off the hallway.

When I got up the next morning, the wind was blowing and there was a foot of new snow on the ground. I climbed the mountain, and it was cold and windy. When I got back to the house at 8 am, Mr. McDonald was not up. I didn't want to wake him up. I didn't know him, so I thought he might have drunk too much. I went back to bed, but I was too cold to sleep. There was no heat in this big building. After two hours, I began to think something was wrong. I got up and dressed. I made a little noise hoping to wake him. Finally, I decided to look in all the bedrooms down the hall. I eventually got to the right door, and I found Mr. McDonald lying in bed. I could see he was dead. His face was already colored. I checked him over to make sure.

The wind was awful outside now, and the lake had whitecaps all over it. I wasn't sure what I should do. There was no phone. I didn't know if that little boat would stay afloat in this storm.

I saw his pants on the chair in his room, and I found his car keys. I put them in my pocket and went out to look at the boat. I looked the boat over and figured out where the switches were hidden. The waves of water were splashing all over, and I really didn't think there was much chance to get the boat all the way to shore where the car was. I thought about waiting until the next day, but the storm might last a few days. So I decided I might as well give it a try. First, I tried to start the outboard motor out of the water just enough to know if it would start, and that I had found the right switches. I didn't even look to see if it had enough gas. I didn't see any gas cans anywhere. Each time I slid the little boat into the water, the waves would throw it back out. I finally got it far enough out to start the motor, and I drove it very slowly into the waves. I just kept the motor going slowly, and the boat went up and over the waves. The whitecaps looked even worse farther out on the lake. I didn't make a lot of headway, but somehow I got to the beach and pulled the boat up and tied it where Mr. McDonald had got it the day before. There was a foot of new snow here, too. I knocked on several doors, but apparently no one lived here in the winter.

I got into his car and started it and warmed the motor. I drove back to the hotel in Polson and told them what had happened. They couldn't believe that Mr. McDonald was dead. These people were very good friends of his. They called the Sheriff, and the Sheriff called the Coroner and others to come and make plans to go out to the island. They didn't want to go out until they could find a big boat; they had a hard time believing I had come across this morning in that little boat.

The Sheriff called the Coast Guard, but they didn't have a boat on the lake that they would take out in this storm, nor would they take a helicopter out. Up and down the streets of Polson the wind was blowing all kinds of debris.

They made the hotel their headquarters for the planning. The Sheriff told me not to let anyone else know what had happened. I took Mr. McDonald's car to go somewhere for them, and a woman ran out and flagged me down. She asked me where Mr. McDonald was; she had to see him. I said he was on the island. She wanted to know if he would be coming back today. I told her he would be in later. She wanted to know how he could get here in this storm and why I was driving his car. I tried to explain, and she let me drive on. I felt like she would report me to the Sheriff, which she did.

While they waited for a bigger boat, a lot of important people started arriving, one a Senator from Montana. I felt a little uncomfortable, as they all knew I didn't know Mr. McDonald until last night, and no one else here knew me either. I was sure some of the people might have it in their heads that I killed him.

It was late afternoon before someone was found with a big aluminum boat. The pilot said if he went

144

he would not take more than two people besides himself. He said in this storm it wouldn't be safe. I said I would be glad to wait until they got back.

The Coroner said he didn't want to go, and the Sheriff said that he had to go. I waited with the Senator and a few others until they got back. I had told them to be sure to bring his pants, as he had a lot of money in them.

When the boat came back, they took Mr. McDonald back to town. The Senator and I had talked a lot while waiting. He was a close friend of the family. I asked him what I should do, and also told him I would be glad to talk to his family if they wanted me to. He said I might as well go on home; they knew where to find me. I talked to the Senator once or twice on the phone after that, but I never found out what Mr. McDonald died of until much later when I was driving through Missoula and stopped and called his widow. She wanted me to come to her house and told me how to get there. We had a long talk. She said her sons couldn't figure out how I found out how to start the boat motor, as they had a secret switch. She said they all thought I was lucky to have gotten across to the car in that storm. She said, "You know what killed him, don't you?" When I said I'd always wondered, she said he'd gotten a clean bill of health from his doctor a few days before he died. There had been a blood clot that came up from his leg and lodged in his lungs.

The doctor told them there was nothing I or anyone could have done if we had been standing by him when it happened. That relieved me, because I'd worried that they might have wondered about me. Mrs. McDonald was a very nice lady, and I was to see her several times again. She invited me to use the island for filming or vacationing any time I wanted to.

34

WALT DISNEY'S WILD ANIMAL FARM CHANGES TO OLYMPIC GAME FARM

The following article appeared in TV Guide, July 24, 1971:

FIND SOMEONE WHO TALKS TO ANIMALS...
TEACH HIM HOW TO HANDLE A CAMERA
AND THE RESULT IS A DISNEY NATURE FILM

By Al Stump

Camped at Point Barrow, 150 miles above the Arctic Circle, a Walt Disney Productions crew had big bear trouble - so much of it that many of the local Nunamiut Eskimos rolled in the snow, going chk, chk, chk! (that, approximately is the sound of Eskimo laughter).

Trouble was that eight screen-tested and supposedly reliable polar bears brought in by the company at a cost of $20,000 refused to perform for the cameras.

Not one bear would dip even a toe into the water. For these were city-raised animals, imported from a heated, comfy European circus and strangers to crashing ice floes, blizzards and 40-below-zero bathing facilities. Taking one shocked look at the boreal hell, they holed up in their cages, snarled, cuffed anyone who approached and wouldn't work.

Filming stopped on Snow Bear - last season's Wonderful World of Disney story of Timko, an Eskimo lad, and his fur-clad but warm-hearted girl friend, Oogala. The scenes called for bears, and since they refused to work, filming had to stop until the problem could be resolved.

For other studios in the nature-adventure field, the delay could have been costly. However, for Disney executive-producer Ron Miller the problem required only one phone call to a trouble-shooter who is part of a small, select group of superspecialists in animal handling and wildlife photography who work for or are associated with Disney. Known as "Disney's Secret Weapon," these people are priceless for their expert knowledge of beasts as actors.

The specialist called by Miller to Point Barrow was Lloyd Beebe, a bounty hunter, logger and all-around woodsman, as well as a skilled 16-mm cameraman. Arriving, Beebe gave orders. "First, get rid of those parkas you're wearing," he told crewmen. "They're lined with wolf and wolverine pelts. The bears smell it and it scares them - which is one reason they've gone into hiding."

With new jackets in use, Beebe easily disposed of the cold-water problem, pointing out, "Back home in captivity these poor things never tasted fresh, raw whale blubber. Bait 'em with it." Crazy about blubber, the bears followed a trail of it into the ocean. Before long, reverting to their blood call, they decided they liked the frigid life.

Shown by NBC last November, Snow Bear was one of the better Disney offerings in an outdoor anthology now in its 18th television year, the winner of many viewing polls and 35 awards. Beebe's rescue job was nothing new at Disney Productions. A few years ago, Minado the Wolverine bogged down at $1500-per-day production cost when Minado tried to eat his fellow cast members. Employing soothing music, gentle coaxing and some secret tricks, Beebe maneuvered the savage wolverine toward civil behavior by slow degrees.

"In the end," Disney's publicity staff was to boast, "he had Minado chasing his tail on cue. He even ate meat off Beebe's cheek. And wolverines are the most vicious killers on the North American continent."

Not by virtue of seniority alone has Disney clung to first place in the fang-and-claw division of entertainment, where independents and other rival studios compete for an audience estimated at 50 million.

Disney explains: "We've reversed the usual procedure of using big-name Hollywood trained cinematographers and gone into the tall timber and elsewhere to find a rare kind of talent. It exists, occasionally, among those who've spent years in the outdoors. They have an extra mystical sense enabling them to draw shy, dangerous beasts into their laps and bring back intimate footage that others can't get. Training them in picture-making technique itself isn't difficult. These people are Ernest Thompson Seton, Audubon and Izaak Walton types. Their very eyes are cameras."

The best tribute paid the backwoods shutterbugs came from the agents of the Society for the Prevention of Cruelty to Animals. Not long ago they walked into the office of producer Winston Hibler and accused the studio of siccing timber wolves, wolverines and dogs on each other to obtain bloody action scenes for a show Hibler made. "The more I denied guilt, the less the agents believed that the animals were friends and were only play-fighting," says Hibler. "They claimed the three species were enemies who never could be mixed."

Hibler had to call in Lloyd Beebe, the Arctic authority, to avoid legal trouble. Beebe explained that by raising wolf, dog and wolverine pups together from infancy, their hate instinct is removed and they love each other forever. This he'd done, and when they play-fought, it appeared that they were tearing each other to bits.

Still he didn't convince the agents until he ran film of the critters sleeping and eating together.

Wonder what the SPCA will say when they see the studio's forthcoming <u>Lefty the Dingaling Lynx</u>? A victim of modern social tensions, Lefty suffers a breakdown and winds up on a psychiatrist's couch.

In real life no one has to abuse Lefty. He fakes it so well because of Disney's backwoods sharpshooters, who can really talk to the animals.

Walt's brother, Roy Disney, was a special friend of ours. Roy and his wife, Edna, came often to see us, and we usually spent a little time

Moose at the Game Farm

147

View of grounds of the Olympic Game Farm

with them when we went to the studio.

One day when Roy, Erwin Verity and others, and Catherine and I were at the studio, we went to dinner in the studio dining room. Roy got up and went over to the counter in conversation with the clerk. Erwin motioned for everyone to look at Roy. They may have known what Roy was up to.

Soon Roy came back and said, "I am disappointed that they didn't have a gold Mickey Mouse watch like mine, so I have to give you this silver Mickey Mouse watch." I was surprised and thanked him. Erwin later told us that Roy had never given him or others at the studio a watch. Roy said, "I wanted to give you a gold watch just like mine," and he showed it to me. He said, "There are not many watches like this."

A couple of weeks later, we saw Roy and Edna drive up into our yard. They were in a brand new gold Cadillac. The first thing Roy did was get out, open up the back trunk and take out his suitcase and get out a gold watch and give it to me. He said, "This watch is just like mine. You will have a lot of fun with this watch; there are not many like it."

We went into the house, and Roy started telling Catherine how one of the windshield wipers didn't work as they got to Portland. They went to the Cadillac dealer to get a new rubber wiper. Edna saw a new gold Cadillac there, and they bought it. He was teasing Edna when he said, "You know when your

148

windshield wiper quits, you buy a new car."

Edna said, "Okay. How about telling what you forgot?" Roy laughed and said, "We are among friends. I forgot my teeth." We all laughed about it. They were just down to earth people.

Roy was the one of the brothers who always arranged to get the money to complete Walt's dreams. He was really happy. He said he had paid off U.S. Steel and everyone on the Florida project and finished all the things he had promised Walt he would do.

He was very relaxed and satisfied with his life. His son, Roy, Jr., had been put in as head of the shows we were doing. Roy said he hadn't wanted his boy to get into this rat race. He wanted young Roy to enjoy his family. When they left

Lloyd and elk friend

to go home, the last word he said was, "Lloyd, keep making my boy look good," and they drove away. That was the last we were to see of Roy Disney. It was five days later that Erwin Verity called with the news that Roy had died. He was a great man, and we still miss him. From that time on, some of the fun of working for the Walt Disney Studio had gone for Catherine and me.

The Bears and I was next. Ron Brown and Al and Ingrid Niemela took the cub bears to Chilko Lake for the picture. Ron had spent a lot of time locating this beautiful spot to film The Bears and I. Pat Wayne was the star actor. Pat is John Wayne's son. John spent time on the job visiting, and we were all there part of the time.

There had been a change in our work for Disney. Roy Disney, Jr. had come to visit us a few times. Roy wanted me to be the boss of six or seven crews, each making a different show. I thought it would be a headache with six or seven different directors. Ron was one. Ron and I were good friends. The other directors I didn't always know.

Most directors care most of all for the picture to be good; the animals staying workable is of secondary importance to them. We trained animals for each show and sent animal handlers with them, who didn't always look after our best interests or those of the animals. They couldn't train the animals for the show, and some directors just spoiled the animals to get a scene and, as a result, the animal couldn't finish the picture. Sometimes the animal was so good that they would keep it and say that they had lost it. It was always the best animal, and we would be left without another animal friend we could have kept tame and valuable to us as long as it lived. The pictures directed by these people were seldom good.

We decided we would not do this any more. We didn't want our names on some of these shows. I think The Bears and I turned out good, and so did a few others. But for us at the Game Farm, it was just a job, and lacked the reward of turning out a picture we could be proud of. Although I went to each filming location to help, I didn't have the authority to insist on doing what I knew was necessary to achieve a quality show.

A young cow elk

The studio had signed contracts for hundreds of hours of television time and they used all the pictures they could get. Walt Disney was not there to say, "It is not good enough, so go back and improve it so I can be proud to have my name on it." The Disneys now have their good name back and are doing great.

We went right on filming one show after another here in Sequim. Everyone called our farm <u>Walt Disney's Wild Animal Ranch</u>. We were a mystery place to people around Washington. People wanted to come in and look around to see what we were doing; they could see wild animals being trained.

That summer Erwin called up and said he and his wife, Aura May, were going to Africa and we wouldn't be seeing him for a while.

The studio had always wanted us to keep people out of the Game Farm and not let any other cameras in. I thought it would be good to know what we could do on our own. It was our place, and the animals were mostly ours, so why not open up to the public for the summer? We did that with guides taking groups of people to see the animals. We only charged one dollar each. People came, and kept on coming.

We kept on filming throughout the summer and letting visitors in at the same time as our own business was going on. We didn't ease up on our filming duties for Disney.

The time came when Erwin Verity arrived back in Los Angeles. I told Erwin what we had been doing, and I was surprised to see that he wasn't mad about it. He just said, "Lloyd, now you are going to find out the problems of dealing with people." It was a kind of warning.

I could tell that he wanted to know how we were doing on the new business. I didn't volunteer any information. We were very happy with what we had done.

A few days later, Erwin called back and wanted to know how things were going, and I told him that everything was fine; Catherine was taking care of the new business. Erwin couldn't stand it any longer. He said, "Damn it, Lloyd. I want to know how much you took in today!" I was tickled about it; it was our best day. I said, "Today we took in nineteen hundred dollars." Erwin didn't speak for a long time, and then said, "What did you say?" I repeated, "Nineteen hundred dollars." He said, "You mean nineteen hundred dollars today? This day?" I said, "Yes, today." Erwin was surprised, and I believe happy for us, but wondered what it might mean to the film part of it.

We told Erwin we were calling our place <u>Olympic Game Farm</u>. He thought that would be a great name if they would let us use it.

I wrote a letter to the Disney Studio and asked if we could talk on our tours about all the things we had done with the studio and the pictures we had made. I reminded them that many people claimed they had worked for Disney Studio, whether they had or not. I said that I believed they knew I would never say anything that was not true, and it would always be something we ourselves had done. I was asking this only in case we wanted to say something on the tours we were giving at the Farm.

Erwin first called back to talk about it. He said it would be a great thing for us, but he didn't think they would want us to do this. It would be up to Bill Anderson and the other bosses at the studio.

A few days later, Bill Anderson, who was taking Walt's place as number one at the studio, came to visit us. He said that they had all voted on what I had requested, and for us to go ahead and say whatever we wanted to about the work we'd done for Disney. It had been a great working relationship with us. Anderson said that after the years of work and all the films we had made for the studio, it was only right that we should be free to get whatever we could out of it. They looked forward to continuing working together with us. The Olympic Game Farm was now a reality.

It was during the many years working for Disney that we recognized the importance of establishing a home for the animal actors. Catherine and I have been working toward that dream since 1960. We had moved so many times that we wanted a new house and a place to keep our old animal friends. We spent all our money on new pens, fenced pastures, training pens and fenced areas where animals could just relax. By 1971, we were ready to begin. We had said goodbye to so many animal friends over the years and replaced them with other animals. We feel that there is no better place to live or raise animals than right here on our Farm; never too hot, and many of the days it is just right. From now on, our animals will keep on getting the attention and respect long after their film work is completed. They will be with us as long as they live. People will now be able to come and see the animal stars like Big Ted of Wahb, King of the Grizzlies, or Charlie the Lonesome Cougar, Ben of the Grizzly Adams series, Tag, the bear that did most of the chase sequences and many seeming impossible things that only he was able to do.

There are many more animal stars that will live out their lives here. I will always visit with them and talk about the times we have had together. I can tell them how much I appreciate the help that they have given to Catherine, myself and the crew. These animals have done so much to build up the Olympic Game Farm. It really belongs to all of them as much as it does to us.

Four young grizzlies have company from the neighboring farm

151

Mother grizzly and her three cubs

Elk welcome guests on Game Farm drive through

152

Lloyd and grizzly

Mother zebra & colt at the Game Farm

Polar bear at our farm.

It is Marinho's turn to ride Mac   Photo credit: Maggie O'Hara

1996 Game Farm crew. Back row, left to right: Jerry West, Joe Mead, Alfie Robb, Lloyd Beebe
Third row: Julie Enzenauer, Andy Langsford, Allyson Keith, Brendan Withey, Bob Rowland
Second row: Catherine Beebe, Michelle Waye, Barbie Paulson, Jennifer Darby
Bottom row: Clark Monroe, Marinho Correia, Wayne Bastrup

Catherine and grizzly cubs   Photo Credit: Tom Thompson, Peninsula Daily News

35

FOR THE LOVE OF COUGARS

After I didn't need the cougar bounty, I would go to the mountains and follow cougars in the snow to learn all I could about them. One time, I followed three cougars in the snow for three days and two nights. I always had my pack sack and plenty of fire starter, so I didn't have to worry about building a fire at night. In my pack, I carried a can with a hole in the bottom and wire bail from top to bottom to carry the can by. When the candle was in the hole, it would make a great light to walk by in the woods. You had to watch the candle and push it up once in a while so it didn't drop out.

I followed these three cougars all one night. I could hear them jumping in the snow ahead of me, and they would go around and around, but I just kept on following them. One dropped out, and then the next. That last one couldn't do that because I could follow the last one. The cougar wouldn't go far, but he kept just out of my way. I could hear him breaking through the crusty snow just ahead of me. I left the last one and went home.

Another time, I followed a mother cougar with three kittens which were about one-third grown. About dark that night, I was still following, and I knew they were keeping just out of sight of me. They went up on a little bench about ten feet above me, and the mother started screaming at me. She wanted me to leave her alone with the kittens. I tried to see them and thought I could just make them out in the bushes. It was too dark now, so I left her with her young ones.

A few days later, I went back and followed her again. That time, I caught up to her before dark. This time, she started making threatening noises sooner than the first time. I just waited there, and I sat down and watched. I could see her moving around. Then I saw a movement in a small bushy fir tree as three kittens came down and ran to the mother, and they left. After sitting there for about an hour, I left for home without seeing them again.

Cougars pull the hair out of the deer with their front teeth, and when they open the skin so they can eat the meat, they pull the skin straight out from the body, and cut it off with their side teeth like a pair of scissors until they can pull the hide back away from the meat.

When I followed cougars one time, I could see in the snow that they were walking along a bench in the forest. They like to look over the bank and down below for deer or elk. Sometimes, I could tell that they had their head around the stump of a tree leaning on the tree and watching and testing the wind. Then they would come away from the bank and make a little circle, and come back to the bench farther along, and watch and wait some more, and finally catch a deer.

Mother cougars sometimes take their kittens

Patience is needed to track cougar

157

Cougars run

to a brushy rabbit patch when they are big enough to catch rabbits, and may leave them there for two weeks or more. When I could come back, there would be no big cougar tracks, just the kittens, and there would be rabbit skins all over the snow. Then, next time I went back, the mother cougar had come back and taken the kittens to a new hunting area or to a deer she had killed.

When the kittens are grown, they like to stay in the area they were raised in. The mother may leave the area when the kittens are about grown to wean them.

I have always loved cougars since

I was a kid in school, and then especially after I had followed them through the forests, I began to understand them and was envious of their patience and hunting ability. I had heard it said that some people believe that when we die, we might come back as an animal. I wished if that happened to me that I would come back as a cougar. It seemed to me a cougar had a great life, roaming through the forest and beautiful mountains, hunting deer and just being lazy.

I learned later that all animals of the forest have tough times in their life. A young cougar, not quite big and experienced enough to catch a deer and not able to catch enough small animals to survive, will die. Then, too, when they grow old and feeble, they may end up starving to

Cougars climb

Cougars jump

death. In the winter, when the snow is icy, they sometimes wear off their pads and start to bleed in tracks in the snow, but must keep on hunting to stay alive.

I once found three half-grown cougars dead in a bunk in a Forest Service Building, and several dead cougar on a deer trail.

GRIZZLY ADAMS AND A HUNDRED OTHER FILMS

We had a nice herd of bighorn sheep. There were four big sheep with a full curl, and three ewes and two young lambs. We had a basement below ground on three sides, but toward the south and the mountains are all large windows. Up at ground level, we have a wooden deck. For a long time, these sheep would spend all their time on the deck overlooking the mountains and creek below. Sometimes, the sheep would rub on the sliding doors, and the door would open and in came the sheep herd. They really made a mess of our deck, but they did look good standing or lying in front of our living room windows.

One day, the light was right and one of the big sheep looked in the window, and it looked like a mirror. He saw his picture in the window, and he butted the big window and smashed it. We decided that they should go in another field, and that is where they went. We could see them down below, but they could no longer see in our windows.

Many of the movies we have filmed have been shot right here at the Olympic Game Farm, and the film crew and I would be busy almost every

Our Rocky Mountain sheep had to be moved to the field below the house.

day. We would be on location in the mountains for a sequence in good weather. In bad weather, we would film a sequence in the barn with studio lights, or we would be building a set for future filming.

Catherine took care of all the business. I tried to keep my mind on Walt Disney filming, so there wouldn't be any questions about us slacking off on our film work, and there never was.

When Walt Disney died, we felt less pride in working for Walt Disney Studio. Then, in 1970 when our old friend Roy Disney, Walt's brother, also died, we lost some of our enthusiasm in the work. Everything went well, however, and the studio was happy with all the films as we finished them. There was always another film waiting for us to start on.

Other film companies kept calling us for help with their films. We had the reputation of being the best in animal photography, and our animals were considered the best to use in films. When we had enough help to handle an extra job, we would send animals and animal handlers to work for two or three weeks on those films. These companies paid well for this, and it helped to build up the Olympic Game Farm and the tourist business.

Chuck Sellier kept calling and wanting me to work with them on the Grizzly Adams show. We had already helped them on its pilot film. Now they were going to create a series of Grizzly Adams. We had the only grizzly bear that could do the show. Chuck knew this, and everyone else knew it, so I finally

Dan Haggerty and Ben, the grizzly, both worked on the Grizzly Adams show. Ben, a life-long resident of the Game Farm, is over thirty years old.

agreed to let our bear be in the show.

I had to work on Disney shows. Chuck called time after time, and each time he offered more money, and it was getting harder to say no. It would mean going to Utah with a five or six-man crew and setting up a camp and compound for animals. I called Chuck back and said no; however, we would send the bear and handlers. We had commitments for Disney. Chuck knew I had been almost ready to say we would do it. Chuck said, "Let me call you back."

The next day, the call came in with a raise in the money. He said, "We all know you people have the best motion picture animals there are, and we feel these pictures need the best animals to make a long series of shows." I couldn't pass up this deal; I felt it was very important to the future of Olympic Game Farm.

I called the Disney Studio and told them about it. I felt I could get animal handlers and send the bears which we were not using. We could keep on with our film crew here at the Olympic Game Farm. I sent Al Niemela down to Utah to find a place to keep our animals, and I went there and joined him a few days later.

We bought thirty acres of land in Utah with plenty of shade trees for the animals.

Al and I returned to Sequim and the big job of training animals for the Grizzly Adams shows, building and trucking take-down pens that we had. We really had to build a new Game Farm at Woodland, Utah. We bought six trailers for some of the help to live in.

I worked with the trainers as much as I could. Terry Rowland was to be the boss. I knew he could do it. When the time came for the animals and trainers to leave at 4 am one morning, it was dark, and we had everything tied on; animals and everything that was left to take. I noticed Terry was not here. I said to the men, "Where is Terry?" Someone said, "Terry said last night he wasn't going to go."

The first year Terry Rowland had worked with the bear in the original pilot show of Grizzly Adams, and in the next twelve shows. In these shows, we furnished the bear only. Terry did a great job.

The animals were not ready to do the show, as it turned out. Each week we worked the animals, they got better. Marinho was to handle the bear. Bozo was a female, but in the show, she was Ben of Grizzly Adams.

Marinho was handling Ben, and Ken was helping. We finished two shows. I was staying at the compound trying to get the animals trained to do a good job. Everything was getting better every day. Then I got a call from the filming location that everything was stopped on the set; Marinho was yelling at Ken. I went right out to the set, about twenty miles away. The work was still stopped. I told Ken to take charge of the bear and had Marinho go back to the compound to work with the wolves. Ken and I worked on the bears for the rest of the week. We got the show finished on time, and Ken finished the next fifty-five <u>Grizzly Adams</u> shows. Ken had done a great job with the bear, as I knew he would.

We were doing one show a week. Once, Dan Haggerty, who was Grizzly Adams in the picture, fell while riding his motorcycle and hurt his leg, so we went home for a while.

On these shows, we met most of the old-time actors from Hollywood. Each week, there would be new guest actors come in for the show. Of course, every show had Denver Pyle as Mad Jack, the Burro #7, Don Shanks as the Indian, Nakoma. I was just trying to keep everything working smoothly.

Dan Haggerty of the Grizzly Adams Show

Whenever I thought we should get new or better animals for the show, I went home and came back with all we needed. Most of the trips would take three days to get back. It was almost eleven hundred miles each way.

I called Catherine every evening to let her know we were doing fine, and found out how things were going in Sequim. I called Roy Disney, Jr., and told him about the mess I had gotten myself into. We decided not to start any more shows until I could be there to look after them, and I knew that was best. I felt like I was letting them down, but there was nothing else I could do.

We tried to do a show every week. We wouldn't get a new script until Thursday, and we would be anxious to see if we had all the animals that the new script called for. There would be a new writer for each script, and a new director.

Directors would study a new script for a week before they would be ready to direct the filming of the show. I would have writers coming to talk to me about the animals and a story that they might write and any ideas I might have. Doing a story a week, they finally would have to stop and take two weeks off and rest, and try to find writers and stories. It was good to let the animals and people rest. We had to work with our animals and be ready to go back to filming.

Whenever it snowed, we sometimes filmed a show in the snow, but it would take longer to finish, and we would get behind schedule. We would move to Arizona, or sometimes to Ruidoso, New Mexico to find a Grizzly Adams type of country free of snow. This would mean a lot of work for the animal people, and we always had to make the move quickly.

One time when filming in New Mexico, Dan Haggerty was at a party and showing someone how to drink a flaming drink. His beard caught on fire and was burned. We had to pack up and go back to Sequim and wait for Dan's beard to grow back. All the expenses came out of our pockets.

Over two years time, we finished fifty-nine or sixty one-hour <u>Grizzly Adams</u> shows. All the time, Catherine was taking care of the <u>Olympic Game Farm</u>. Several times, we would be home for two or three weeks. When the last <u>Grizzly Adams</u> show was finished, we went home expecting to be called back, but the show was cancelled.

We started working to make the <u>Olympic Game Farm</u> better. We also worked on jobs for almost every film company. Many film companies called wanting us to do the animal part of films and commercials. By now, we could see we were doing well enough with the <u>Olympic Game Farm</u> so that we could get by

This bear has learned to throw rocks

without filming any more. The Olympic Game Farm was more interesting to us.

I have been trying to say no to film makers, but it isn't easy. About a month ago, I got a call from Alaska. After much talking, I found out I was talking to a Korean who was working with a film crew. It was hard to hear, and this man only knew a few words of English. I knew he was asking me to help them get some bear pictures. They had been in Alaska for two months filming this picture; they had to have bear pictures. I finally found out that the script called for a big Alaska brown bear to chase an actor, and finally the actor would stop running and shoot the bear with his rifle. I told this man I didn't have time to help him. He told me they were making this film for the little children of Korea. He said, "You help us?" I told him, "No, we don't do this kind of work any more, and we are very busy and can't help you." He kept repeating that it was for the little children of Korea, "You help us? We need you help us." This man finally said he would call back tomorrow. The next day, the same talk, and I said, "No."

Marinho, who works with the bear, had an accident and wouldn't be working for a while, so the next time this man called, I told him the bear man was hurt and we couldn't do it. This man said something about motels in Sequim; they would need three rooms. I still said that we couldn't do it. A day or two later, a lady at a motel in Sequim called to find out about the Korean crew that was coming. She could not understand them. I sent word to them in Alaska not to come, because we couldn't help them.

The Koreans came to the motel, and there were eighteen people going to stay in three rooms. The motel lady found the rooms they needed, and the next day the film crew came to talk about us helping them. Only one knew any English words, and he would then turn to the rest of the crew and talk in Korean whenever he could understand what I said. It took a long time for us to understand one another. I began to think it might be easier to go ahead and help them film what they wanted. He said, "We need shoot bear. We can shoot bear?" I said, "No, you can't shoot the bear." He said, "Can we buy bear?" I said, "No, I won't sell you a bear to shoot." "What we do then? No can shoot bear." Then he said, "You have bear bladders?" "No, it is against the law to sell or have bear bladders." This is highly priced medicine in Asia and Korea. It can cure anything, they say, worth a lot of money. They said, "You can help us? We need you help us for little children."

I decided to help them finish their picture so I could get back to our work. We filmed for two days of bears traveling, chasing the actor. When it came to shooting a bear, we had our bear stand up. They filmed the top half of the bear as the bear fell out of the picture. Then for the part of the bear being shot, I took a bear suit we had, and they glued a plastic bag of fake blood to the forehead of the bear suit. This fake blood is made of

Rock throwing bear

berry juice. The flat bag of berry juice had an explosive inside and a wire coming out of the bag to be connected to a battery when it is time to see the bullet hit. This would be timed to coincide with the rifleman's shooting at the bear. I found the crew some bear hair that matched, and they glued it around and over the plastic bag. It looked good. I think the scene will be the way they wanted it, very bloody. When they shot the scene there was a cloud of blood in the air and on the bear suit. It took a long time to clean up the bear suit.

The Korean film crew left Sequim happy and said next time they might make a picture with tigers. They said, "You help us make picture with your tigers." I said, "No." They said, "We need you help us." I said, "No," but I am not sure they understood even with my head and hands shaking "no" too.

One day, a lady who was driving around stopped where I was working and said she had been watching the most interesting thing for about thirty minutes. As she was passing a field of bears, there was a bear in the creek. This bear was spending his time throwing rocks at the electric fence. He was digging rocks out of the creek and throwing them at the fence because he was afraid to touch it. When a rock would hit the fence wire, the bear would get excited and jump up and down, then get another rock and throw it. I went over there to watch and, sure enough, this bear was throwing rocks. It didn't matter what size, whether they were marble size or football size. There was a big pile of rocks on both sides of the fence and under it as well. I took some pictures of her throwing rocks. Then, when she threw the next rock, I said, "Good girl," and clapped my hands. The bears were used to us training them, so she knew what I meant and threw the next rock over to me, and I caught it. I threw it back in the creek, and she got it and threw it back, and kept getting more accurate as she found out what we were doing. We played catch for a while. She really thought that was fun. I kept telling her, "Good, good girl."

I had been gone, and when I told some of the workers about it, they said that lately there had been clods of dirt and bones and other debris all over the road. The zebras and yaks walk up and down that road. The bear had been throwing these clods of dirt and bones at them. We put a sign saying to watch out for the rock-throwing bear. People didn't believe it. There was a camper or two that came out with a bone through a window. Then they believed it. That bear was in a field with five other bears, and the other bears always chased her, so she stayed by herself and had to amuse herself, and rock-throwing was a game she learned by herself.

A year later, there were two more bears throwing rocks. They apparently learned from each other. We used the first rock thrower in more than one movie. When Grizzly Adams was building a fireplace or piling wood, he would catch wood or rocks that the bear threw to him as he put them in position. You had to do something with the rock quickly, as there would be another coming. We renamed that bear Rock Thrower, and that is her name even today.

If Rock Thrower gets a shock from the electric fence, she goes down to the creek and throws rocks at the fence.

In a scene from "Grizzly Adams", "Ben" gives a ride to a little girl & her doll.

This wolf and grizzly liked to play together until the bear sat on the wolf and wouldn't let him up

WE BOUGHT A MILE OF THE DUNGENESS RIVER

We bought the Seamands farm that was between us and the Dungeness River, then we bought a mile-long strip on the opposite side of the Dungeness River from us. The Dungeness River is considered a private river. The land on either side has a property line in the center of the river. If you own land on each side, you own all the way across the river. The land belongs to the land owner; the water and fish belong to the State.

We kept working for film companies from many countries.

While working on the Grizzly Adams show, I missed some of what went on at our Game Farm. We knew a friend of ours, Maggie O'Hara, had written about the Olympic Game Farm during that time. Catherine and all the Game Farm crew helped Maggie on her project. Catherine suggested that, since I was not here much at that time, why not use some of Maggie's story in our book? Catherine had let Maggie use some of our pictures and helped in other ways. As Maggie has agreed, I thought it would help our story to have someone who knew about writing a story write some of it.

Catherine chooses some of Maggie's story starting now:

WILD ANIMALS & GENTLE PEOPLE
by Maggie O'Hara

If questions are put to Lloyd Beebe about his animals, location shooting in the wilds of Canada, and what it was like filming scenes for Disney's True Life Adventures, the owner of Olympic Game Farm is enthusiastically vocal. His eyes light up, expressing the keen interest he feels. But focus the attention on Lloyd the man and suddenly the easy talking gives way to reluctant monosyllables. With people other than his immediate family and close friends, he still retains a shyness from his early years, a reluctance to talk about himself.

"Lloyd was always shy; that's just the way he is," says Catherine.

Basically, this man with an affinity for handling wild creatures and a skill in recording their actions on film comes through as being quiet, reflective, persistent, patient and perhaps above all, extremely knowledgeable in his specialized field.

"Lloyd's outstanding characteristic is film maker," says Ron Brown, who worked for Disney for ten years directing people and animals, as well as acting. "He's creative like Walt Disney. He's the best animal trainer/photographer there is. Lloyd is a very exceptional man."

Not long ago when Big Mac, a four-year-old Kodiak bear born at the farm, was out in one of the training compounds, he inadvertently stepped on Lloyd's foot. Now, a bear shifts all his weight from one foot to another as he walks. That's what gives him that lumbering gait. Anybody else would have yelled or at least said, "Ouch!" Not Lloyd. He said, "Boy, we're going to have to weigh him!" And he proceeded to do so. Big Mac weighed in at one thousand two hundred pounds.

Tour guide Chuck Crary witnessed this byplay. "I've never seen Lloyd excited. He's very low-keyed, but handles a crisis so fast you wonder if it really happened at all," Chuck said.

Although educated for the most part in the School of Life, and formed by his environment - mountain country - Lloyd's undefined dream of combining his love of animals with his interest in filming them took shape.

"He's amazing," says Bill Robb, tour manager at the Game Farm. "When Lloyd talks with wild animals, they are quieter. He has a special quality. A lot of people would like to have that quality, but they don't. Wild animals come up to him - trust him. He believes in leaving the animal as it is, with its claws and teeth. (Some places don't; they remove the animals' dangerous weapons.) He never gets scratched," Bill added.

Living on a dairy ranch in the shadow of the Olympic Mountains - the habitat of deer, black bear and cougar - Lloyd spent much of his time in the back-country. He became familiar with the wilderness - its silence, its majesty and above all, its wild creatures.

As a young man, he hunted cougar for the bounty money they brought. That was during the Great Depression. The hunting was motivated by a need for income to survive, not trophy or sports hunting. Lloyd has not carried a gun for a long time. He preserves life.

As he worked with Sam the cougar, Lloyd provided a capsule explanation of his thought on animal training - and, without being aware of it, a demonstration.

"Take the animals, you have to think like they think. You have to be like them not to upset them. I talk with the animals...I want it to be a happy experience for them."

Meticulously, prior to the picture-taking session, Lloyd had taken out his penknife and scraped off some lichen that would have shown up white on film. Years of movie making have given him that special eye for detail, for detecting even the most trivial flaw.

Lloyd talked to the cougar, whose muscles rippled under his sleek, tawny coat, and he caressed him. Every motion was slow and gentle. Cougars are shy and seldom seen in the wilderness, although they may be nearby; hence the name "ghost cat" often applied to them. Being on the shy side himself, Lloyd recognizes the same trait in Sam.

Lloyd makes everything as easy and natural for the animals as possible. For instance, in this case he reserved the flat portion of the log for Sam - "more comfortable," he says.

Lloyd and Sam the cougar

"You almost never see cougars in the wild, but they are curious and will follow you," Lloyd continued. "If there's mud or snow you can see their footprints. They don't attack people without provocation. They almost never attack domestic animals in this region because their favorite food is venison, and there are plenty of deer on the Olympic Peninsula. They'll skirt a farm but seldom stop. The cougar does not like the scent of man and will avoid his dwellings. Only a cougar that is old and feeble or for some other reason can't make a living in the normal cougar way will take a domestic animal," Lloyd explained.

Four-year-old Sam - all one hundred seventy-five pounds of him - was posing like the professional he is. It was difficult to remember that he was, after all, a wild (even if trained) animal. The trainers never lose track of this fact, however, and are always alert to anything that might spell danger.

Suddenly, there was an electric charge in the air.

Catherine and animals around our new house

"Peacock coming up on the right." Ken Beebe spoke the words softly.

The cougar had not seen the foolish bird make its ill-advised entrance on stage, and before Sam spied the strutting peacock, Lloyd cupped the big cat's chin in a gentle hand and turned the animal's head in the opposite direction. Simultaneously, with his other hand, he picked up a stone and tossed it at the advancing peacock. The bird beat a retreat before Sam could ruffle its beautiful feathers. It had taken Lloyd only a second or two to handle the emergency.

"Sam was born at the farm, very reliable, very nice," Lloyd said as he caressed Sam. "It depends a lot on how much attention the animal gets. And we don't take too many chances. Someone asked me once if I had a special relationship with animals. I'd never thought about it until I realized that I do get away with things other people couldn't." Sam gave one of his little short meows and licked Lloyd's hand as though corroborating his human friend's statement.

Man and cougar sat quietly on the log. It was the kind of peaceful relationship many people hope of having with a wild animal; a reminder of the ancient hopes of humans living in harmonious coexistence with wild animals.

One cannot help but wonder if Lloyd and Sam's special relationship is mystical. Mystical or not, it is quite obviously rooted in mutual respect and a sense of dignity not to be violated by either party.

On a hilltop overlooking the Game Farm and the Olympic Mountains stands the Beebe home - the headquarters and lookout for the busy operation. It also serves as a nursery for future animal stars.

At the foot of the hill is a meandering creek, home to a variety of waterfowl. Adjacent to the creek are pens and runs where Albert, the polar bear, and other large bears reside. There is a studio barn where filming takes place, as well as an outdoor set which includes a log cabin and old wagons - frequent props appearing in many movie productions. Beyond are runs for wolves, coyotes, foxes, bobcats, cougars, jaguars, tigers and lions. Badgers, wolverines, raccoons and smaller animals reside in other compounds nearby.

There are spacious grassy enclosures where grizzlies wander, loaf, stand up and wave for treats and dig holes that accommodate their ample, supple bodies. Ricky, the rhinoceros, lives nearby in his private stockade. Pasture land stretches for many acres for the grazing bison, elk, yak and many varieties of deer. Zebra and guanaco (a relative of the camel and llama) roam in their own playground bordering the winding creek.

It is on these grasslands a drive-through tour has been designed, so visitors may mingle with the hoofed wild animals. From their vehicles people can photograph and observe them at close range.

Back at the headquarters on the hill, Catherine is the trouble-shooter. In between phone calls and megaphone messages she relays from her deck to Game Farm personnel below, she manages to finish her doughnut and coffee (breakfast and lunch).

Messages are received and relayed to and from location crews in Alaska and other parts of the United States as well as Canada. Shortly before, a caravan had taken off for Utah where a pilot film, The Capture of Grizzly Adams, is being shot by Taft International Pictures. The caravan consists of several trucks and trailers bearing the animals that will be acting in the film - Ben the grizzly, Number 7 (a burro) and some raccoons.

Lloyd and his son, Ken, and trainers Debbie Coe and Gayle Bartlett make up the crew from the Farm. The destination is near Woodland, Utah, where Lloyd owns acreage and where permanent pens and runs are already installed. Maintenance man and mechanic, Joe Janssen, left ahead of the caravan to begin building enclosures and props that will be needed for the production.

For the moment, the nursery phase of the home on the hill is getting the attention. It's time to mix another batch of formula. The Beebes' living room - lived in to the fullest - harbors four twenty-day-old timber wolves cuddled in a box under a hand hair dryer. Catherine had bathed them that morning. A young apprentice trainer comes in to give them their ten o'clock feeding. He holds the wolf pups gently as they wolf down their formula.

Over by the huge, stone fireplace two bobcat kittens are playing. Their mealtime is scheduled for a little later. Playtime is NOW, and it is engaged in with great gusto.

Armed with five bottles of freshly prepared formula, Catherine slides open the glass doors leading to the patio. Just outside struts a peacock, his tail feathers spread out in an immense and brilliant fan. As his feet tap out a martial rhythm, he pivots in precise circles in front of the glass doors.

"That's his favorite spot," remarks Catherine, edging past him. "I don't know if he sees his reflection in the glass or what it is, but you can be sure to find him there - always in the way."

Catherine enters a large cage where more wolf pups eagerly await their surrogate mother. This time it is five-week-olds. As she gives them their bottles, she talks to them. "Has her had enough?"

When the last of the wolf pups has "filled its little tummy" with formula, Catherine gives them a pan of solid food.

"When they're older, wolves can change real quick - can't trust them," warns Catherine, a comment the scene in that room would make unbelievable if it came from someone less experienced.

After getting their faces wiped, the pups waddle over to their bed and flop down and are fast asleep in seconds.

"I never get through making formulas!" exclaims Catherine. It's for the bobcat kittens this time. "Their little claws are like needles," Catherine notes as she bottle-feeds two very active kittens.

Between phone calls, nursery feedings and the many trips, Catherine trouble-shoots emergencies. And she has been involved in quite a few, both at the Farm and on locations. The hectic schedule must not fluster her over-much, because the smile is always ready to break through - especially when she is baby-talking the young ones in the Beebe nursery.

Another cup of coffee and another doughnut and Catherine is fortified for the next eventuality. It is a call from the Utah-bound caravan. Did they forget something? No, but one of the trucks broke down at The Dalles outside Portland, Oregon. This means sending a mechanic with necessary parts to the breakdown site. Also, the other trucks would be phoning the Farm at the next relay point to find out what happened to the missing truck. When they do call, Catherine gives them the time of the breakdown and the location so a new relay point can be decided on. Because the moving caravan can't be contacted by Catherine, it's a matter of the caravan always keeping in touch with her.

When trainers and handlers leave on location, that's when Catherine must be ready to go to Seattle, about one hundred miles away, to put animals on a plane to join the crew. She has had to make three round trips in twenty-four hours to accommodate a location crew. Film production is very costly, and the filming better not be held up by any member of the production, whether animal or human.

Visitors taking the walking tour through the Game Farm see many animals on the endangered list, including tigers, jaguars, spotted and clouded leopards and golden cats. The guides are well versed on the characteristics of the various species, pointing out camouflage features, physical traits that distinguish one animal from another, behavior patterns, natural habitat and other interesting information.

Bozo has her (yes, Ben is a girl) own furniture - a table and stool where she often sits in a meditative mood while the guide relates her spectacular achievements in the world of motion picture and television.

Before the gates are opened to the public, the "Game Farm Gang," as tour guide Chuck Crary calls the animal trainers, handlers, maintenance crew and tour guides, are busy with such routine chores as cleaning pens, checking electric fences, mowing grass, cleaning water pumps and inspecting the animals for any abnormalities in appearance or behavior.

The Game Farm Gang shares the diversified jobs. There are animals to be transferred from one enclosure to another. And there are those that are taken for walks. A visitor coming face to face with a grizzly being moved to a compound for filming might be more than a little startled. So these activities generally take place other than during tour times.

When all is ready, the gates open and the walk-through tours begin.

And guess who's first in line?

None other than Frank Walker.

Frank is a Canadian goose. Television viewers will remember him as the star of the Wien Alaska Airline commercials, peering out of a plane's cockpit through old-fashioned goggles attached to a Lindy cap pulled down over his head.

"Last year Frank began joining the tours," guide Maureen McDougald explained. "If the tour got ahead of him, he'd wing it, coming in for a dramatic landing right in the middle of all the people. When the tour ended, he'd zip back into the Petting Farm (an area where people, especially children, can handle animals). This year, he apparently decided he could get almost as much attention by alternating tours with resting in the Petting Farm, so except when he is on tour, he can always be found there, hobnobbing with kids, calves, fawns and children.

"All the other geese socialize among themselves, as normal geese should, either swimming in the pond or circling the Farm in a great flapping of wings. But for some reason, Frank prefers to associate with people. That's just the way he is.

"Frank Walker was born with a mission: to be sociable with people," is the way Maureen summed it up.

A marvel of animal life is its uniqueness. And when a Frank Walker comes along, the speculations about what is going on in an animal's head are revived. Man's ego is deflated at such times because he realizes how far he is from fathoming the mental processes of the creatures.

169

Whatever the reason, Frank dedicates his daylight hours to accompanying visitors on the tours, pausing when they do, being attentive to the guides. Occasionally he will switch from one tour to another, but wouldn't think of abandoning his self-imposed walks. Not Frank!

He stands tall the better to see the Siberian tigers, leopards, jaguars and others - tall but silent, never interrupting the guides.

On a typical sunny day, Frank may join Maureen's tour group in front of the fenced enclosure of Natasha, the tigress, as the guide tells the visitors: "Camouflage is very important for survival. On the back of the Siberian tigers' ears you'll see their false eyes. The false eyes reflect light from the moon and the sun and are an aid to the babies when following their parent. The false eyes also protect a sleeping tiger from predators, who mistake the false eyes for real ones, giving the impression the tiger is awake. All of the large cats have these false eyes."

Natasha strides over to Maureen. The big cat wants her cheek scratched. Frank waddles over to be close to Maureen, but not too close to the tigress. "Natasha is one of the magnificent tigers whose numbers have dramatically decreased since man has been taking over their land. It is estimated that only from fifty to one hundred of them are left in the wild. There are about five hundred living in captivity. The tigress weighs five hundred pounds. During the breeding program at the Farm, eighty-six tiger babies were born. The young are born every third year. The tigers' life span average twenty-five years."

To be born beautiful is to be coveted. The object of human desire that is causing the extinction of the tigers is their fur, sought for coats.

"Among the other big cats at the Farm are the jaguar, clouded leopard and Asian leopard," Maureen continues. "The jaguar has the most powerful jaws. Its coat has spots inside the rosettes, whereas the leopard does not have the spots," the guide points out as she moves down the lines of the air animal enclosures.

Frank Walker bobs his head on his long neck, as if in agreement.

The clouded leopard has an interesting camouflage coloration. When it is up in a tree, its stomach gives the appearance of a cloud because the fur is white. Its black markings elsewhere imitate those of the boa constrictor - a very useful camouflage indeed. They are the only cats that have a wrist-like action on the back legs. This permits them to run down a tree head first.

Moving to a small dog-like fox, Bill Robb tells the visitors and Frank, "The alert and swift red fox is a frequent actor on the silver screen." Bill picks up Sly, a cuddly fox. "He likes to be held. Originally imported from England to New England, the fox is very adaptable. It has, however, a high mortality rate in the wild, and that is in spite of exceedingly sharp hearing," Bill adds.

Fickle Frank again takes to the air to glide over to another tour group to hear what Chuck Crary has to say about coyotes as he stands at one of the roomy enclosures.

"The much maligned coyote lives in security here at the Game Farm," Chuck is saying. "Smiley over there has acted in movies, including the Disney productions Country Coyote Goes Hollywood and The Nashville Coyote."

The rosy glow of twilight backlights the jagged Olympic Mountains, and Frank Walker seems to know the tours are over for that day. Exhausted, the Canadian honker just barely clears the fence of the Petting Farm, where he rejoins his hoofed and horned comrades. Tucking his head securely under a wing, he recuperates from his strenuous tour of duty, dreaming, no doubt, of tomorrow's journey - a goose again on safari.

"When going down their row, whether feeding, cleaning or conducting a tour, we know which animals like to come into their house to 'talk' to us as we approach their enclosure. When they don't follow the usual pattern, we take another look to see if something is wrong," Bill explained. He has been affiliated with the Farm since 1968. His father, Alfie Robb, has been working with the Beebes since 1966.

Chuck says, "I enjoy the intellectual stimulation that entails. I've learned I have a lot to learn about animals." Chuck added that although he has learned a lot from the animals, he has also learned a lot from watching Lloyd Beebe. "He has a fantastic fund of knowledge. He's a very deep man."

And the owner of the Game Farm puts that knowledge to work in his credo: Patience and Reward.

His concept of human-animal relationships follows the same precepts, whether at the Farm or away on location. When an animal is in constant association with people, it is able to adjust to a different environment and different situations much more easily than one that is not getting his daily attention. The staff at the Farm adheres to Lloyd's philosophy. The association they have with the animals is without carelessness, ever mindful that the animals are wild. The staff must constantly be aware of how their actions appear to the animals.

"Someone who can raise an animal to trust him and keep on trusting him is number one with me," explained Lloyd Beebe. "Such an animal is more apt to look like he's doing things on his own during the shooting of a movie. If an animal has confidence in you, you can arrange his environment for a scene so he'll do what you want in a natural way. He must feel friendly toward you.

"Even after the feel for an animal has been acquired, the person's actions - outside as well as inside the enclosures - should always be unobtrusive, never pushy or over-confident," said Lloyd, whose voice is ever quiet and whose motions are slow and easy. Only in a crisis does he move fast, and that is very fast! "I don't like any rough business; there are ways of getting what you want without that. We don't do things that spoil an animal - that takes away his trust in you."

One of Lloyd's basic principles is to work bare-handed when around an animal. "Wearing gloves creates a false sense of security and can lead to a handler behaving in a careless manner. Handlers are more conscious of what they're doing if they are bare-handed - much more alert. You should behave in such a way that the animal will come to you. It takes more time, but you've established the fact that you trust the animal. He knows whether you trust him or not.

"To put on heavy gloves and grab a young animal for any reason, even if you're in a hurry, is a sure way to lose his confidence. An animal that's been spooked by a 'glove-grabber' whose moves and mind are bad, is not an animal you can depend on to work confidently with an actor."

Wearing gloves is a little like feeling a necessity for carrying a gun, according to trainer Al Niemela. And no guns are carried at the Farm. Al was an animal trainer with Walt Disney Studios and is now with the Game Farm.

The talk about poor methods reminded the trainer of an incident that occurred during the filming of the picture, Snow Bear, at Point Barrow, Alaska. The Game Farm didn't have polar bears at the time, so bears and their trainers from Holland were flown to Alaska.

"Those trainers were herding their polar bears much as a dog herds sheep, using hazel sticks. This kind of training works all right in circus work, but it doesn't work in filming because the trainer can't be on camera. Well, they couldn't get the bears to do what they were supposed to do unless they were right with them. Two polar bear babies were then flown in from Holland.

"Meanwhile, the trainers had been watching us working our wolves by means of the buzzer-reward system. They'd never seen this training method before - a method where the trainer can be well removed from the animal he is working.

"So they asked us if we would show them how to use this system of training with the baby bears. They were amazed at how well our method worked and how quickly they could train the polar cubs. Best of all, they saw how they could direct the bears without being on camera themselves."

"There is no such thing as an easy script when it comes to directing animals," says Ken Beebe. "Scriptwriters are not usually familiar enough with the animals to know what kind of behavior comes naturally to them."

Getting a grizzly to pick up a bunny without hurting it is a scriptwriters' fantasy. It is certainly unheard of in nature. But that was what a script called for Ben to do. And, as though that were not enough to boggle the trainer's mind, the bear was also supposed to rock this baby rabbit on its stomach.

The bear-bunny scene was filmed successfully after many attempts. But no sooner had that unbelievable Madonna and child illusion been fabricated than along came another scriptwriter with another fanciful scene. This time, Ben had to express tender feelings for a newly-hatched gosling. The tiny goose had to be trained to follow the giant grizzly wherever the bear went. And poor Ben had to suppress all natural impulses to have a small, feathery dinner and instead play Mother Goose.

Matching these whimsical, contrary-to-nature scenes is one contrived by a writer whose flights of fancy led to animals carrying small fruits and vegetables to a mother rabbit and her babies.

While an animal is still young, it is introduced to the buzzer-reward method of training. It doesn't take the animal long to learn that where he hears the sound of a buzzer, he can expect to find food at that spot. Once the animal understands the connection between food and buzzer, the trainer can move him around from one buzzer to another. He can also regulate the speed of the animal. If he wants the animal to run the buzzer goes fast. When the animal should pause at a location, the next buzzer is delayed.

"During the filming of Never Cry Wolf, the buzzer - an extra loud one - was a mile away. Those wolves went for it," recalled Debbie.

During actual filming there are no treats at the buzzers, because if it were otherwise, the audience would see an animal stop and eat at each location instead of going where he is supposed to go. However, the expectation of finding food at the buzzers is maintained by having treats there during training periods. Not only is the buzzer-reward system very efficient; it is a very rapid training device. When an animal does not understand what he is supposed to do, it is almost always the trainer's fault, the Game Farm staff agrees. Training, to be effective, must be done with kindness, reward and repetition.

Voice commands should be firm or cajoling, but always in a conversational tone. On the movie set, hand signals are used instead of words almost exclusively. When voice signals must be used, the film editor can scrub them out later. Some sounds, like a bear growling, can be dubbed in.

"Training is an achievement," explained Al Niemela. "Like climbing a mountain, you take it step by step. Once you are winning - getting closer to what you're looking for - it's like getting closer to the top of the mountain. You can't get discouraged. You have to have faith - faith you'll get the results you've been looking for...reach to the top of that mountain."

"My most fascinating experience was working with director Carroll Ballard as wolf trainer on Never Cry Wolf, adapted from Canadian writer Farley Mowat's book of the same name," Debbie Coe writes. "I had read the book four times. I couldn't believe my luck to be working on the same picture with the man who had directed The Black Stallion, a film I saw five times.

"When Lloyd came and asked me if I thought there were any wolves that could work on Never Cry Wolf, I must've jumped fifteen feet in the air and said, 'Sure there are!' I would have done anything to get on that show."

This ends the excerpts from Maggie O'Hara's book.

WE REBUILT THE OLD FARMER'S DIKE ALONG THE RIVER

When Catherine and I got married in 1939, the Depression was still on, and the logging camp was shut down. My father gave me fifty dollars to go with a little money I had saved up. Catherine and I got married. We went to Seattle for two days and returned to Forks, Washington.

We had very little money. We both knew what it was like to be broke. We never bought anything until we had the money to pay for it. That is the way we built our first home, just finished it as we had the money. That is the way it was until 1983. We decided to rebuild the farmer's dike we had worked on when we first moved to Sequim.

In 1964, after many meetings in the Schoolhouse at Dungeness, about a mile from our place, the County and the Corps of Engineers decided to build a dike on each side of the river. Because there were more people at the Town of Dungeness, they wanted to build the east side dike first. The west side people agreed to that. As soon as the east side dike was built, the Commissioners and the Corps of Engineers promised to build the other dike to protect us on the west side. The Clallam County Commissioners and Corps of Engineers never did build the west side dike. The water wasn't running through Dungeness and farms on the east side, where most of the people lived. Whenever west side people would get flooded and demand that the west side dike be built as promised, there would be a new study of the river, and all the money would be used to hire Engineers to study the river. This would shut the people up for a few years; then there would be another study.

The flood couldn't go to the east anymore, and the river just kept building up more gravel, as all the surveys told them would happen. When a flood would come, the water got worse on our side and flooded animal pens and buildings. It would knock down our fences where the water came into our place, and again when it had to go out back to the river. Catherine and I and our crew would be wading hip deep in water trying to fold up the wire mesh fences before they came down. Most of the time, the water seemed to come up in the dark. We had to watch that buffalo and deer didn't get out before we got the fence up again.

During each flood, we had to put piles of baled hay in houses and pens so the animals could get out of the water. Each year the flooding got worse.

When we bought the Seamands farm, that gave us ownership of the old Seamands dike along the river that Mel Seamands had built. My father and I used to help Mel build the dike whenever we had time.

The County wouldn't let us connect our dike to the high ground about one hundred feet from the river, so the high water from upriver would run around our dike. I knew we would have to buy the next twenty acres along the river to the end of the old dike. I knew Mr. Sapp who owned it needed to sell. He had offered it to me for fourteen thousand dollars three years before. I didn't need it then. It wasn't any good to Mr. Sapp or me at that time. He sold it to a man for forty thousand dollars. The County wouldn't let him build anything on it, so he moved to Idaho. He had built a nice garage on it when they stopped his work. I called him in Idaho; he wanted eighty thousand dollars for it now.

We were out of money, but summer was here, and we would have our tours going soon. I told him that I would give him a little now, and would pay the eighty thousand dollars off in the next three months, and that I couldn't pay him any interest. He said that would be all right. Catherine and I drove to eastern Washington and signed the papers. We got it paid off on time, and by then, we had done some work on the farmer's dike to the high ground. It wasn't a good dike, but now we saw what we could do.

The County finally put a stop work order on us and had a Court Order to make us take out a road we had put in to the dike at Mr. Sapp's line. We took all the riprap out on this road. The County also wanted us to take out a culvert. We had our Fisheries permits. It was a little funny that the Fisheries wouldn't allow us to take out the culvert. FEMA had started to force the County to make us take out our dike and road.

The County officials wouldn't let us talk to the Planning Department and other offices while there was any litigation going on. Catherine and I went to the Courthouse and asked for papers on trials that were similar to what we were doing that the County had lost. The County told us we would have to hire a Consultant to help us get permits; it would be too complicated for ordinary people to do. We hired a young man named Louis Torres. Louis turned out to be a good choice, and he went to work on trying to get more permits. Louis said we needed the best lawyer available, and he checked with the University of Washington to see who would be the best lawyer to handle this for us.

We had first called a good friend of ours who was a lawyer. When we told him our troubles, he said, "I am not the lawyer you need. When you mentioned FEMA and the Corps of Engineers, that scared me, and I just couldn't help."

Louis got word back from the University that John Ederer was the lawyer we needed. By this time, FEMA had threatened the County that they would take away all flood insurance from the County if the county did not force us to take out the dike on the west side of the Dungeness River.

We hired Mary Rowland to look up laws of the State of Washington as well as any other laws that we could think of. Mary is the wife of Bob Rowland, who works for us. Mary was really good at doing this kind of research. She went to the Courthouse, and under the Freedom of Information Act, got all letters to or from Bob McDonald. Also, from the Department of Ecology, Corps of Engineers, Fisheries, Game Department and others.

The Prosecutor said there had never been a Seamands dike. The Prosecutor lied many times. I knew of times the County had put big rocks to protect the Seamands dike. We had Mary look up these papers in the Courthouse, and she did, and they showed the money that the County spent saving the Seamands dike. Whenever the dike broke, it washed out Ward Road, too.

Mary was in the Courthouse so much that they were wondering who wanted all the information. Mary finally had to tell them. They felt relieved that there wasn't a new lawsuit.

The County got a Court Order for us to remove the dike, and we started a damages suit for two hundred fifty thousand dollars against the County. Soon the County wanted to make an agreement that we could do anything on our dike that the State Laws said we could do. There were exemptions for farmers. We agreed, and we dropped our suit.

We went back to work on our dike. Bob McDonald found out about the agreement and called FEMA. FEMA got mad at the County and gave them ninety days to get Beebe's dike out from along the river. It was the Seamands dike before we got it; but from now on, it was the Beebe dike.

The County Prosecutor sued us to make us take out the dike and redo the agreement. The Judge ruled for us, and then, again, we won. They appealed and said that Federal law was higher than State law. The Judge said that FEMA is not a law; it is a federal insurance company. The Beebes had done no wrong, and all the State laws said the Beebes had a right to do what they did, and they could continue repairing their dike.

I was plowing on the hill with the tractor when Catherine came to tell me that we had won, and the whole thing was over. What a relief!

One of the County Commissioners put an article in the Port Angeles paper a year before about his efforts to force us to take our dike out. In it he said, "Suing Lloyd Beebe was just like suing Santa Claus." When we won, the paper had an article titled, "Santa Claus Won Again," and went on to report the Appeals Court's last decision.

174

REMEMBERING OUR OLD FRIENDS - ANIMALS & HUMANS

We have a few acres of old growth fir trees out from the house. It is on a hill, and the ground is dry. Water never stands on it. My very best animal friends from over the years are all buried there. I have a little book that shows me right where each of them are resting in their last long sleep. Once in a while, I walk over to each grave and just stand and look down at the ground thinking of all the great work they did for me, and how it helped our lives. They are deep in the ground, so that if trees ever blow down, the roots will not disturb them.

There is Charlie, the lonesome cougar, Seeta, the mountain lion, Big Ted, the king of the grizzlies, Minado, the wolverine, and sister Tava, Lefty, the dingaling lynx, and many more animal stars.

There is a spot waiting for Tag, the best Kodiak grizzly bear ever. Tag is getting old and stiff and can't last much longer. He built much of this Game Farm with the money from his shows. Tag is Big Ted's son, and is thirty years old.

Another spot is there waiting for Bozo, the gentle grizzly bear - Ben - Grizzly Adams' bear. Bozo or Ben is almost thirty years old.

When I visit the animal friends that are gone, I can't help but go down to the animal pens and talk to some of the animals in the compound. There is the son of Charlie the lonesome cougar, whose name is Sam. Sam is getting old, too. He loves to have me sit with him, and when no one is listening, I talk to him and pet him. I tell him of the great things his dad had done for me and for the Game Farm. Sam is a great cougar and will be with his dad on the hill some day.

Lloyd and Sam resting on the film set

I always talk to the daughter of Seeta the mountain lion, and Tag, who has many offspring at the Game Farm.

I appreciate all the work these animals have done for us. They have helped us to succeed, given us a good name, and I will never forget them.

One day, Catherine said she had promised to come to a dinner in Sequim, and she wanted me to come with her. We always help each other, but I didn't like the looks of this. It would be all right as long as they didn't call on me to speak. I usually stay on the farm and work with my animal friends instead of going to town, as we always have problems about the shows we are doing. Everything was going well. We had finished our dinner. A speaker got up with a plaque to present, and he read what it said: "Citizen of the Year, Lloyd S. Beebe, for Outstanding Service and Contribution to the Community, 1987."

Catherine had told them before that if I found out about it, I wouldn't come. I got up and tried to thank them, and it did make me proud that they gave it to me. I mumbled a few more words and sat down embarrassed that I wasn't able to do a good job of thanking them.

That is the way I am, and I have said to myself many times, "I am glad I am shy. It has helped me to understand wild animals. There is not much difference between them and me." I have never been pushy

Grizzly bear and cubs born at the Olympic Game Farm

around animals. We always make an agreement to be friends. We each have the same rights.

When we got home, we put the award up on the wall, and there it will stay.

When I stop to look back, I think of a lot of little things that were interesting to me.

The elk and deer have been in the Olympics for thousands of years. They are the gardeners of the Olympics. They clear the brush under the trees to make meadows so that the grass will grow. Then the bears and all other grass-eaters can enjoy the grassy meadows under the trees.

I think of all the things the cougars and dogs have shown me. Many times my dogs have shown me where a bear den was as we traveled through the forest.

The winters in the Olympics are mild in most places, and would seldom force the black bear to hibernate in order to deal with severe cold. But for a female bear not traveling with cubs from the year before, finding a den in the winter has many advantages.

Bear cubs, when they are born, weigh only a few ounces and are quite helpless. But safe within the den, in midwinter the female will have her cubs. During the next two months until spring, she will tend their every need, not leaving the den, drawing heavily on fat stored in summer to nourish herself and supply milk to her cubs.

From two to four cubs are usually born in January. They are about nine inches long and weigh six to eight ounces. The cubs are covered with very fine black fur.

A mother has six nipples to feed her cubs with. When the cubs are very small, the mother will gently move them to a position to nurse. When not nursing, she keeps them folded in her thick layers of fur for warmth.

After about forty days, they open their eyes. At this time, they are about twelve inches long and weigh about two pounds. A month later, if the weather is mild, the mother may take the cubs for a walk around the den area.

When the cubs are about three months old, the bear family will leave the den and travel together for the next year.

When my dogs let me know where a bear den was, they would stand back a ways and look excited, but they knew they should not bother the bears. The dogs knew I wanted to know that the bears and den were there.

I always go very close and listen to see if I can hear cub bears in the den. If the mother is not disturbed, very small bears will nurse every few minutes, and you can hear the sound of nursing. It is a kind of mmm, mmm, mmm, mmm sound. If the mother is disturbed, the cubs will cry out in a loud squawking sound. You can tell how old they are by the sound.

I have had mother bears come part way out and look at me and the dogs. Once in a while, they will come all the way out and look, then go around the stump, or whatever their den is in, and go away for a little while. I think they stayed close, watching to see if I was going to follow them or go away.

One time when I was just a kid, a bear came out and went behind the stump. I took a look behind the stump and couldn't see the bear, so I quickly went into the den and took the two cubs and carried them home. It was five miles to the road, and the mother bear followed all the way to the car.

I felt so sorry for her that time that I never did that again. It would have been

1800 pound grizzly "Big Mac"

bad if she had come back to the den with me, but at the time I thought it was worth the chance.

When my family came to the Olympic Peninsula to live and I started high school in 1930, I had four friends and we always stayed close. They were Wayne Hathaway, Chet Binkie, Hollum Hunley and Perry Brackett. We hiked the mountains and camped out when we could, and enjoyed bows and arrows. Perry was as good a young man as I've ever seen and one of the most honest. He tried to keep the rest of us that way.

After getting out of school, Perry was manager of a savings and loan in Port Angeles. Everyone in Port Angeles trusted Perry Brackett. He got married to a very nice girl and had some children. Perry bought an airplane. Everyone was stunned when it crashed with Perry, his wife and son on board. They were all killed. It was a sad day for everyone, and they would be missed.

Wayne Hathaway was with me when he and I first worked in the logging, and other jobs later on. Wayne was the first of us boys to get married. They had a daughter. I stayed with Wayne and Margaret for several months in Port Angeles, while we were working in the logging near Port Angeles.

Wayne's dad, Erwin Hathaway, was with us cutting logs. We were working in the hills. It was a very hard time, and we didn't make much

Lloyd and his grizzly bears

177

Wayne Hathaway with black bear taken with bow and arrow

money, but were very lucky to have a job.

There were a lot of blue grouse and rabbits there, and I was able to get a grouse or rabbit almost every day with a rock or stick. The grouse were always in trees. I found out if I was uphill from a rabbit, I could take a short stick and run downhill in great leaps, and the rabbit would get excited and dodge back and forth, and with long jumps downhill, I could often get him with a stick. That helped a great deal with our food bill.

Wayne and I thought it would be nice to mount our next season's deer head. I sent for a book that taught taxidermy. Wayne was more interested in it than I was, and became the best taxidermist in Washington. Wayne stayed at that work until he died in 1979. The doctor had told him to quit smoking his pipe. He just had time to make his daughter promise to quit her smoking, and then died as she was promising, and I believe she did quit.

Chet Binkie was a great fisherman and has been living in Sitka, Alaska for thirty-six years. There are only seven or eight miles of roads there, so Chet doesn't have a car, just a boat. Chet had to have a heart bypass two years ago, and came to Seattle for the operation. We went over to see him in the hospital. It was great to see Chet. He got along fine with the operation. The next year, he came down to stay with us for a week. We tried to catch up on the thirty-six years since we had seen each other.

The Gravenstein apples were ripe, and Chet loved them. We send Chet and Terry a box each fall. Chet just couldn't get over the changes in the County, the cars and everything. He was afraid to ride on some of the roads we used to travel before he left. Chet and his wife, Terry are doing fine now.

Hollum Hunley was living alone in Port Angeles in the same house that his parents lived in until they died. Hollum was not too well, and needed a lot of medicine. We called each other often. Hollum was ten months older than I. He called me whenever we were the same age for two months to tell me that I was getting old, and two months later when his birthday came and he was one year older than me, I called him to say how young I felt. Hollum passed away August 31, 1994.

Hollum's cousin, Sigel Silcox, my old friend who took a trip one winter cougar hunting with me, died of liver cancer two years ago.

I have been lucky all my life because I have never gone to the hospital for a day in my life, other than to get a cut sewed up a few times - never spent a night there.

Chet Binkie with "Drum"

Alfie Robb wouldn't come out too well if he tried pitting his strength against Ricky's 4,500 pounds so he scratches Ricky's back instead.

Olympic Game Farm film crew: Dell Ray, Lloyd Beebe, Ron Brown, Al Niemela and Marinho Correia

THIS WILL BE OUR LAST WILDLIFE FILM

I have always wanted to make a film of our Olympic Mountains at the time the wolves roamed there. Also, I would like to tell the story on film that led up to the disappearance of the wolves. The fur trade, bringing with it hunters from many countries, had an enormous impact on this most northwestern part of our state, and was responsible for much of the change that took place.

The arrival of the homesteaders who settled the land and were, for the most part, farmers and cattle ranchers, also played their part in the disappearance of the Olympic wolf.

Ever since 1938, when I saw the footprints, undeniably those of a wolf, I've wanted to trace the origins that led to his vanishing from our mountains. With this in mind, I've saved some very good film over the years for telling the story. I know it will be undertaken with dedication to the truth, and the finished film will bring its own rewards.

The foreign ships, coming for fur trade, worked their way from the east coast and arrived on the west coast by the 1800's. Here they discovered the sea otter skins. The sailors wiped their tarry hands on them for lack of towels, and generally treated them as something useful, but hardly precious. Then, landing in China, they were astonished when offered a good price for even a torn or damaged skin. They had not known that the sea otter hide was the royal fur of China. They didn't foresee the day when a single sea otter skin would bring thirteen hundred forty dollars at the London fur market.

There was no longer any uncertainty about the value of the furs coming from the Pacific coast. Fortunes were being made and continued to be made.

The Indians would gladly trade a sea otter hide for an iron nail or an abalone shell. The fur traders soon found out that the best way to get sea otters was to hire Indian hunters and take their canoes aboard the ships. The ships had goods to trade for any furs or hides. It was the only way the Indians had to get metal, guns and tools they needed.

The Olympics was the first land on the west coast to be reported by explorers and the last to be mapped, "The Last Wilderness."

The Olympic Peninsula has the thickest part of the evergreen forest that extends from northern California to the Alaska Peninsula.

The Indians were not people of the forests. They looked to the sea, beaches and the steep dangerous salmon-choked rivers for their living. They seldom ventured into the deep forest.

With the passage of time through the centuries, the Olympic Peninsula had reached its own particular balance of nature. The Indians along the coast with their relatively small population and primitive hunting and fishing methods had little effect on the wild animal population until the time the ships arrived in 1800, and then the settlers arrived in 1850.

Before that time, the number of wolves was controlled by the amount of prey that was available.

One thing was certain, though. In this time period, the wolf pack was the dominant animal group, and all others, prey and predator alike, did their best to keep track of the wolf packs and avoid them if possible.

In 1850, the United States sent homesteaders to win the land. The wolves could not know what this would mean to them. Many homesteaders were without money and had to live in stump houses, split cedar or bark lean-tos.

The settlers learned from the Indians how to live on this new land. The settlers had to leave their homesteads for several months at a time to work in logging camps and mills that had started up in the Olympics. They returned to their land after earning money to buy food and tools, going back when they needed more money.

The land had to be cleared of the big trees before it would produce food. The trees were like weeds to the homesteaders.

By 1870 the sea otters were about gone, and the foreign fur traders with larger sea-going ships with Indian crews and canoes aboard started after the millions of seals, following the seal herd far out into the ocean. The Indians had been getting a new rifle for each sea otter hide. Some of the fur traders and trappers became homesteaders, and Indians and whites trapped on land for the fur traders.

Wolves killed farm animals and pets, and the settlers fought back. When the wolves killed stock at a homestead, all the neighbors were notified and were ready to shoot the predator. The wolves paid a high price when they came back.

In 1905 the State of Washington put a bounty on wolves, wild cats and cougars. The bounty was fifteen dollars for each wolf. The bounty was to protect the elk, deer and the struggling homesteaders' stock. This same year, Washington passed a law preventing the shooting of elk with guns. Most of the elk were gone now after years of market hunting for elk hides, teeth and meat.

According to history, the Indian tribes have always fought wars over land and possessions, just like most other people of the world, trying to take over each other's land. The people came from many countries on ships from around the world. Ships came for buffalo hides until the buffalo were gone. Ships came from all over the world to get fur and hides on the east coast, and traded for furs all the way to the west coast by the 1800's. Ships also came from many countries in the world to get the old growth forests; now the old growth forests are about gone on much of the land.

Now ships are coming from many countries in the world with the finest fishing equipment to catch our salmon, with many nets thirty or more miles long. Our country has not been able or willing to stop them. It seems whenever ships come from many countries, they can wipe out anything. We, too, have been hungry and have been willing to sell almost anything.

You can't blame other countries that are hungry for making profits. Our country, however, should protect its resources. We may not have anything left that they would come for.

Other countries have furnished the market and so far we have been willing to sell. The people at the head of the market know what is happening. The workers, trappers, fishermen and farmers are too busy just making a living to know what is really taking place until it is too late.

It is easy to look back in history and decide what should have been done. Under the same circumstances, things would most likely have ended up exactly the same as they have, even with different people. People will do what they believe they have to do to survive.

I plan to use some of the film I've kept, and it will go into this movie to show how the wolves disappeared, and how other animals came back from the pressure of the fur trade and from the people who settled on the Olympic Peninsula.

The war between the settlers and the wolves came to an end in the 1920's. There were only three wolves bountied after 1920. The last wolf was supposedly shot and bountied on January 17, 1929.

I know there was one wolf that I followed for three days starting on November 18, 1938. I have always wondered if that was the last Olympic wolf, or if it was a visitor from the Cascades or Canada. It would not be far for a wolf to come from Canada. They might come back on their own some day. The Olympic Mountains don't have much low land around them.

When the snow comes in winter, the elk and deer come down where the settlers live. There is nothing easier than settlers' stock for wolves to eat. In winter, there is not enough room for both people and wolves to coexist in the low country.

I want to finish this show, and that, I believe, will be my last wildlife film.

LOOKING BACK

As I think back on my life, I remember that ever since I was a kid, the State Patrol and Sheriff have called on me to look for lost people in the mountains and forests. Almost any logger or homesteader would be glad to go looking for anyone who was lost. Even after moving to the Farm in Sequim, I would get calls to go look for someone.

One day, several Army trucks came to my father's house. They said they were doing some work along the coast of the Pacific Ocean north of the mouth of the Hoh River, and one of their soldiers had gotten lost, and the Commander would not let any of their men leave the trail to look for this lost soldier because he didn't want to lose any more men.

They asked us for help. Hollum Hunley was there at our house, so Hollum and I said we would go. We got our equipment and pack sacks ready, and the Army trucks took us to where they had lost their buddy. We followed him for two days before we caught up to him. This soldier's feet got sore and swelled up, so he couldn't get his shoes on. We found the shoes first. It turned out okay. He just had to spend one day in the hospital.

We found all the people that I ever helped look for except one. That time, the State Patrol called me at the Farm in Sequim, and Catherine told them that I was on my way to Forks. They put out a call to stop me on the highway.

I was using elk hunting as an excuse to get out into the forest for a while. Looking for a lost elk hunter was a much better reason. Catherine found out on the radio later where I was.

This elk hunter had left the Hoh River to hunt and was last seen a mile or so from the river. The Patrolman said the hunter was wearing a new pair of caulk shoes. These were the shoes all loggers used. They have short spikes in the shoe soles to keep from slipping as you walk logs. I said I would be glad to go.

It was a rainy day, as most elk seasons were at Forks. Gene Fraker was there, and he said he would go with me and asked about sleeping bags and supplies. I told him we couldn't take sleeping bags through the brush; there wouldn't be a trail. I said we would have to build a fire to keep us warm at night. Gene didn't think much of going without a sleeping bag. I said, "I am not going to take a sleeping bag, and we will be fine." Gene said, "Okay, I will go," and we left with a few things and food enough for two days.

We started into the forest near where the hunter had. We were sure he must have gone over the hill, or he wouldn't have gotten lost. We finally found tracks of a man with new spike shoes and began to

Lloyd and Catherine overlooking their home at the Olympic Game Farm.

follow him. We could see that if he kept going he would end up in Goodman Creek. We kept on his trail until it was too dark. We built a fire and chopped wood to last all night. It wasn't too long until we were warm, if not dry. It had rained all day, and the brush is thick in this area. We had on raincoats and kept the fire going.

The next morning, we started out on the trail again. We came to Goodman Creek, and went on down the creek toward the ocean. We crossed the creek many times before we reached within one half mile of the Pacific Ocean. We had waded the flooding creek many times chest deep in fast water not knowing if we could stay on our feet.

Charlie Anderson was there on the trail that comes back from the beach. Charlie had come from where he lived on the Hoh River along the beach trail. Charlie was one of the people always called out when someone was lost in this area.

The hunter's trail went down the creek a little more, and there he left his shoes, rifle and some clothes. He was a good swimmer, and he apparently felt he could swim down the creek in the backwater to the ocean beach. It was very rocky on both sides of the creek. The hunter had crossed the beach trail without seeing it. We took the trail to the beach and looked up and down. The only sign was his shorts washed up on the beach.

We left his shoes, rifle and other things for the officials to see and went down the trail to LaPush. When we arrived, there was a group planning the search for the next day. They had been searching along the beach all day. We told the men what we had found, and that the hunter had drowned in the Ocean.

The State Patrolman was there and wanted me to come to a meeting that night at the school. There were many friends and relatives and search parties that had come about one hundred fifty miles to look for the hunter. I just had time to change my wet clothes and go with Boyd Roup, the Patrolman. He took me to the meeting, and I told my story about trailing him for eight miles and crossing Goodman Creek twenty or more times up to our armpits, and that the end came in the Pacific Ocean, and how I wished I could have had better news for them.

These people had come a long way to this meeting and to help with the search. The school auditorium was crowded. When the meeting was over, the relatives and friends wanted to talk and all lined up. The men wanted to shake hands and thank me. The women and kids wanted to hug me. The look in their eyes told me they thought I had done a great thing, and they appreciated it. All this made me think I was taking credit for something I hadn't done. Other than worrying about the lost man, I had enjoyed the trip.

The things they said to me did make me feel good. I'd had my trip to the forest, so I decided to get back to the Farm and the animals. I would save the elk hunting excuse for another time.

When I was still a kid, I started bringing wild animals home with me. I thought I knew how animals felt. Wild animals are shy and wary, almost like I was.

I started right in wondering about what animals were thinking, are they afraid, do they trust me, are they getting to know me? I always watched and studied the animals as I worked around them, and came to recognize that there was a sign language that animals use to tell you what they think of you. Their language shows you the changes in their feelings as they begin to trust you.

When you watch them and learn their expressions and actions, you should talk in a low, friendly voice all the time, learning what they are telling you, never doing anything to startle the animals or frighten them. In the beginning, you might only be able to talk to them in a low voice. If you watch closely, you will know when to dare to do more.

Let animals know you will not do anything that will worry them, even if you don't do anything except talk softly. Don't ever overstep your welcome or take short cuts; be satisfied with what an animal will permit you to do.

The first wolves I had were too old to tame easily. I could take them for walks on a chain, but they didn't trust anyone. I spent a lot of time with them. I learned it was hard to tame more than one wild animal at a time.

One of these wolves would reach up and pinch my arm or leg. She didn't bite hard enough to make holes in me, but it did hurt. I thought about this problem for a week. When I sat on the ground on a log with the wolf, she would pinch my arm once in a while. After agonizing over the problem, I finally decided to slap her a little next time she did this. I knew it might frighten her; she was already afraid of things. She pinched my arm again, and I slapped her on the nose a little. That did frighten her, and I could see she was almost ruined now. I finally found out if I sat down with the wolves near a bear or some animal they were afraid of, they then got interested in making friends with me. In that way we became friends, but I learned not to be rough with wild animals, just enjoy the company of the animal and the changes in them, like lying down, going to sleep or relaxing.

Many animals get nervous when you look into their eyes. If this happens, look off to the side a little until they trust you. You must have a lot of patience. My first animals were always wild.

I started out right because I only wanted an animal to be my friend. When you have a new animal you shouldn't trust the animal, and that animal doesn't trust you, so be afraid of getting bitten. If he bites you, you have already made a mistake and the animal trusts you less now. It will be harder to make him trust you again. Biting is a bad habit for an animal to learn. When you are training an animal, the animal will learn good things or bad things, depending on how careful and thoughtful you are.

All my life in training and taming wild animals, I have never, that I can remember, been bitten. I always keep watching what the animals are telling me. I wait to pet them until they want me to. There have been a few times during filming animals, however, that I have gotten a few bites. At these times, I knew I was going to be bitten because of what the script called for. This happened when I doubled for an actor, pretending to fight with a wild animal.

One time on a high mountain, we were filming a wolverine. The wolverine decided he was tired of being filmed, and ran down the hill like he wasn't coming back. After going through the forest for three hundred yards, I saw him. I had some small bites of meat with me, so when the wolverine looked at me, I threw a piece of meat close to the wolverine. He ate it; then I threw one closer to me. It looked to me like I could grab the wolverine by the neck with my bare hands. If I did catch him and couldn't hold on to him, I knew we would lose this wolverine. I knew I would get bitten, but I caught him by the loose skin on the back of the neck, got my other arm around his body and started up the mountain. I got tired and went to my knees a few times, but kept his head turned away from me. His claws were stuck in my clothes by now, and when I got close to the crew, I shouted for them to come part of the way with a cage to put the wolverine in.

When the wolverine was back in the cage, I could see that I had a few small bites and scratches, but nothing to what I had expected when I decided to grab him. We got to be friends again, and if he hadn't been a little friendly before, I would have been worse off.

After my father died in 1965, and then in 1987, years later, when my mother died, I often thought and I wished I had spent more time with them both. You cannot spend too much time with the ones you love.

I have been so lucky with my parents. It just couldn't have been better. After I was born, I made every move with my mother and father. Even after I was married, Catherine and I lived within a stone's throw of my parents. That might seem like a drawback to some; we never had any trouble from living close together.

I think it always helped them, and they also helped Catherine and me. They may have had doubts about some of our decisions, but I believe they knew that Catherine would always do everything she could to help it work out. They both lived on our Farm until they died.

We always wished they could have known how the Farm developed, and we wish they could see it now.

We have been just as lucky with Catherine's family; we couldn't have been luckier. Although they were our parents, they were also our best friends.

WE ARE SO HAPPY WITH HOW WE SPENT OUR LIVES

We have several poems on the wall where we can see them every day as we enter the kitchen. I read these poems often and think of our parents and friends, and think of how fortunate we have been.

LEST WE FORGET

Around the corner I have a friend,
In this great city that has no end;
Yet days go by, and weeks rush on,
And before I know it a year has gone.
And I never see my old friend's face,
For life is a swift and terrible race.
He knows I like him just as well
As in the days when I rang his bell
And he rang mine. We were younger then;
And now we are busy, tired men:
Tired with playing a foolish game,
Tired with trying to make a name.
"Tomorrow," I'd say, "I will call on Jim,
Just to show that I'm thinking of him."
But tomorrow comes - and tomorrow goes,
And the distance between us grows and grows.
Around the corner! - yet miles away...
"Here's a telegram sir...Jim died today."
And that's what we get, and deserve in the end:
Around the corner - a vanished friend.

I believe our parents' and friends' answer would be the same as mine will be.

I'M FREE

Don't grieve for me, for now I'm free
I'm following the path God laid for me.
I took his hand when I heard Him call
I turned my back and left it all.
I could not stay another day
To laugh, to love, to work or play.
Tasks left undone must stay that way
I found that peace at close of day.

If my parting has left a void,
Then fill it with remembered joy.
A friendship shared, a laugh, a kiss
Ah yes, these things I too will miss.
Be not burdened with times of sorrow
I wish you the sunshine of tomorrow.
My life's been full, I savored much
Good times, good friends, a loved one's touch.

Perhaps my time seemed all too brief
Don't lengthen it now with undue grief.
Lift up your hearts and share with me
God wanted me now; He set me free.

There is a third poem next to the first two, one to remind me of how fortunate we have been all our lives. No matter what happens to us in the future, I don't see how we could feel anything but happiness with the way we spent our lives.

"Today, upon a bus, I saw a lovely maid with golden hair.
"I envied her, she seemed so gay, and I wished I were as fair.
"When suddenly she rose to leave, I saw her hobble down the aisle;
"She had one foot, and used a crutch, but as she passed she had a smile.
"Oh, God forgive me when I whine; I have two feet, the world is mine.

"And when I stopped to buy some sweets,
"The lad who sold them had such charm. I talked with him, he said to me,
'It's nice to talk to men like you. You see,' he said, 'I'm blind."
"Oh, God forgive me when I whine; I have two eyes, the world is mine.

"Then, as I passed along the way, I saw a child with eyes of blue.
"He stood and watched the others play; it seemed he knew not what to do.
"I stopped for a moment; and then I said, 'Why don't you join the others, dear?'
"He looked ahead without a word, and then I knew he could not hear.
"Oh, God forgive me when I whine; I have two ears, the world is mine.

"With feet to take me where I'd go,
"With eyes to see the sunset's glow,
"With ears to hear what I would know,
"I'm blessed indeed.
"The world is mine.
"Oh, God forgive me if I whine."

"A small businessman from the old country kept his accounts payable in a cigar box, his accounts receivable on a spindle, and his money in a cash box. One day his son stopped by and offered, 'I just don't see how you can run your business this way. How do you know what your profits are?' 'Son,' the father replied, 'when I got off the boat, I had only the pants I was wearing. Today your sister is an art teacher, your brother is a doctor, you are an accountant. I have a car, a home and a good business. Everything is paid for. So you add it all up, subtract the pants, and there's your profit.'"

This is pretty much the way we have lived our lives. We never went in debt; we paid for things as we could pay for them. We did go without for long periods of time, but never had anything repossessed, because if we couldn't pay for something, we would rather not have it. We were patient and waited until we could afford it.

Catherine and I always enjoyed each other's company, and it was fun to work on the same jobs together. The fun was finishing a project successfully and starting a new one.

We are going to take time to return to some of the beautiful locations that we worked in, like Banff, Alberta, Canada, Sedona and Payson, Arizona, and many others. We will take a little time to stop and reminisce about the great times we have had and try to find some of the friends we haven't seen for a long time.

We have always been so busy we have seldom returned to visit our friends. We can do that now, but it will be too late for some.

There will always be many things for us to do here. Just across the road from the Game Farm we have a mile of property along the Dungeness River, with roads all ready for people to drive through. We have been building a picnic area for our customers.

It is fun to work on improvements to the Farm. It can be almost like looking into the future, to see how much better it will be. Catherine and I will keep on working and enjoying the beautiful scenery and animals at our Farm. We will be remembering the great life we have lived; also, the good people and friends who have worked with us, on the Farm and in motion pictures.

Catherine and Lloyd after 56 years of happy marriage

Ken, Mel and Alice (Mel and Alice Richmond Bromley were married April 19, 1992) will be here to do the work we decide that we will not have time to do.

Catherine and I may just want to live in our house on the hill, enjoying the beautiful view overlooking the Game Farm, without shouldering much responsibility for running the business.

Catherine and I have always been happy to just be together, and we are still in love with each other. We know that is the way it will continue to be.

THE END